Religion
as
Poetry

ANDREW M. GREELEY

Religion as Poetry

Transaction Publishers
New Brunswick (U.S.A.) and London (U.K.)

Library of Congress Catalog Number: 94-16035
ISBN: 1-56000-183-6
Printed in the United States of America

Library of Congress Cataloging-in-Publication Data
Greeley, Andrew M., 1928–
    Religion as poetry / Andrew Greeley.
        p. cm.
    Includes bibliographical references and index.
    ISBN 1-56000-183-6
    1. Religion and sociology. 2. Storytelling—Religious aspects. 3. Secularization (Theology). I. Title.
BL60.G725 1994
306.6—dc20   94-16035
                                                          CIP

For Jim Coleman

Contents

Foreword ix

Acknowledgments xiii

Prelude xv

1. Introduction 1

2. Social Science Theories of Religion 5

3. Religion as Poetry 23

4. The Faith We Have Lost 57

5. The Persistence of Religion 83

6. Testing the Links 111

7. Different Poetry for Different People 123

8. The Pragmatics of Prayer 157

9. Religious Stories and Political Stories 179

10. Religious Stories and the Environment 191

11. Religious Stories and AIDS 205

12. Religious Stories and Contact with the Dead 217

13. A Story of Two Religious Imaginations 229

14. The Development of a Religious Story 257

15. Conclusion 263

References 271

Index 277

Religion is poetry which intervenes in life. Poetry is religion which supervenes on life.

—Santayana

I must go where all ladders start
The foul rag and bone shop of my heart

—Yeats

Foreword

Contemporary sociologists, political scientists, and economists pay little attention to religion. The neglect by economists may not be surprising because of the continuing emphasis in economics on markets and material aspects of life. But the neglect by sociology is not easy to explain, given the important work on religion by Durkheim, Weber, Parsons, and other giants in the intellectual history of sociology.

Greeley's explanation for the neglect, which I find persuasive, is that most intellectuals are hostile to religious belief and religious behavior. And it is no longer possible to study religion through a "modernity" framework that predicts that religion will become less important as societies become more secular and "modern." For the empirical evidence contradicts this prediction for the United States and many other countries. Yet whatever one's personal attitude toward religion, it is an extremely important social phenomenon that merits extensive and serious social science research. In this provocative book, Andrew Greeley proposes a theoretical framework for understanding religion that emphasizes religious stories that "we tell to ourselves and to others to explain what our life means." Most of the book, however, is empirical; it examines the relation between religious beliefs, experiences, and practices to attitudes on many important social issues.

Let me whet the appetite of the reader by citing a few of the many interesting findings. Greeley presents evidence that shows conclusively that Americans are very religious: 65 percent pray weekly, 44 percent attend church regularly, 78 percent believe in an afterlife, and many even believe that the dead sometimes return to life. The evidence suggests that such religious beliefs are also common in West Germany (but not in East Germany), Great Britain, and many other countries.

Even more fascinating is the evidence on the revival of religion in the formerly communist nations of Eastern Europe. Although the revival has been uneven, it has been surprisingly rapid and extensive in the Russian Republic. Despite seventy-five years of communist rule, destruction of churches, and extensive propaganda against religion, already 30 percent of all Russians state that they believe in heaven, and one out of eight pray weekly. This is a powerful testimony to the appeal of religious beliefs in the modern world, no matter how secularist or hostile are state policies.

Greeley shows that religious beliefs correlate with attitudes on many social issues. For example, individuals who pray tend to be opposed to the death penalty, to be sympathetic to the poor, and to be more honest in dealing with the government. Catholics who pray frequently are more sympathetic to victims of AIDS.

I would like to see Greeley's emphasis on religious stories and experiences placed within a rational choice framework, for there is no inconsistency between a rational choice approach and coping with eventual death through religion. In recent years rational choice approaches to religion have brought economists and sociologists together in one of the more exciting developments in interdisciplinary cooperation. This framework provides additional important implications about religious behavior; for example, it has been shown that religious beliefs are strongest in environments where governments do not have favorite religions, but allow open competition among different religions for members.

I would also like to have seen more attention paid to the problems raised by what is called "selectivity" in econometric analysis. Greeley fully recognizes that correlation does not prove causation, and that unmeasured variables may explain why the attitudes of religious persons on many social issues systematically differ from those of others. But it is desirable to probe further to determine the causation behind the relation between religious beliefs and other attitudes.

However, the questions I have about the theory and empirical results do not weaken my conviction that this is a valuable book that deserves to be read not only by other sociologists, but also by economists and everyone else interested in social behavior. For what Greeley does do is significant. He shows that religion still has a powerful attraction, that religious beliefs correlate with attitudes on many social issues, that the type of beliefs also affects these attitudes, and that the implications of the theoretical analysis are consistent with the signs of many of the correlations.

The challenge to other social scientists is to recognize the importance of religion in modern life, and to carry both the theory and the empirical analysis further. I hope that this book will succeed in prodding others—not only sociologists—into taking religion more seriously as an important subject for social science investigation.

—Gary Becker

Acknowledgments

In addition to Jim Coleman, whose powerful support for this book I note in my dedication, I am grateful for help to the following (in alphabetical order): Gary Becker (to whom thanks is also due for the Foreword), Albert Bergesen, Norman Bradburn, Michael Carroll, Liz Clement, Jim Davis, Elizabeth Durkin, Mary Jule Durkin, Sean Durkin, Paula England, Debra Friedman, Clifford Geertz, Michael Hechter, Michael Hout, Mary Kotecki, Douglas McAdam, Manuel Pacheco, William McCready, Martin Marty, Robert Michael, Julie Montague, Walter Powell, Peter Rossi, Ingrid Shafer, Tom Smith, David Snow, Ross Stolzenberg, David Tracy, Linda Waite, Zdzislawa Walaczek, and Conor Ward.

Prelude

In starkly beautiful mountains of northern New Mexico around the city of Taos and especially south of it in small towns in the Mora area, one encounters low adobe or stone buildings—sometime in ruins—with crosses on them, some kind of Catholic chapel perhaps, but hardly a church. They are *morados,* the prayer site of some of the members of an extraordinary religious and ethnic group. Its congregants will tell you that they are not Mexican, not Hispanic, but *Hispano.* Nominally and often devoutly Catholic, they are apparently descendants of *conversos* or *maraños,* Spanish Jews who were forced to convert to Catholicism in the fifteenth and sixteenth centuries but secretly continued to be Jews. Many of them, it is said, migrated to New Spain to escape the Inquisition and then moved as far from Mexico City, the center of power and of the Inquisition, as they could. The group that settled in northern New Mexico seems to have been sufficiently large to possess the "critical mass" necessary to become a distinct community. Through the years, most of this community seems to have drifted from Judaism to Catholicism, though to a special kind of Catholicism that kept alive Jewish practices—such as the "bread of the Semites" during Holy Week—and combined this tradition with the tradition of fiercely penitential popular Catholicism. For two and a half centuries until the coming to Santa Fe of Archbishop Lamy (the real life counterpart of Willa Cather's archbishop in her novel *Death Comes for the Archbishop*), only an occasional wandering friar visited their mountain villages. The *hermano major* of the Third Order Franciscan *fraternidad* in each village presided over weddings and baptisms and acted as the religious as well as the civic leader.

Little is known of the history of this community in the years between their settlement in northern New Mexico and the arrival of Archbishop Lamy; hence, it is impossible to measure the speed of the drift from secret Judaism under a mask of Catholic orthodoxy to popular Catholicism with surviving Jewish customs. It does not seem unreasonable to speculate that the blend of Catholicism and Judaism might have already begun before the migration from Spain. It is often said that those Spanish names ending in "ez" are Sephardic (Jewish) names.

The *hispanos* reside in an area that encompasses the mountain range known as the *Sangre de Cristo* (Blood of Christ) that runs from southern Colorado to seventy-five miles north of Santa Fe. Most of the present community consider themselves to be Catholics and many of them are intensely Catholic. Some of them have memories of a different past about which they do not want to talk or that they prefer to ignore. A few of them may still claim to be Jewish.

From the folk Catholicism of Spain they brought with them a peculiar Catholic devotion: In the Spain of the era of their ancestors' departure, devotion to the sufferings of Jesus—His wounds, His scourging, His crowning with thorns—had become very intense. One aspect of this devotion was the emergence of "confraternities" (groups of laymen) dedicated to reenacting Jesus's sufferings during Holy Week. The *hermanos penitentes* even performed ritual crucifixions in which the Christ-figure on occasion died. The official Spanish church, harsh as it might have been, had not approved of such rituals, but seems to have been unable to stop them. These penitential devotions continued in New Spain and continue in some forms even today, though often in thoroughly pagan contexts such as the rituals of the Yaqui tribe of northern Sonora and southern Arizona.

The custom of processions of flagellants, possibly revived from an earlier era or possibly brought with them as part of religious baggage from Spain, became popular with the *Hispanos* living in the *Sangre de Cristo* range (an appropriate name for the mountains). We do not know why this community, whose origins were Jewish and whose Catholicism initially was a veneer, came to adopt this practice of folk Catholicism and to make it in some sense the center of their religion.[1] But the confraternities provided the binding force that held the community together. The Church opposed the penitentes bitterly and eventually the members of the confraternities were excommunicated from the Catholic church. A half century ago, a skilled New York Irish man named Edwin V. Byrne became Archbishop of Santa Fe (1943–1963)[2] and finessed a compromise by which the excommunications were lifted and the penitential confraternities readmitted to the Church with the promise that the Holy Week processions would involve neither flagellation nor crucifixion. It would seem that the terms of the compromise have been adhered to, though one hears rumors of occasional bloody outbursts up in the hills. Today in the *Sangre de Cristo* area many families maintain intense and devout holy week devotions; according to some anecdotal reports, the numbers of young people involved in such devotions has increased.

Thus, the *Hispano* Catholicism of the community continues today, still semisecret, in part because some of the people do not want to talk about their past, either Jewish or Penitential, but mostly because no research has been done on it.[3] In late twentieth-century America, with its mass public education, its scientific and technological progress, and its ever-present television tube, the community in the *Sangre de Cristo* with its bewitching history continues to survive and in some fashion to keep alive its curious mixture of customs and traditions.[4]

It cannot possibly continue, some will say. But such an assertion begs the question. It *has* continued as have many other small and unusual religious collectivities. When a sociologist of religion predicts the future not on the basis of trend lines but on the basis of his own implicit assumptions, he is no different from the most dogmatic of theologians.

The pertinent question about the *Sangre de Cristo* Catholics, one that sociology of religion in the United States today could not possibly consider, is how two very different stories, one Jewish and the other folk Catholic, could have blended through the course of time into one story, a story that is the cement of this fascinating community. Manuel Pacheco has suggested to me that the one-time Sephardics of the *Sangre de Cristo* turned to the penitential *Fraternidads* because these Third Order Franciscan groups were the only community groups available to them. One belonged to what was available—an appealing sociological explanation to be tested against data that remains to be collected.

I begin this study in the sociology of religion with a description of the *Sangre de Cristo* Catholics, not because I am an expert on them or even qualified to attempt confidently a description of them, but to emphasize the enormous durability and flexibility of religious heritages and their fundamental nature as poetic rather than prosaic affairs. The northern New Mexico community, for weal or woe, had no theology, very little propositional religion, no overarching religious institution, and almost no religious "education" as that term would be understood today. It did have, and still has in abundance, metaphors, stories, and rituals that both endured and changed. If one strives to understand its Catholicism by probing for doctrinal convictions, one misunderstands it completely. Its central story is in fact a blend of two seemingly contradictory stories, one from folk Catholicism and the other from a remnant of Judaism. The secret of its survival is the story.

Its college-educated members graft onto the traditional story of contemporary Catholic interpretations. They are thus able to keep alive their heritage and still seem both orthodox and rational, which is surely legitimate and perhaps even necessary for their personal identity. Nonetheless, the origins and the power of the faith of the Taos community, as complex and as intricate as it may be, are to be found not in prose propositions but in poetic rituals and stories.

So, I will argue in this book, it is with all religion.

Notes

1. The migration of Spanish religious symbols and devotions to New Spain is a fascinating story and one that has not yet been told in any elaborate detail. For example, there is a shrine in Spain to Our Lady of Guadeloupe that is clearly the ancestor of its Mexican counterpart. In Spain the image of the Mother of Jesus is imprinted on a rock, not a cloak. The shrine was probably a pre-Christian place of devotion before it became Christian. It does not follow that present Mexican and Mexican-American devotion to Our Lady of Guadeloupe is pagan or mostly pagan—though that issue is surely a researchable question. Later in this book I will try to understand the mix of Christianity and pre-Christianity in past and present popular Catholicism.

2. President Manuel Pacheco (a Sephardic name) of the University of Arizona tells me that Byrne was a hero to his family and to all the devout *Hispano* Catholics of the area for whom an intense piety was built around the *morado*—the meeting house of the *fraternidad*. He described to me a funeral for a relative thirty years ago that began with prayers in the morado and then adjourned to the parish church for the requiem mass. He also showed me a prayer book of his grandfather which was flaked with dried blood. It appears to me from President Pacheco's stories that the piety of the confraternities after the flagellation had been abandoned was both intense and thoroughly Catholic.

3. My information is based on one book, two articles, and several conversations, especially with President Pacheco. At dinner in his house one night, he introduced me to his sister (a psychiatrist) whose flaming red hair reminded me of some of the heroines of my novels. He told me that half of the children in his parents' family had such hair. Since I knew about red-haired Sephardic Jews in the past and something of the story of the *Sangre de Cristo*, I asked him what his mother's maiden name was. "Lopez," he said with a smile that indicated he understod the implication of my question. In a subsequent conversation he expressed (pleased) surprise that a community that he had taken for granted when he was growing up would be interesting to others. So perhaps it is with all the places from which we begin our journeys.

4. For the record, on the basis of my limited knowledge it stands at some distance on the Catholic side of the permeable border, which separates popular religion that is fundamentally Catholic from popular religion that ceases to be Catholic.

1

Introduction

I propose to develop in this book a sociological theory of religion. By theory I mean a set of propositions that generates hypotheses that can be tested against data, a model or provisional picture of reality that can be corrected when examined in the light of empirical findings, a perspective that can be kept in mind when exploring phenomena, a set of questions that can be asked when one is confronted with an unexplored data set. In the next two chapters I will consider first the classical theories of the sociology of religion and then drawing on them I will explicate my own theory. In the next two chapters (4 and 5) I will make a forced detour to consider the "secularization theory" that religion is declining, a theory that stands in the way of persuading sociologists that religion is still worth studying.

In the remaining chapters I will test my theory against empirical data. I do not propose to prove that my theory is "true," that it is the only or the best theory with which the sociologist can explore religion. I intend rather to suggest that it is useful in helping the sociologist to explore the complexities of human religion because it provides perspectives on religion that other theories might not provide.

I would rather not define religion now because in my experience a definition at the beginning of an investigation runs the risk of excluding phenomena that ought to be included and bogging down in endless bickering about the meaning of terms in the definition. It would be much better to investigate the phenomenon and then define it at the end of the investigation. We know what religious phenomena or near-religious phenomena are when we see them. Investigate the phenomena and then work out a definition.

While I am convinced that this is the way the human search for understanding actually operates, I doubt that I can get away with such an approach in this context. In most of my conversations with academics, particularly with fellow sociologists, definitions are demanded at the beginning—often with angry outbursts about all the harm religion has done to the world or to one's own personal life and arguments about whether everyone has or needs a religion or whether something like Marxism might be defined as a religion. It is demanded that I define religion up-front and answer such questions.

So, against my better judgment, I make my own the definition of religion proposed by Clifford Geertz in a lecture I heard in 1962, a definition that has the merit of having come at the end of his early investigations and hence being in part data driven and that, as he says in the published version of the lecture, establishes at least a useful "orientation, or reorientation of thought, such that an extended unpacking...can be an effective way of developing and controlling a novel line of inquiry."[1]

Therefore, Geertz's definition:

> A religion is a system of symbols which acts to establish powerful and long—lasting moods in men [sic] by formulating conceptions of a general order of existence and clothing conceptions with such an aura of factuality that the moods and motivations seem uniquely realistic.

Thirty years later, in addition to changing "men" to "humans" so that Professor Geertz and I might not be charged with being politically incorrect, I would make two changes to the definition. I would add the adjective *narrative* before symbols—perhaps unnecessarily since it is in the nature of a symbol to imply a story. Nonetheless, I want to make the story dimension of the definition explicit. I would also add to his explanation that religion enables humans to cope with joy and grace as well as suffering, injustice, and death—marriage and birth as well as sickness and death.

Geertz's definition may at first seem to finesse the question of whether a "transcendental referent" is required for a proper definition of religion: do you have to imply that God, should She[2] exist, is involved? But in fact I think that the words *uniquely realistic* are addressed to precisely that question. Whatever the images are that gives one an explanation of what life means and (as Geertz subsequently says) how one is to cope with injustice, suffering, and death (the last being the worst injustice and the ultimate suffering), they become unique in their "aura of factuality."

In the two chapters following this introduction, I will first discuss various contemporary theories of religion and then, in response to the classics, develop my own model in detail. Next, I will make a forced detour to consider the "secularization theory" that religion is declining, a theory that stands in the way of persuading sociologists that religion is still worth studying, and present an argument against the secularization approach from both the *terminus ad quem* and the *terminus a quo*. Finally, in the remaining chapters I will report how the use of religion as a poetic predictor variable opens up the possibility of deeper understanding of the effect of religion on human life, *an understanding based on empirical evidence that in the absence of the theory would have been harder to fashion.*

Notes

1. The paradigm in Professor Geertz's definition has influenced my thinking on the sociology of religion ever since and I am grateful to him for the orientation he has provided.
2. In my own religious heritage God is both male and female and neither male nor female and therefore may be pictured with either gender (or neither, though that is difficult for human imagination). Therefore, I reserve the right to describe Him as possessing either gender in the course of this book—as did Bernard, Anselm, Julian of Norwich, and Pope John Paul I.

2

Social Science Theories of Religion

Serious, critical, and nontheological reflection on religion has presumably gone on as long as there has been religion. But such reflection as a formal activity that preoccupied many thinkers and writers was a late nineteenth-century phenomenon. The men who engaged in such reflection, all of them brilliant and some of them geniuses, provided the raw materials out of which came contemporary social science.

One could divide them into two categories—those who sought to explain religion and those who sought to explain it away. Marx and Freud and perhaps Durkheim can be included in the latter category while Weber, Simmel, Otto, and especially William James belong in the former.

Many of them were concerned about the persistence of religion, its ability to survive despite the onslaught of science. Some, most notably Freud, thought religion would slowly disappear. Others, Durkheim for example, thought it would survive but with a very limited area of competence. Still others, Weber and Simmel, found it hard to imagine a world without religion.

Most of these men were at most agnostics, Freud and Marx atheists. Only William James asked a question which sociology (and his psychology) as such cannot answer: is religion true? James's answer in effect was, "I think so, but if you don't think so, I can't force you to agree with me."

The search for the meaning of religion in these classic thinkers (as interpreted and clarified by their contemporary disciples) continues to define the terms of sociology's attempt to understand religion. They are to be read, not because they were right, not because what they said is the last word, but because it is within the context of the questions they ask— perennial questions perhaps—that our search continues.

Opiate of the People: Karl Marx

Karl Marx (1818-1883) was a dialectical materialist; he combined the Hegelian notion that reality emerges from an endless series of contradictions with Ludwig Feuerbach's materialism, the belief that matter was the only and ultimate reality. Hegel was wrong, Marx argued, not about dialectics but about making the dialectic spiritual. The ultimate reality is not spirit (or Spirit) but matter. Political and social reality is shaped by struggles between social classes over control of the material means of production.

Since there is no such thing as spirit, religion must be an illusion, part of the "superstructure" of reality generated by underlying reality of the material substructure. It is one of the techniques that the ruling class (whoever controls the means of production) uses to keep the subject class under control. It is an opiate, a drug that immobilizes the subject class with the hope of a spiritual reward as a substitute for material possessions.

Marx was more than just a philosopher, however. He was also a messianic prophet who preached to the workers of the world the need to throw off the chains of oppression with which the bourgeoisie (the ruling class) had bound them. It was therefore not enough to reveal that religion was an illusion. Religion must be denounced as the enemy of the working class. To throw off its chains, the working class must dispose of religion. Hence the prophetic fervor of his attack on religion. Curiously enough his own Marxist philosophy would eventually become a quasi religion in its own right and Marx himself the Moses of the new faith. In a nice historical irony that faith was used in Eastern Europe to control the people; and, in its promise of an eventual materialist paradise, Marxism itself had become an opiate for the people, one that worked only when enforced at gunpoint.

Obviously, Marx was not completely wrong. Religion has often been a tool in the hands of rulers and a means for cowing people into submission. However, religion has also frequently been a motivating force for those people who feel that they are oppressed: the Fundamentalist Shiite Muslims in Iran, the new religious right in the United States, Solidarity in Poland, the civil rights movement in this country.

Marx owed his popularity to the incisiveness of his historical analysis, the toughness of his materialism, and the enthusiasm of his vision.

Precisely because he admitted only material reality, his doctrine was considered to be scientific; and precisely because of the seeming inevitability of the dialectic he described, those who followed his faith believed that they would triumph. They would "bury" capitalism as Nikita Khrushchev, Soviet party boss in the late 1950s and early 1960s, once boasted.

After the collapse of the Iron Curtain in 1990, the weaknesses of Marxism were revealed to everyone. But Marx's notion that religion was a means of social domination and control can stand alone and does not need the rest of his philosophical system to sustain it. Religion still seems to promise "Pie in the sky when you die" as a substitute for social justice while you are still alive. Much of the skepticism of many intellectuals about religion is based on an implicit Marxist premise: men and women would like to believe in God and therefore they do. In fact, however, these observers would say, religion is nothing more than wish fulfillment, and indeed wish fulfillment that blinds men and women to injustice.

This argument has appeal to some clergy, particularly Catholic clergy for whom liberation theology and "identification with the poor" is an effort to prove that there is more to religion than just spiritual promises and pious devotions. It may be that the last Marxist in the world will be a Catholic priest, perhaps even a Jesuit, and one with a tenured faculty appointment at a Catholic university.

Reading Marx's attack on religion as the opiate of the people (in his essay, "Contributions to the Critique of Hegel's Theory of Right"), one is struck by how "unscientific" it is by the standards of contemporary social science. He asserts but does not prove. He attacks but does not provide evidence. He argues fiercely but his arguments are aprioristic and deductive. If science requires the possibility of falsification for verification to become possible then Marx's comments on religion are hardly scientific. But the passion of his moral outrage can still stir the emotions.

Religion as Neurosis: Sigmund Freud

In a certain sense Freud and Marx are at the opposite ends of the argument about human suffering. Marx saw suffering as the result of the oppression of one social class by another. Freud (1856–1939) saw it as the result of unresolved childhood conflicts. Marx called for revolution,

Freud for psychoanalysis. Marx wanted the workers to throw off the chains of bourgeoisie oppression. Freud wanted the patient to throw off the domination of the neurotic superego. Marx exhorted his followers to social action, Freud prescribed long and painful self-examination.

But both were atheists, both were materialists, both rejected the spiritual, both believed that materialism was necessary for science and that their respective analyses were "scientific," indeed the only possible science. Both began movements that often have looked like substitute religions, even substitute churches. Both often looked and acted like the Moses of their new faiths. Both have had enormous influence on how men and women, including many who are anything but Marxists or Freudians, think about religion.

For Freud religion is essentially neurotic, a regression to childhood behavior patterns of guilt and dependency, based either on humankind's collective guilt about the murder of a father by the primal horde (in *Totem and Taboo*) or on the human need to transfer control of life to a father figure (as in *Moses and Monotheism*). Religion therefore reinforces the control of the superego—the childish self with its feelings of guilt—over the reality principle, the mature self. In the process of discharging guilt and breaking free of dependency, psychoanalysis should free a person from the religious illusion.

Freud no more proved the truth of this analysis of religion than Marx proved the truth of his analysis. The brilliance of his insight is taken to be sufficient proof, a posture that no responsible modern scientist could possibly accept. Yet it is certainly clear to both clinicians who must work everyday with the emotionally troubled and to ordinary people that religion is often the focus if not the cause of much neurosis, especially if religion is linked to conflicts with one's parents. God becomes the father, the Church becomes the mother, and guilt over one's failures to be what parents want one to be becomes the source of neurotic feelings of "sinfulness."

Some religious leaders often seem to be only too willing to become substitutes for parents and thus targets for neurotic guilt and anger. Just as Marx was entirely correct that religion often was (and is) a drug to narcotize the oppressed, so Freud was entirely correct that religious faith and fervor are often the result of guilt and dependency.

The question remains, however, of whether that is all religion does. Is religion ever radical instead of reactionary? Are religious men and women ever relatively free of neurosis? Freud never really bothered to try to respond to the latter question just as Marx never bothered to respond to the former question. For both men the questions never arose because on apriori grounds there was no point in asking them.

Religion as Society's Self-Worship: Emile Durkheim

Marxism and Freudianism in attenuated forms pervade the atmosphere of modern thought and shape, however implicitly, the response of many men and women to religion: it is an illusion, created either by the infrastructure of society (the means of production) or the superstructure of the self (the rigid, controlling superego). Emile Durkheim (1858–1917) is not so well known and certainly not so influential. But among sociologists who study religion, Durkheim is far more influential than either Marx or Freud. The latter two discuss religion in passing as part of their larger theories of the human condition and dismiss it as an illusion. Durkheim, however, made religion the central concern of his sociology and can be considered in many respects the founder of not only sociology of religion but also empirical sociology. In his book *Suicide* (1897) he begins with an empirical question: why are suicide rates lower for Catholics than for Protestants? His answer is that Catholicism as a community exerts stronger social control than does Protestantism. Catholic suicide rates are, by the way, still lower than Protestant rates, almost a century after Durkheim's analysis.

In his *Elementary Forms of the Religious Life* (1915) he considers the religion of the Australian aborigines and asks what role it plays in their lives. Durkheim's startling, original, and creative explanation of religion is that it is society worshiping itself as it experiences itself in the "effervescence"—the emotional enthusiasm of religious rituals. The experience of the ritual creates religion instead of vice versa.

Durkheim calls these rituals "collective representations" because in them the community becomes conscious of itself as a reality that transcends the personality of the individual members—as, for example, in a football pep rally. The energies released in such situations become or seem to become a reality distinct from that of the participants. When the rituals are religious—a Catholic Mass, a Jewish high holy day ceremony, a Protestant revival service—the celebrants encounter what seems to be a religious reality and assume that it is a "supernatural" figure. In fact they merely encounter society as a collective agent, generating enthusiasm and fervor. Thus, Durkheim says, worship of God is nothing more than society worshiping itself. Durkheim has had a tremendous impact on both sociologists and anthropologists. Religions with strong ritual systems have more control on the behavior of their members than do other religions. Thus, Eider (1992), in a study of elderly people, showed that those who practiced Catholicism or Judaism (as opposed to Protestantism) had better health and that Jews and Catholics even "postponed" their deaths until after their important religious festivals (Christmas and Easter, high holy days and Passover). Durkheim established beyond any possibility of doubt that ritual and imagery were of enormous religious importance and that to a very considerable extent they shaped religion and religious response.

Like Marx before him and Freud after him, Durkheim was ultimately a reductionist: in explaining religion he explained it away. Unlike Marx and Freud, however, Durkheim was not hostile to religion. Quite the contrary, he was perfectly prepared to see religion as useful and necessary. It could and should continue, though it should abandon the field of explanations about the world to science. He seemed unwilling to face the fact that those who, like himself, saw what religion really was—society's self-worship—would have an insidious effect on the faith of less sophisticated people. It is fair to say that religion as something more than ritual has survived despite Durkheim's analysis. While no serious social science student of religion today can ignore Durkheim's conclusions, there are relatively few who accept his analysis without considerable qualification.

The Function of Funerals: Bronislaw Malinowksi

Bronislaw Malinowski (1884-1942) was a Polish anthropologist who worked in the Tobriand Islands in South Pacific during the First World War. His approach to religion is "functionalism." He was not so much concerned with explaining religion as a global phenomenon as he was with describing the function of specific religious activities in society. His description of a funeral ritual is a classic in social research and could as easily be applied to a funeral service in a contemporary American church or synagogue as to a primitive people in Melanesia. The ritual reintegrates the social network after the trauma of loss and enables life to continue. Malinowski built on the work of Durkheim who also described funeral rites, though not so precisely or powerfully, but he did not fall into reductionism. The dangers of functionalism are that the analyst plays God, explaining what people are doing from the point of view of one who understands their "real" if unperceived motivations. In unskilled hands, functionalism can become supercilious and arrogant. However, Malinowksi was far too sophisticated to succumb to such a temptation. His "primitives" are more or less deliberately creating emotions that reintegrate society. Their ritual is not so much producing a "supernatural" that they can adore, but attempting to heal wounds in the social fabric.

The Irish wake—now infrequent in Ireland but persisting in somewhat more modest form in the United States—is a spectacular example of "mortuary ritual." The drinking and singing and dancing in the cottage where the dead body rests (described in the Dublin ballad "Tim Finnegan's Wake") to say nothing of the love making in the fields around the cottage were deliberate acts of defiance aimed at death. The social network was reintegrated by shouting at the top of one's lungs, "screw you, death!" It is one way to deal with grief.

Religion as a Feeling of Respect: Georg Simmel

The classic authors read so far were at best agnostic. They sought to explain religion by explaining it away. They began their research with the conviction that there was (probably) no supernatural reality and then explained how religion came to be. Ultimately religion was an illusion, though perhaps a necessary illusion.

Georg Simmel (1858–1918) was more of a believer than an unbeliever. He argues that religion grows out of a generalized piety, a respect for those on whom we are dependent. As creatures who need not exist and eventually will not exist, humans are not merely dependent on one another; they are dependent on forces far superior to them over which they have no control. The piety of a child for a parent, of a spouse for the other spouse, become the paradigms for piety toward these superior energies that are perceived to be at work in the cosmos. In Simmel's social-psychological view of religion, there is no need for spectacular collective rituals; finitude, a sense of dependency, and the resultant piety are enough to make humans wonder about and indeed hope for an ultimate power.

As to the issue of whether there is indeed an ultimate power, possibly one that is as loving as a tender spouse or generous parent, Simmel quite properly insists that sociology cannot answer that question. Is the impulse to piety with which humans are endowed a revelation by which the ultimate (arguably the Ultimate) reveals itself or is it merely a highly functional form of self-deception? That he distinguishes sharply between the sociological and the religious question (as would most sociologists today—in principle at any rate) shows that Simmel does not believe that explanations and answers to the first question automatically constrain a specific answer to the second question.

If his distinction between the two issues is accepted as valid, then sociology of religion can neither prove nor disprove the existence of an Ultimate Reality and hence can neither prove nor disprove the validity of religion or of any specific religion. It cannot defend religion in general or any specific religion nor can it, whatever the particular sociologists' personal beliefs are, prove that religious sentiments, experiences, and convictions are illusions.

Simmel hints that another set of criteria are required to address the religious question, criteria that may well concern the sociologist as a person but to which as sociologist he must respond with an agnostic shrug of the shoulders. Sociology as such simply does not provide the tools with which to essay an answer.

A Reply to Marx: Max Weber

Max Weber (1864–1920), according to most sociologists, is the giant who did more to shape contemporary sociology than any other of the founding geniuses. Much of his life's work was an implicit dialogue with Karl Marx in which Weber argued against materialistic determinism. His best known work *The Protestant Ethic and the Spirit of Capitalism* (1922) argues that while religion may be shaped by social institutions (such as the means of production), it also shapes them. The "work ethic" ("inner-worldly asceticism") is perhaps the result of capitalism but also shapes it. Capitalism is in part the product of a religious ethic.

There is much debate about what exactly Weber meant. Indeed the production of books purporting to explain Weber has become a cottage industry among sociologists. A number of conclusions about what Weber did not mean seem, however, to be generally accepted:

1. Weber did not believe that Protestantism caused capitalism. Something very much like the capitalist system of plowing profits back into the enterprise already existed in the medieval Italian city states.
2. He did not believe that all forms of Protestantism encouraged the "vocation" of the work ethic. Indeed the reformers themselves were diligent in their condemnation of greed.
3. He did not believe that religious affiliation still necessary correlated with the work ethic—though his evidence did show that there was more emphasis on education in the Protestant regions of Germany than in the Catholic.
4. He did not believe that without the Reformation, capitalism would not have emerged.

What did he mean?

Weber believed that there was an affinity between the kind of work habits that capitalism requires and the ethical emphasis of certain kinds of Protestantism, particularly Calvinism. This affinity created a situation in which those who possessed such an ethic would become leaders in the capitalist enterprise and to some extent shape its development. Eventually the ethic (which Weber did not like) would become so powerful and pervasive in capitalist society that it would no longer correlate with religion.

His analysis then is cautious, complex, and low-key. Marx said the economic organization of society shaped religion, that the latter was little more than an epiphenomenon. Weber did *not* reply that the truth was the other way around. Rather he replied that matters were more complicated and that both religion and economic organization were capable to some extent of shaping one another.

Such an analysis does not provide the sort of rallying cry around which revolutions are organized. But it does correspond to the gray, problematic nature of ordinary reality and to what a common sense answer would be to the question of whether religion shapes economic structure or economic structure shapes religion.

Weber's reply, in language much simpler than the heavy Teutonic academic rhetoric that he would have preferred, is that both are capable of influencing each other. It is an insight that seems so self-evident as to be trivial except that since Marx, millions of people have rejected it. Moreover, it completely recasts the issue of religion in modern society. In Weber's view religion was not merely the result of collective experiences of higher powers (though it surely could be that, too). Religion was also a road map which explained the meaning of life and provided directions for how men and women ought to live,It is fair to say that this understanding of religion has shaped sociology and the sociology of religion ever since. There are still reductionists, men and women who insist that religion is "nothing but...." However, after Max Weber that position is a difficult one to take.

Religion as a Search for Meaning: Talcott Parsons

Talcott Parsons (1902–1979), who taught at Harvard University for several decades, was the most influential American sociologist of his generation, due to both his books and his classroom work with many who later taught sociology in major American universities. He did his graduate work in Germany and studied Max Weber there. When he returned to the United States he translated some of Weber's writing into English. Using Weber as source and inspiration, he developed an elaborate theory of human social behavior as "purposive social action"—an approach that was directly antagonistic to materialism and determinism, especially of the Marxist variety.

His literary style was, alas, opaque and sometimes virtually unintelligible. His Marxist critics, especially during the 1960s, took glee in ridiculing and satirizing Parsons, whom they accused of underwriting the social order and of providing no room in his system for social change, to say nothing of revolution.

His essay on sociology of religion, written in 1944,does not suffer from heaviness of style (which students insisted did not affect his classroom lectures). Moreover, it foreshadows his later theory that human behavior is shaped to some considerable (though not total) extent by the meaning that humans attach to their lives. Humans, to anticipate Parsons's student Clifford Geertz, are interpreting animals. Their behavior depends on their interpretations.

The 1944 essay also neatly and deftly combines the work of the classic theorists with that of Weber to develop a theory of religion as providing an answer to the "problem of meaning." The "function" of religion is to give meaning to life—a notion with which most humans would have little trouble agreeing but which seems to have escaped the classic theorists.

If life needs explanation, if humans require meaning to shape their lives, then there will always be religion, if not for everyone then for most humans.

Parsons's brief synthesis has itself provided meaning for sociologists of religion ever since. While they have often been content to look at devotional statistics to see whether the influence of religion is waxing or waning, they cannot pretend finally that those are the important issues about religion. To study religion as a sociologist finally means to ask how religious meaning systems influence human behavior.

The "Holy": Rudolf Otto

The classic writers, for all their emphasis on experience in religious rituals, paid very little attention to religious experience as such. Even Geertz, whose theory of religion as a culture system is the most important work on the sociology of religion in the final half of this century and whose other work brilliantly analyzes religious experience (in Bali, for example), does not integrate into his theory a view on how experience shapes the symbols that explain the "real" or how these symbols in their turn shape further religious experiences. For the German theologian Rudolf Otto (1869–1937) the essence of religion was the experience of "The Holy" (The Idea of the Holy, 1958), the "totally other,"the "numinous" that was both fascinating and terrifying. Human beings are religious because they encounter, sometimes intensely, sometimes very gently, the numinous that both frightens them and fascinates them. Such experiences may occur in collective rituals, in relationships with others, or in personal and solitary encounters. Once one has encountered the "totally other," all questions about the value and validity of religion are swept aside. Nothing that is merely an illusion can be so intimidating and yet so attractive.

Otto neatly describes human ambivalence toward the sacred, which is both intimidating and appealing but from which humans cannot escape once they have encountered it.

For some people (about a third according to my research on such experiences in contemporary America), the experience is spectacular, time stands still, the whole cosmos rushes into the person and she/he perceives the unity of the cosmos and the person's place within it, she/he is filled with light and love and laughter and knows that everything will be "all right."

For others the experience is less spectacular but still powerful enough to confirm religious faith. Yet for still others the experiences of the numinous are so mild that they are hardly noticed.

Does everyone have at least mild experiences of the numinous? Perhaps not, but it seems safe to say that most people do. The question then arises as to whether this terrifying and intriguing totally other is real or merely a creation of the imagination and the needs of the one having the experience. The classic writers in varying degrees would be skeptical of such experiences. They would admit the power of the encounter with the numinous but suggest that there is no need to postulate an actual numen or Numen to account for the experience. Biological, psychological, and sociological dynamisms provide adequate explanations.

One would have a hard time winning an argument on that point with one who had been, for example, knocked off a horse by the numinous. Nonetheless, while sociology cannot accept on its own terms the existence of the totally other, neither can it prove that experiences of the numinous are either wish fulfillment or self-deception. An understanding of the dynamics of such experiences does not necessarily establish that there is not a Numen at work that chooses to reveal itself through such dynamics. To Otto, the sociologist must reply, perhaps, and then again, perhaps not. If she/he is wise and sensitive, however, the sociologist will not ridicule those who claim such experiences, but like Otto listen carefully to what they say and try to learn what kinds of people have such experiences and what impact they have on human life.

Voltaire said that man creates God in his own image and likeness. Perhaps it would be more accurate to say that humans create God in the image and likeness of the numen they have experienced.

The Pragmatics of Religion: William James

William James (1842–1910) may have been the most important thinker that the United States has ever produced. He surely was one of the most imaginative and creative. A physician, psychologist, and philosopher, his work has had tremendous if not always acknowledged impact on American life. His philosophy of pragmatism articulates in philosophical terms an important part of the national ethos. His brother was Henry James the novelist; and it has been said, with only some exaggeration, that Willy James was a psychologist who wrote like a novelist and Harry James was a novelist who wrote like a psychologist.

His classic work on religion is *The Varieties of Religious Experience* (1961). It was originally presented as the Gifford Lectures in Edinburgh in 1900. In the concluding chapter he asks the question of whether all the religious experiences he has considered in two years of lectures should be taken as a description of a reality beyond nature. In James we face a very different kind of mind than that of the other classic writers, not only because he is the most sympathetic to religion of any of them but also because the criteria he advances for possibly accepting religion are of an utterly different sort than would satisfy Durkheim, to say nothing of Marx or Freud.

The benefits of religion, he argues, enable one to break out of the trap in which the scholar finds himself, if not indeed as a social scientist, then as a philosopher and as a human being. To choose spiritual reality is the decision of most ordinary people and with what they think is good reason. Their decision ought to be taken seriously as a hint of what reality is like. If religion has a pragmatic payoff, would not the reason be that such is the nature of reality? In the payoff we discover the real.

It is not an argument that will convince everyone; and clearly James had no illusion that it would. Nor is it a social science argument as we understand social science today. But James's conclusion does show how one extremely gifted social scientist went beyond data analysis and tried to decide for himself what decision he should make (or long ago had made) about reality beyond ordinary human consciousness.

No one has improved on William James's *Varieties* as a description of the mystical experience. It is for him above all an experience of *knowing,* "noetic," in his term. Passive, transient, beyond description, it conveys powerful and exciting insights into what existence means. Such experiences do not by any means guarantee personal stability or mental health. They do not make a person easy to live with or a devout and regular church member. But they are nonetheless profoundly religious interludes in the basic sense of the word: religion explains what life means. James believed that something positive must be said about the mystic's knowledge. Neither mystics or nonmystics can claim a monopoly on truth. Both must listen to one another. The scientist must realize that it is possible that the mystic knows something about reality that is important in the search for truth even though the methods of science cannot attain it.

James is very "catholic" in the *Varieties.* He seems to revel in the fact that there are many different forms of knowledge, each of them with its own validity, and each with the responsibility to acknowledge the domain of the others. He concludes that while the mystic cannot constrain the nonmystic to agree with him, neither can the scientific skeptic claim rights to superior knowledge than the mystic possesses.

Curiously enough, contemporary sociology of religion pays little attention to William James. In the second half of the twentieth century it almost seems that "variety" no longer exists, especially in sociology and most especially in the sociology of religion. The journals abound in articles about small religious cults, about "secularization," and about the alleged rise or decline of religious devotion. Yet sociologists have paid very little attention to either William James (although the offices of Harvard University sociologists are in a building named after him) or the ecstatic component of religion.

The World as Pale Reflection: Mircea Eliade

Mircea Eliade, Romanian by birth as well as by young adult life, was a novelist, a mystic, a linguist, a diplomat, and perhaps the most brilliant student of the "history of religions" in the twentieth century. Unlike some of his predecessors (in a field that was for many years called "comparative religion"), he was not interested in either debunking Christianity or arguing that all religions were essentially the same. Unlike Joseph Campbell, he did not see a single hero with a thousand faces. Rather he saw many heroes with similar faces but very different stories. Jesus and Buddha are both saviors in a certain sense, but their stories are very different. Mary, Venus, Brigid, and Aurora are all spring goddesses, whose youthful faces and bodies represent the promise of new life. But their stories are very different. (Brigid was assimilated to Mary by the early Irish Christians who called her "Mary of the Gaels" and thought she was the mother of Jesus reincarnate). So there are many water ceremonies and they are all about life, but they tell different stories about the origins and meaning of life.

Among the many phenomena that impinge on human consciousness there are some that because of their enormous importance and power have usually been interpreted by humans as revealing in a special way the work of the deities—water, fire, sun, moon, food and drink, sex, birth, death. These realities become "sacraments," that is, hints of the gods at work, and around them humans build their rituals by which they join in the original creative activity of the gods. Thus, humans may plant their fields as part of a ritual dance and husband and wife may even make love in the fields to link their crops with the ultimate powers of fertility that "in that time" created the earth and its fertility.

Note that there is a certain "fiction," an act of "make-believe," a kind of "fantasy" at work in such sacrament making. The love making in the fields, for example, is an act of physical union between a man and a woman, indistinguishable in the act itself from other acts of love between them; that it represents in this particular case a link to the gods' life-giving actions depends on their "pretense" that it is a very special kind of sexual congress. Such a pretense may well make it special. The sacred tree is merely a tree. An outsider would think it is a tree like any other tree. But the members of the tribe "pretend" that it is the *axis mundi,* the link between heaven and earth, and thus make it special.

Such "pretense" is not an attempt to deceive. It is rather the investment of certain objects, events, and persons with a special interpretation. Myth making and sacrament making is interpretative behavior.

For Eliade this world was but a pale reflection of what happened *in illo tempore* ("in that very special time") and human religion is in substantial part an attempt to maintain contact with the Real that exists "in that time." In the present worldly time, we exist as if trapped in a labyrinth, cut off from the source of life. I felt for many years that Eliade's radical Platonism was more a metaphor than a statement of his literal belief. However, he autographed a copy of his autobiographical novel *The Forbidden Forest* for me with the words, "who is also trapped in the labyrinth."

It is not necessary to adopt Eliade's radical Platonism to learn from his vast erudition how the sacred can lurk everywhere.

Rational Choice Models

A more recent approach to the sociology of religion is the so-called "rational choice" model advocated, for example, by Iannacone (1991), Finke and Stark (1992), and Warner (1993). These theorists propose a model of "religious competition" to account for the fact that religion prospers in countries with religious pluralism (like the United States) and does not prosper in countries where there is either an established Church or a religious quasi-monopoly. The model, which Warner proposes as a replacement for the secularization model that he considers bankrupt, does not try to explain away religion but rather to explain why it is stronger in some parts of the world than in others.

The "rational choice" model, based on a convergence of concerns between economics and sociology, is used at the present time as a paradigm for the consideration of many traditional sociological problems. It will not serve my purpose in this book to address the controversy over the general use of a "rational choice" approach to sociology. Its great merit when applied to religion (and to the rationality of churches trying harder when they are forced to compete) is that it does not attempt to explain religion away but, forsaking the secularization ideology, address itself to a specific empirical question without prejudice based on the presumed disappearance of religion. John Durkin and I (1991) have also found it useful to explain why so many people invest in religion and in particular in the religion in which they were raised.

Nonetheless, while giving due credit to those who work with this paradigm for their contributions, my interests in this book are more in explaining what religion is than why some of its external forms flourish more in one country than in another.

Moreover, the "rational choice" theorists have failed to convince me that their model fits Ireland in which (in the twenty-six counties) there is indeed a quasi-monopoly on religion and yet high levels of religious practice. Moreover, research done on religious change in Ireland by Whelan (1994) and his colleagues gives little evidence of a decline of religious devotion in Ireland, despite dramatic changes in sexual attitudes and behaviors.

Conclusion

My theory of the sociology of religion, which I will propose in the next chapter, owes something to each one of the classic theories propounded in this chapter.

With Marx, I believe that religion is profoundly influenced by the social context in which the believer finds himself, including the context of his own religious heritage.

With Freud, I believe that religion is in substantial part shaped by the family of origin. My analyses will show that religious devotion is influenced by the devotion of the parents, particularly the father and by the quality of the relationship of the parents with the self and with each other and that relationships with parents substantially influence the narrative symbols, the religious stories with which one attempts to explain the meaning of life.

With Durkheim, I believe that the experience of the collectivity in ritual behavior has an enormous impact on religious faith and is one of the primary means of passing on religious heritages.

With Malinowski, I believe that religion is often the binding force that holds human communities together in times of crisis.

With Weber, I believe that religion provides values and meaning that shape human behavior in society as well as being shaped by society.

With Parsons and Geertz I believe that religion is essentially a meaning system.

With Simmel, Otto, and James I believe that religion takes its origin and its raw power from experiences—of respect, of the holy, and of the transcendent.

And with Eliade I believe that "triggers" for religious experience lurk everywhere—in the objects, events, and persons of everyday life, which can, on certain occasions, lead to experiences in which hope is renewed.

3

Religion as Poetry

In social science and mass media discourse, religion frequently seems to mean a religious institution or denomination and the doctrines for which that institution demands acceptance from its members, as in "Catholicism is in crisis because Catholics no longer accept the teachings of the Catholic Church."

Such an assertion is often made in news stories and television "specials" about the "Catholic crisis," a crisis which by definition must exist and which therefore in fact does exist even though the available evidence shows that ordinary Catholics don't feel any such crisis.

It is not my intent to reject the sociological study of religious institutions or religious dogmas. But the theory with which I am concerned in this book does not focus on such subjects. I am convinced that both institution and dogmas are derivative from religious heritages, though they are certainly necessary for the preservation of heritages. If I therefore pay little attention to the voluminous literature on religious institutions, the reason is not that I think that institutions are unimportant but that I am interested in that which is more primordial and more fundamental to religion—its poetry.

My model or paradigm is in fact a five-phase sketch of what might be called "religion-genesis"—the origins of religion in both an individual's life and in the history of a religious heritage. Religion, I propose, begins in *experiences* that renew hope, is encoded in the preconscious (creative intuition, poetic dimension, agent intellect, call it what one will), in *symbols,* shared with others in *stories,* which are told to and constitute a story-telling community, which enacts the stories in community *rituals.*

I describe this sketch as though it were a linear model but in fact it might be more helpfully viewed as a circle with five points on the circumference and influence lines running from each point to the other four points. Hope renewal experiences, logically the first step in the model, are in real life influenced and shaped by the religious heritage of the person who undergoes the experience, a heritage that includes overarching experiences (Sinai, Easter) as well as symbols, stories, community culture, and rituals (all of which could be lumped under the rubric "religious language" or "religious poetry"), which are the religious matrix that a person brings to a hope renewal experience and which impose interpretations on the event in the very act of experiencing it. There are no generic hope renewal experiences. On the contrary every experience contains its own interpretation.

Thus, the Sinai experience of the Hebrew peoples was interpreted in the religious vocabulary and the symbols that the peoples brought to that experience. Their religious language was transformed in the experience and their subsequent reflection on it, but the experience itself was not imposed on a blank slate. Perhaps one could say that they experienced the desert warrior God whom they had known before their encounter at Sinai (whatever that encounter might have been) but now they experienced Him as *their* God and that awareness transformed forever their religious language.

So too the apostles' experience with Jesus, who was dead and now alive again, was an experience of men steeped in the religious language, the religious poetry, of Second Temple Judaism and interpreted in the very experience itself in the poetry of that heritage, a poetry that was forever transformed by that experience. Their attempts to explain it afterward made use of all the rich imaginative resources of their own heritage (Adam, Moses, David, Suffering Servant, Son of Man, Anointed One) but put a new "spin" on the meaning of these resources. They used the same metaphors but with meanings drawn from the metaphors (whether legitimately or not is not relevant to this discussion) that had not been drawn from them before and that created new trajectories for the future use of the metaphors, trajectories that in the absence of their experience would probably have not emerged.[1]

Or in the case of an individual, if an experience of a woman or by a woman renews a person's hope because that person encounters the mother love of God, the encounter is shaped in the act of experiencing it by the religious metaphors that the person brings to the encounter, for example, the Madonna imagery of the Catholic heritage. So the person will use the metaphor from this tradition to describe to others and to herself what has happened, but in the act of using that description she will be possessed by resources of story, ritual, and community contained in the Madonna metaphor that she had not before perceived. The May crownings of her youth, for example, may mean both something different and something much more than they did at the time.[2] God *really* is like a woman holding a newborn babe in her arms. From that reinterpretation of the metaphor (which need not be formal or conscious or explicit), a new trajectory of meaning for both woman and God will take possession of the person's life.

The person may reflect on this experience and the insights contained in it and express these reflections in prose, perhaps even theological prose (as I did in my book *The Mary Myth*), because as a reflecting person, a person with intermittent needs to explain where and why one stands and to tell one's story in "rational" terms, such prosaic expression is often necessary and always useful—especially because it helps to formalize, to "lock in" the experience. Nonetheless, the experience is antecedent to the formal reflection—though of course not to past formal reflections which have helped to shape the person's religious personality (reflections perhaps on Mary as the "guarantee" of the humanity of Jesus).

Thus, I will describe my model in a linear format (almost as though it could be expressed in LISREL computer terms) because I do not know how else it can be described; the reader, however, must understand that in life it is circular rather than linear. Thus, it becomes sociological in the strict sense of the term and not merely psychological because it is shaped by and shapes the self's relationship with the objects, events, and persons of its life. It is out of the previous experiences of life and the inherited and acquired metaphors with which the person attempts to explain life that a new hope renewal experience is shaped and interpreted.

To some extent the model is a paradigm of assumptions borrowed piecemeal from other theorists (James, Otto, Weber, and Geertz most notably). It constitutes a perspective for examining religious phenomena and will be seen as a worthwhile perspective so long as it provides new questions and unexpected answers that otherwise would not have been asked or sought (a relationship between frequency of sex, for example, and image of God as a spouse). The links in the model are more postulated than proven; assumptions stated for heuristic purposes, rather than assertions subject to proof; propositions that might generate testable hypotheses rather than hypotheses themselves to be tested. However, the model itself can be subjected to some empirical testing should there be data available to examine the links that are postulated (as I will show in chapter 6).

An Experience that Renews Hope

Religion, I assume, is the result of two incurable diseases from which humankind suffers: life, from which we die; and hope, which hints that there might be more meaning to life than a termination in death. Humankind in the form in which we now know is the only being of which we are aware that is conscious of its own mortality and is capable of hoping that death is not the final fact in human life.

Thus, religion becomes possible when a being is conscious of the inevitability of its own death and becomes inevitable when the being has experiences that suggest that death does not have the final word. We know nothing about the consciousness of mortality among *Homo habilis* and *Homo erectus*. But our immediate predecessors in the human family tree, *Homo sapiens neanderthalensis,* had not only developed sufficient consciousness of death but also hope in immortality if we are to judge by their burial sites. Whether there was religion before them we cannot say. But there seems little doubt that religion existed among them.

Should there exist a species whose members know they must die and yet, for reasons of genetic hard wiring or soft wiring or cultural conditioning, have no experiences of hope, then that species would not create for itself a religion—and would probably not survive for long. There are few if any evolutionary advantages in despair.

The issue here is not whether every human hopes, much less whether, as Lionel Tiger (1979) suggested some years ago, there is a gene that creates hope even though the situation is hopeless. To explain religion, it is not necessary that *every* human have experiences that renew hope any more that it is necessary to contend that *every* human has a religion of some sort. It is enough merely to say that *most* humans have experiences that renew their hope, and therefore humankind has religion.

Hope, however, is not certainty. Certainty precludes religion just as despair does. Should there exist somewhere in the cosmos (or in other cosmos) a mortal being that has absolute certainty that it will be victorious over death, that being will not need religion either. Hope and therefore religion exist only in conditions of uncertainty, of possibility, of relative degrees of probability. Hope and hence religion emerge only when the data are inconclusive. Mortality, uncertainty, possibility—these form a triangle of factors out of which religion comes.

It is not necessary for the purposes of my model that the content of hope be specific. Hope can remain vague. It need not specify a God (who, as I will argue later, is a derivative and reflective hypothesis) nor an explicit conviction of personal survival. Hope may involve nothing more than an uncertain sense that things will get better or that tomorrow will be different, even when today is the last day of one's life.[3]

Hope therefore permeates the human condition and not merely the last day of life, though some of the research on dying and death suggests that it increases in intensity as life approaches its end.[4] Nonetheless, because the data are inconclusive and the outcome uncertain, hope wavers. Religion exists to confirm and reinforce and renew hope through its crises, major and minor, daily and lifelong. More precisely religion grows out of those experiences, major and minor, in which hope is confirmed, reinforced and renewed. Therefore, religion arises and continues because of the human propensity to experiences that renew hope.

I will assume that such experiences are common in the human condition and defer proof that they are common until a later chapter (when I examine some of the evidence about the links between the factors in my paradigm). My discussion of the dynamics of the hope renewal experience (which others call the "limit" experience or the "horizon" experience) is indebted to the work of Thomas Fawcett (1971) and David Tracy (1973).

By way of illustration: I am walking through the chaos of O'Hare International Airport a week before Christmas. The weather is terrible, flights are delayed, the crowds are irritable and impatient. No one is smiling, I least of all. I reflect that many of these Christmas travelers are moving about the planet because of an obligation that they cannot resist and that their tense, hasty visits are likely to be unsatisfactory both to them and those whom they are visiting. Humankind, I continued to reflect, is adept at folly. It turns arduous family festivals into situations in which it punishes those it loves. Old Qoheleth (a.k.a. Ecclesiastes) was right: all is vanity. This mob scene at O'Hare, a search for love, is, to quote him again, nothing more than chasing after the wind. As is the whole human enterprise. Why bother about anything, why bother about Christmas, especially why bother about Christmas?

Then, coming out of the American gates, in the midst of a particularly frantic troop of descendants of *Homo habilis,* I see a lovely young mother with a tiny infant in her arms. She is so proud of her child (blue means little boy, doesn't it, I ask myself), so determined to protect him, so overwhelmed by his wonder, that she seems oblivious to the crowds, the noise, the electricity of tension and frustrations in the airport. She is unable to restrain a radiant smile at him and the miracle that he is. I pause to revel in this snapshot of beauty and goodness. She notices my admiration and, mother-like, assuming that it is for her son, she smiles at me, as though I have joined her in admiration for her sleeping babe.

She disappears with the crowd and I go through the security check point, a Christmas carol in my head, a smile on my lips, and a sense that Qoheleth had it only half right at best and that neither Christmas nor life are merely an exercise in chasing after the wind.[5]

Some immediate comments before I analyze what has happened:

1. The smiling-mother-with-tiny-boy-child phenomenon is interpreted in the very act of experiencing it. Indeed an interpretation is waiting even before the experience because I carry around in my preconscious a Madonna model[6] waiting to be activated, especially at Christmas. My Madonna image is a sensor scanning for a corresponding reality.

2. While there is a preconscious interpretation waiting for the experience, the initial effect on me is unreflective. I do not try to get any meaning from it, not at least until later. Rather, I am absorbed by it, possessed by it, transformed (however temporarily) by it in the experience itself.

3. The experience itself is purely secular. It is not formally religious. It does not occur in church. It is a commonplace, utterly ordinary event. The statistical chances of encountering a young mother with a baby at O'Hare at Christmas are probably close to 100 percent. I am indeed inclined to experience such a renewal of hope by my own religious heritage and its repertory of vivid symbols, especially Christmas symbols. But Catholic Christianity has no monopoly either on mother goddesses or on wonder at the miracle of new life.

4. Because of the secularity of the experience, I need not be detained in subsequent reflection or in this book by the question of the sacred versus the profane which so concerns anthropologists. Every object, event, and person in life is potentially an occasion of hope renewal and hence potentially sacred. The secular or the profane—words which for my purposes mean the same thing—becomes sacred when it occasions

a hope renewal experience. Some realities may be more sacred than others in that they are especially disposed to occasion grace renewal experiences. On the other hand, for all its beauty and all its solemnity, a reality (like *San Pietro in Vaticano*), which seems especially designed to hint at something or someone beyond itself, may leave me cold, unimpressed, and perhaps less hopeful.

5. In the course of far too many ventures to O'Hare, I might have encountered hundreds of thousands of mothers with newborn children. The same woman with the same child may have earned no more than a passing glance any other day of my life. Today they occasioned a hope renewal experience, that is, a "religious" experience, though they might not have done so on any other day.

6. I experience the woman-and-child event as purely gratuitous (one might almost say "graceful"). It is a result of, as it seems, an improbable concatenation of contingent circumstances. She didn't have to be there. I didn't have to notice her. She didn't have to smile at me. It all "just happened." It was a "surprise." If I had reflected on the meaning of that surprise and the joy it has restored to my being as I was emptying the coins from my pockets into the tray at the checkpoint, I might have realized that I had spontaneously reacted to it with an emotion that contained the feeling that in a world in which such a surprise is possible there are still some reasons for celebrating Christmas.

7. I have deliberately chosen a small and low-key, though delightful, religious experience, one on which I might hardly reflect at all if I were not writing this book, to emphasize that there is a gradient in hope renewal experiences, from the very small to the very large about which William James wrote in his *Varieties*. As I will argue later it may be that the critical hope renewal experiences occur at major transitions in the life cycle.

8. In response to the sociological voice, which I have carried from many seminars into my head and hear and respond to often in this book, that insists, "you don't have to be religious to have that kind of experience," I reply that such is precisely my point. Of course you don't. The experience is not so much the result of religion (though a specific interpretation may be the result of one's heritage) as the cause of it.

Technically, my encounter with the Madonna of O'Hare is a disclosure. As Thomas Fawcett observes, a disclosure of any kind is only possible when something within a person's experience confronts him in such a way and at such a time that a response is invoked within him. The mob scene at O'Hare, the woman, the child are merely "things" that I might otherwise pass without any experience at all (other perhaps than Sartre's *la nausee*). The woman and child become a "sign" for me only when they produce a reaction in me at the level of emotion and imagination that seems to grant something new in my life, only in fact when they subtly infiltrate my consciousness and take it over, skillfully but violently, to transform that consciousness, almost it seems, without any willingness on my part for it to be transformed and perhaps against my stubborn determination that it not be transformed.

Fawcett sees three "moments" in such experiences: (1) the presence of an existential need (my Qoheleth-type mood); (2) the moment of disclosure or perception itself; and (3) the embodiment of the experience in symbolic form.

The Madonna of O'Hare and her child invade, unwanted and uninvited, and modify the structures of my perception, the linguistic models, the operating metaphors by which I explain to myself the everyday reality in which I am immersed and the ultimate reality that seems to lurk behind it. On that particular day I am interpreting the world around me with an ad hoc paradigm of which Qoheleth would be proud. It's all absurdity, vanity, chasing after the wind: foolish, anxious, angry people doing foolish, anxious, angry things in the name of a festival of joy and new life. What idiots we all are, what a sick joke life is, how absurd everything is. What purpose is there in a celebration? How ridiculous is that huge pagan *Tannenbaum*, how empty the carols. Will they ever stop playing *Adeste Fideles* and muttering "have a nice holiday!" In theory I may still believe that there is something more to be said about life, or I may have other metaphorical resources available to explain it to myself. But just now my dominant metaphor for life is the grim, nervous, unsmiling crowd at O'Hare.

Then, mother-and-child shatter my operating paradigms and demand that I consider other metaphors and integrate them into my structure of perceptions, perhaps despite my wishes in the matter. For a time my image of them becomes the dominant metaphor by which I explain life, particularly my life, to myself.

In his description of the phenomenon, Fawcett speaks of two phases, Descent and Ascent. In the former my existential need exists, I recognize the need, and feel "ontological anxiety." In the latter I encounter the occasion of grace (if I may call it that), I am seized and transformed by it, and I integrate the experience and the metaphor it represents into my personality (at least temporarily).[7]

Many, if not all,[8] of the objects, events, and persons of life may in the right time and the right place and for the right person occasion such an experience.

The "revelation" at O'Hare does not produce certainty. It does not eliminate anxiety or fear of death. It merely is a sign, a hint that there might be something more to life than my pessimism. In the religion-producing triangle, mortality and uncertainty remain, but there now seems a little more possibility, a tilt, as it were, in the direction of possibility. I am yet aware that I will die, that the lovely young woman will die, and eventually her child will die, too. Life goes on but lives end. I have experienced good all right, not unmixed with "un-good," but nonetheless still good. That is precisely where religion begins and what religion does.

In effect I have bumped up against the outer "limits" of my life, I have seen what appears to be its final "horizon," yet I sense, because of the wonder and surprise and the gratuitousness (gracefulness) of the woman's smile, that there might well be something beyond the limits, something lurking beyond the horizon, voices, perhaps rumors of angels, faintly audible beyond the wall I have encountered.[9] I am not altogether sure I hear the voices and I am perhaps inclined to doubt that I do hear them. On the other hand, I cannot be absolutely sure that I do not hear them. So I pause, as it were, to listen.[10]

My experience is not merely emotional because I am not merely an emotional being. I interpret it in the act of having it. I reintegrate (or permit to be reintegrated) my perceptive structures, which surely involve my intelligence, especially if I reflect on the experience after the fact. But the experience and its afterglow are not propositional or reflective. Rather they occur in that dimension of my knowing self, which is dominated by the free play of images, by that scanner within my personality that is constantly playing games of *bricolage* with images of past experiences—the creative intuition, the preconscious, the creative faculty, the metaphor maker, the poetic self. It is the need for metaphor, the openness to metaphor, and the irresistibility of the proper metaphor, especially when it crowds itself into my conscious, which constitute the genesis of religion.

In addition to the "sociological voice," which complains in my ear that it never has had such an experience (which I doubt) or that the experience is not religious (though the way I define religion it is),[11] there is also a "theological voice" which insists with grim determination that I am paying no attention to the doctrinal content of religion or, as Andrew Sullivan did in a review of an earlier version of this theory (Greeley 1982) in *The New Republic*, that without a cognitive system of belief there can be no religion. The voice continues to argue this position even though I have insisted that my theory does not exclude reflective religion but rather concentrates on examining the poetry that precedes reflection while of course admitting that previous reflections shaped my Madonna "sensor" that was operative at O'Hare and shape all my hope renewal experiences.

The theological voice wants doctrines, creeds, and moral obligations, and, more recently, obligations toward social activism and "concern for the poor." I reject none of these. I merely insist that experiences that renew hope are prior to and richer than propositional and ethical religion and provide the raw power for the latter.

Moreover, for most of human history there was little if any doctrinal and philosophical reflection on religious experience. As I shall contend in the next chapter, doctrinal convictions and devotional habits become necessary for a religious culture at a certain point in its development, but if they are to be of any use they must build on experiences that renew hope. Otherwise, those who propagate them may well become either bishops or full professors, but no one other than their colleagues will be listening to them.

Religion, either in the individual or in the heritage, then begins in experiences that renew hope. These images are stored in symbols.

Encoded in Symbols

Symbolic language, Fawcett (1971) tells us, attempts to

> reach out to grasp that which is not immediately known. Symbols do not denote things which are already understood, but attempt to…grasp the reality of things, the real nature of life, the stuff of existence itself…by taking images derived from the world of sense experience and using them to speak of that which transcends them. (29-30)

Humankind, according to G. E. Wright (1964: 163) "does not encounter the world directly." Rather, it "creates or has created a world of symbols through which he [sic] experiences, interprets, and perceives 'truth' in the objects, processes, people, nations and cultural heritage in the midst of which he lives."

If a sign is a reality that stands for another reality (a red light for the obligation to stop), a symbol is a reality that attempts to bestow meaning on another reality by recalling a person or an object or an event that provides that meaning (the Fourth of July ritual recalling the foundation experiences of our republic). To avoid a long discussion of symbolism, which would not serve the purpose of this essay, a symbol is a metaphor that is retained in the memory of either a heritage or a person because the experience it recalls gives (new) meaning[12] to the events of life. A religious symbol recalls some person or object or event that bestows ultimate meaning on life.

There are two kinds of symbols that correlate one with another; the first I call the primary symbol and the second the activating symbol. The Fourth of July symbol recalls with rich resonances of meaning—the Declaration of Independence, Liberty Hall, the Liberty Bell, Ben Franklin—the beginnings of our republic. A Fourth of July event, a potentially activating symbol, has greater or lesser importance in the life of an individual, depending perhaps on his existential needs to recall what America *really* means. Thus, the Madonna symbol in Catholic Christianity and the mother god symbol in most religions recalls (at the risk of trying to interpret the ineffable) the life-giving, life-nurturing love of the ultimate (or Ultimate). A particular image of mother-love, which flashes, perhaps briefly, across a person's consciousness (as did my Madonna of O'Hare), may activate—with all its comforting and reassuring power—the primary symbol, in this case Mary and her babe.

Note that after the encounter in which the (potentially) activating symbol does indeed correlate with the primary symbol, the former is integrated into the structure of the latter with the memory and resonances of the experience itself and the (however temporary) transformation of my perceptions and my consciousness that occurred at the time. Mary and the mother at O'Hare are assimilated one to another in what is now a more elaborate and more powerful symbolic paradigm and an even stronger sensor to scan for hope renewal at some future time of existential need. My memory of her smile, at the babe and at me, is not merely an ordinary memory to be stored on the hard disk of my brain, it has now become a memory that is stored in the subdirectory c:\memories\symbols\Madonnas. Assimilated to the pre-existing symbol of the Madonna, it recalls a hope renewal experience, gives a renewed meaning to my life, and disposes me for other hope renewal experiences. The experience has become a symbol.

Not everyone has a functional equivalent of a primary Madonna symbol lurking in their preconscious, the sociological voice says to me; for example, I haven't.

Many people do, I reply, and that's all that's necessary to make my point. Besides I'm not so sure that you can be part of our cultural system and not possess such a symbol, but I won't argue with you about it.

But what about the doctrine of the Immaculate Conception of Mary, says the theologian, or (if she/he be of the Left) Our Lady of Guadalupe as patroness of the poor and the oppressed.

I might, if I've had it with the theologian, say something like "gimme a break!" Or I might reply that one should revel in the illumination the symbol provides before trying to reduce it to prose.

What of the God symbol? Voltaire argued that humans create God in their own image and likeness. My theory would rephrase his epigram somewhat: humans create God in image and likeness of the goodness they encounter in their grace (or hope renewal) experiences. Since the moments of grace (like my encounter with the young mother at O'Hare) seem like pure gift, one begins to postulate a giver. God is therefore the agent to whom humans assign responsibility for their experiences of hope renewal, God is the author of grace. The symbol of God—a metaphor suggesting that someone is the giver—for most people is the central and primary religious symbol, the one in which all the metaphors are combined and into which all are projected. If I learn what your image of God is I may have a good indicator of what your religion is because your God symbol tells me the story of what you feel life is about, far more powerfully in fact than do your doctrinal convictions about God.[13]

If you claim that you do not believe in God, which is your privilege of course, then I must probe further to find out what image ties together all your ultimate metaphors for what life means.[14] But I find it difficult to believe that you do not have memories of experiences which become permanent metaphors that explain to you (still on the pre-propositional level of the personality) what life means and that these experiences and metaphors are not bound together by some privileged metaphor (and the experience it reflects).

Finally, I must insist that such phrases as "only a symbol" or "only poetry" are obsolete. If we were Cartesian ghosts in a machine or if we were disembodied angelic spirits,[15] pure ideas, devoid of emotional and imaginative resonances, would be the more satisfactory means of explaining reality and, should there be one, Reality. Even for the ghost and the angel, God-talk would still necessarily be metaphorical if prosaic. However, for humans, images that appeal to the senses as well as the mind are necessarily the most powerful and effective form of religious language, although as a reflecting being, a human must reflect on her/his images and experiences, if only to re-present them to her/himself and "harden" them in her/his personality by lifting them from the imagination and "freezing" them in the propositional memory.

Moreover, the experience that the symbol implies is shared with others in stories that are reflective, either in careful propositional narration (plot) or in carefully thought-out expansion of poetic imagery. Humans need both experience and reflection, both poetry and prose, both fiction and nonfiction.

Shared with Others in Stories

A story is an attempt to share with someone else an experience by activating in the imagination of the other a similar experience that the other has had. It seeks to tell the other about one's own experience, not by recounting to the other all the details so as to imitate as fully as possible a videotape replay, but by describing the strategic and significant details that remind the other of parallel experiences the other might have had. (It is irrelevant what kind of coat the young woman is wearing save when I decide—as in fact I did not in the above account—that the coat, which is cloth, not fur, is crucial to my narrative.) The skillful storyteller persuades the listener to identify with the protagonist of the story so that what happens to the protagonist reminds the listener of an event or a series of events in the latter's life. If the listener is constrained to murmur to her/himself, "I know what that experience is like because once something like that happened to me," the storyteller has been successful.

Thus, the fairy tale about Cinderella might recall, to the mind of one who is reading it, times in childhood when it seemed that parents were discriminating unfairly in favor of other siblings. The most common plot of all, "boy meets girl, boy loves girl, boy loses girl, boy finds girl again,"[16] appeals to the universal human experience of finding love, losing it, and (maybe) finding it again.

The storyteller is bent on doing more, however. Not only does she/he want to enthrall the listener by leading her/him into the world of the story and "hooking" her/him on it by stirring up in her/his imagination a recollection of a previous experience, she/he also wants to provide for the listener a touch of illumination (sometimes a very small touch) that offers to the listener the possibility of a return to the world beyond the story with an awareness of (perhaps only slightly) expanded possibilities for his own life. Maybe it is possible, for example, to find that girl again, even if you have been married to her for a quarter of a century.

Thus:

"Did you hear the story about the Yuppie who made a lot more money when he acquired a mistress as well as a wife?"

"How come?"

"After work his wife thought he was with his mistress and his mistress thought he was with his wife and actually he was in his office getting more work done!"

The listener is intrigued by the odd premise. There might, after all, be something to be said for having both a wife and a lover. But how could anyone, even a Yuppie, turn such a situation into a profit? The explanation makes fun of the success-crazed culture of the young urban professional, calls to mind the experience of being caught between work and family, and warns the listener of how badly such an obsession can pervert the joys and pleasures of human relationships.

The last paragraph is superfluous in most circumstances. The story does not need to be explained. The listener "gets it" immediately. In the circumstances of this essay, however, an explanation serves to illustrate how stories work.

Or:

"I had a fascinating experience at O'Hare this morning."

"Yeah?"

"I was really discouraged and pessimistic about Christmas and everything else."

"So what else is new? Why should you be different?"

"Then something happened."

"Yea? What?"

"I met a Madonna."

I could have streamlined the story and merely said, "A funny thing happened to me at O'Hare this morning: I met a Madonna." The effect would presumably have been the same. In either case, I probably would not have had to explain what happened. My listener would recall similar experiences of hope in life renewed by a new mother and a new child. He would know exactly what I meant without another word being said.

Moreover, stories illumine and renew not only the listener but the teller. When I tell the Yuppie story, I remind myself of the folly of work obsession; and when I tell the Madonna of O'Hare International story, I renew in myself the afterglow, as it were, of that religious experience.

Similarly:

"And the Prince and Snow White lived happily ever after."

Or:

"Michael Collins said to the British General, 'I'm not seven minutes late. You're seven centuries late.'"

Or:

"Abraham Lincoln freed the slaves, won the war, and then they killed him on Good Friday."

Or:

"Upon hearing that General U.S. Grant was drunk, the President asked what kind of whiskey he drank so he could send some of it to his other generals."

Or:

"Our father was a wandering Aramaean whom the Lord called into Egypt."

Or:

"He went before us with a pillar of cloud by day and a pillar of fire by night."

Or:

"A child is born to us in Bethlehem."

Or

"Jesus who was dead is alive."

Huge volumes of psychology or history or sociology or theology could not tell the stories so well—though the volumes are necessary too.

No one has ever denied the fascination of stories nor their ability to make a point. But until recently both preachers and professors, critics and columnists, literalists and lecturers have thought it essential to turn the stories into nonfiction as quickly as they can, either to explain the "point" of the story or to protect the unwary from thinking that the story has said all that needs to be said.

More recently, however, scholars from a wide variety of disciplines have come to believe that the story *is* the truth and that the exegesis of the story, however necessary it may be, invariably deprives the story not only of its wonder and its fascination but also of some of the resonances and nuances that lurk in the periphery and the penumbra of the tale.

We tell stories, it is now understood, to explain ourselves and our lives, first of all to ourselves and then to others. Story telling is humankind's primary meaning-bestowing activity. Without stories nothing makes sense.

This notion is extremely difficult to explain to the products of the American educational enterprise, (perhaps especially) including the products of Ph.D. granting institutions. Is not truth contained in the precise and measured sentences of the professional scientists? Are not clear and concise ideas the stepping stones to truth? Do not the messy and imprecise components of narrative—plot, character, atmosphere—risk inaccuracy, misunderstanding, self-deception?

But many of science's most fruitful terms are metaphors that tell stories: black holes, great attractors, big bangs, double helix, survival of the fittest, $E=MC^2$. Is not the closest thing to a paradigm that sociology has—the social mobility model of Robert Houser et al.—a story (and a very interesting one at that)?

There is a time, in other words, for precision and a time for narrative. The story provides the big picture; precision is necessary for the details. In the case of the social mobility model, the precision comes after the first story (children of rich parents have a greater chance of success than do the children of poor parents) and before the second story—or perhaps as the second story evolves (in the United States, a college education levels the playing field).

The French philosopher Paul Ricoeur has applied the same model to religious stories—critical analysis of the story intervened between the "first naiveté" ("Remember, O most gracious Virgin Mary...) and the "second naiveté" ("This morning at O'Hare I met a Madonna"/ "A mother's smile reminded me of the life-giving love of the Ultimate").

The most drastic and radical (and I believe the best) description of the power of story comes from what might at first seem an unlikely source—a cognitive psychologist who is an electrical engineer specializing in computer models for Artificial Intelligence. Professor Roger Shrank[17] (1990: 219) of Northwestern University puts it bluntly:

> People think in terms of stories. They understand the world in terms of stories they have already understood. New events or problems are understood by reference to old previously understood stories and explained to others by the use of stories. We understand personal problems and relationships between people through stories that typify those situations. We also understand just about everything else this way as well. Scientists have prototypical scientific success and failure stories that they use to help them with new problems. Historians have their favorite stories in terms of which they understand and explain the world. Stories are very basic to the human thinking process.

Understanding, then, does not proceed from the general to the particular, from the abstract to the concrete, from the theoretical to the practical. Rather, it proceeds from the particular to the particular, from story to story—with intermittent forays to the general and the abstract:

> The issue with respect to stories is this: we know them, find them, reconsider them, manipulate them, use them to understand the world and to operate in the world, adapt them to new purposes, tell them in new ways, and we invent them. We live in a world of stories. Our ability to utilize these stories in novel ways is a hallmark of what we consider to be intelligence. (Schank 1990: 241)

Schank also notes that it is the purpose of the story to forget as well as remember, to eliminate unnecessary details (okay, she was wearing a cloth coat but I don't remember the color and it's irrelevant anyway) so as to remember the telling details (she smiled at me!).

In Geertz's definition of religion, as I have said before, there is no mention of narrative. At the time he formulated the notion that religion is a system of symbols to explain the ultimate, the current understanding of the importance of story in the human condition had not yet developed. However, religious symbols (perhaps all symbols, but that is beyond the point of this essay) are inherently narrative. In the symbol of the Madonna that dwells in my preconscious there is an inchoate story— or rather many inchoate stories. I tell these stories to myself and to others to explain what life ultimately means. If I know your stories then I'll know how you explain life. If I ask you who you are, you will tell me where you come from, what you are doing now, and what the trajectory is for your future, immediate future most likely. If I ask you what your life means or why you are where you are now, there is a good chance you will tell me of some decisive event in your life, which has given it direction and purpose. Whether this decisive event (or these decisive events) is encoded in a formally religious story and whether you will not be too embarrassed to talk about ultimate meaning will depend on the circumstances. But the stories you tell about what endows your life with meaning are your religious stories, narratives about past hope renewal experiences, which in turn predispose you perhaps for future experiences of grace.

In Schank's (1991)[18] words:

> Human beings are naturally predisposed to hear, remember, and to tell stories. The problem—for teachers, parents, government leaders, friends, and computers—is to have more interesting stories to tell. (p. 248)

He might have added religious leaders and teachers (as well as lovers) to his litany of storytellers. Implicit in such an addition would be the understanding that his sentence could end, "Or more interesting ways to tell old stories."

Here then is the core of my theory, its very essence: Religion *is* story, story before it is anything else, story after it is everything else, story born from experience, coded in symbol, reinforced in the self, and shared with others to explain life and death. Religious stories—while they must be subjected to analysis and criticism because humans are analyzing and criticizing beings—are elemental religion, religion pure and simple, religion raw and primordial.

The important question is not whether the story is true (though in some religious heritages that is a legitimate question) but whether it is True,[19] that is, what explanation it offers for the meaning of human life and whether that explanation corresponds to one's own experiences of hope renewal. Nor does it suffice to dismiss something as "only a story." There is no such thing as a story that is only a story.

In its nuances and resonances, its shadings and allusions, its suggestions and its hints, its density and its ambiguities, its many levels and its multiplicity of messages, the story appeals to and discloses the total human person, soul and body, intelligence and senses, reason and intuition, reasoning and instinct—or whatever other metaphor you may wish to use to divide up the seeming duality of human knowing.

Precisely because of its multifaceted possibilities and the richness of potential interpretations, a story may have depths that are recognized only with time. Paul Ricoeur writes of the "meaning in front of the text" of a story, that meaning we may legitimately find in the story although the one who first told it and those who have repeated it through time have not been aware that such meaning lurks in the story. Thus, when I say that the Madonna story reflects the mother love of God, I am finding in the story a possibility that actually lurks there, but which I would not have recognized without knowledge of the history of religion and anthropology that was not available at earlier stages of the story's life.

Not every meaning can be claimed to be legitimately discovered "in front of the text." Thus, a claim that the Madonna story supports sacred prostitution (as did earlier stories of spring goddesses) would be an illegitimate violation of the text of her story.

For the social scientist who wants to study religion—not necessarily religious institutions—there is no escape from a study of religious stories, from the poetry of religion that antedates its prose. While I believe in a catholicity of disciplinary boundaries, I cannot see, at the present stage of our understanding of religion, how an enterprise that ignores the narrative dimensions of religion can define itself as sociology of religion.

In the language of the 1992 election campaign, "it's the *story*, stupid!"

Stories that are Told to and Constitute a Story-Telling Community

One does not tell a story to someone who is not likely to "get it." Thus, I would not tell the following story to someone who does not know that Quakers are also called "Friends":

> A Rabbi in Washington complained that since Chelsea Clinton had enrolled at a Quaker school in the city, that school had become fashionable for many of the members of his temple. "Some of my best Jews," he lamented, "are Friends."

The nuances and resonances of that pun need not detain us. Rather, the point, for my present purposes, is that a person who does not know that the formal name of the Quakers is "Society of Friends" is doomed to miss the joke. Such a person is excluded from my story-telling community.

Similarly, I would not say, "Today at O'Hare I met a Madonna" to a Fundamentalist or Evangelical acquaintance. While the mother-and-child image is an important component of Western religious culture, it might be too much for him to absorb, given the differences between our religious cultures, especially on the subject of the proper place in the Christian heritage of Mary the mother of Jesus. He might well know what I mean and might be tolerant of my mode of expression. Or again he might not. He could misunderstand me and think that I had encountered the pop singer (arguably in one of her advanced stages of undress!). Since we feel vulnerable (at least in most circumstances in our culture) when we tell religious stories, I would more likely—should I want to talk to him at all about my experience —describe it in more prosaic fashion. I would, however, feel much more at ease in describing the wonder of my experience to a person, or better a group of persons, who would know what I meant.

Such a group would not necessarily be Catholic. Thus, I could describe the experience to my colleague Martin Marty with serene confidence that he would "get" my story. On the other hand, I would not want to share my story in cryptic symbolic language with a Catholic who thought that the Mary symbol was excess baggage in an ecumenical age or a nun theologian (such as Sister Elizabeth Johnson) who thought a male priest had no right to use feminine images.

One picks one's story-telling community carefully, particularly if the story to be told is a religious story. The story is too precious to be wasted on those who are so insensitive to the imagery that they cannot comprehend it or so hostile to the storyteller that they cannot permit themselves to recall parallel experiences or to those who are so caught up in ideology that they must search a story for signs of absence of a politically correct storyteller. Indeed, the prospect of recounting the experience to a listener or a group of listeners who will understand ("get it") is perhaps on the periphery of consciousness in the very act of experiencing hope renewal, just as a travel experience is enhanced by the prospect of recounting it to those back home when the trip is over.

Religious heritages constitute story-telling communities or perhaps, in the case of a heritage as multifaceted as Catholic Christianity or Islam, a congeries of storytelling communities. They are at root a group of humans who share a common repertory of symbols and a sufficiently common interpretation of these symbols so that it is relatively easy to tell them the story and relatively reasonable to expect that they will "get it"; that is, when they hear my story, memories of parallel experiences in their reservoir of memories will be readily activated.

Religious story-telling communities may become much more with the passage of time, indeed grow into massive worldwide bureaucracies. But in essence they remain groups of people who one can expect will understand one's stories. Thus, the early preachers of the Jesus movement could expect that those to whom they offered comparisons of Jesus with Adam, Abraham, Moses, and David would know what they were talking about; and they would not use those comparisons when speaking to gentiles for whom the metaphors would be so much gibberish.

The stories are told to the community and it is the common storehouse of stories that constitute the community. Catholicism (or Islam) is the aggregation of people who can be expected to understand Catholic (or Islamic) stories.

Moreover, the story-telling community also can correct you if you get the story wrong. Thus, when the child says (often in outrage), "You didn't tell it right," she is objecting to the fact not that the story has been told differently but that it is has been told in such a way that it has no resemblance to the story she knows and about which she feels confident and protective.[20] On the other hand, when the kid hears a story told differently and announces, "I *like* the story when you tell it that way," she is testifying that in her judgment the story fits the paradigm as she comprehends it.[21] She is saying in effect that the second version of the story is orthodox and the first is not.

If Ms. Marple doesn't solve the crime, her fans rise in protest: the story has been violated; there is no room in the story-telling community for such violation.

The story-telling community therefore develops its own methods for determining which versions of a story are acceptable and which are not. It is indeed the nature of the community that it should do this. When in certain stages of development a group within the community claims the right to make this judgment, it is not thereby excused completely from listening to what the rest of the community thinks of a new version of the story.

A Jewish group that changes the ritual of the Seder so that it can hardly be recognized (*per absurdum*, "next year in New York" or "next year in Dublin") can hardly be expected to be taken seriously. Nor if I were to report that my lovely Madonna of O'Hare shouted curses at all male chauvinists could I expect instant approval from the rest of my story-telling community, to say nothing of that group (bishops) that claims to constitute the "magisterium."[22.] The story-telling community, therefore, in the nature of things is both an audience and a critic of one's story. Or to put the matter more precisely, perhaps, the story-telling community is a critical audience.

The story-telling community also introduces a distinctively sociological component into my model. The poetry of religion is group culture, not merely individual psychology. It is in the story-telling community that one first hears the stories and it is as a member of the story-telling community[23] that one uses the stories as prisms through which life can be viewed and as templates that guide and shape one's responses to the problems and tragedies of life—as well as its hopes and joys. It is in the story-telling community that one learns how to correlate one's own personal experiences and stories about them with the overarching experiences and stories that constitute the religious heritage of which the community is the custodian.

Stories are told by the family, by the local community, by friends and lovers, by neighbors and relatives, by teachers and clergy persons, sometimes in community rituals, more often perhaps outside of the ritual context but with a nod in its direction, sometimes formally, more often informally, sometimes by explicit words, more often implicitly by the way the relevant storyteller leads the life of the story in his personal behavior and relationships with others.

The research evidence, to which I will turn in a later chapter, suggests that there are two key relationships that are situations *par excellence* of religious "socialization," of passing on the story-telling tradition—the family of origin and the family (so-called) of procreation. Parents and spouses are the primary religious socializers. They tell the stories in what they say, in what they do, and in who they are for the child or for the beloved. In answer to the question of where the stories come from, one replies that they come from the heritage, from the community that has custody of the heritage, and especially from parents and spouse. The same stories can be heard differently depending on the kind of person the intimate storyteller is and the quality of that relationship. The implications of these differences for a person's religious life and hence for his whole life are enormous. If a relationship is punitive or loveless, the story told in the context of that relationship will tend to be rigid and vindictive. For someone whose two socialization relationships were harsh (harsh parents and/or harsh wife), my claim that I encountered a Madonna at O'Hare is likely to conjure memories of a cold and punitive mother or an unresponsive wife or a list of negative rules about sexual morality or rigid silence in the school yard after the bell has rung or a deity who is more concerned with justice than mercy or finally, as Michael Carroll observes (1992), a wicked womanly power who demands penances such as self-flagellation in her honor. Such a person will not want to listen to my story. Moreover, while he may still have some claim to be a member of the story-telling community because he "gets" part of the story, he understands the story only in a fatefully incomplete version.[24]

The Stories in Community Rituals

Community rituals—stories in drama form, poetry in motion—are crucial to the handing on of stories, especially in the context of participation in the rituals with the intimate other (parent or spouse). Thus, a mother takes the child over to see the crib newly erected under their Christmas tree,[25] a drama that the child loves because it has everything: a mommy, a daddy, little kids, angels, animals (sorry, no dinosaurs), shepherds, wise men in funny clothes (multicultural wise men at that), and all at Christmas time.

"Who is the baby?" she demands.

"That's Jesus."

"Who's Jesus?"

Her mother hesitates, wrestling with theological issues still perhaps unresolved in her own mind.

"Jesus is God."

"Oh."

The kid has no problem. Everyone was a baby once, why not God as baby?

"And who's the lady holding the baby?"

"That's Mary."

"Who's Mary?"

The mother hesitates again, not too sure about the proper rules of the "communication of idioms."

"Well, she's God's mommy."

"Oh!"

The kid has no problem with that at all. In her experience everyone has a mommy, why not God too?

In later years it will be only a small narrative step for her to understand that God loves like a mommy as well as like a daddy.[26]

It would be an interesting research question to study how much of the Christian heritage is transmitted to the very young at Christmas time and how much of the Jewish heritage is transmitted at the Seder. Or to put the same question in a different perspective, how much of the bonding of a young person into a religious community is accomplished at festivals in which the young person is given a major role to play—inspecting the crib scene in Catholic Christianity or reciting the narrative at the Passover dinner. After both events the child has much yet to learn about the heritage, but may also have learned everything that is important to belong to the heritage.

Durkheim was right when he saw the "effervescence" of a ritual experience as essential to the religious enterprise. The little girl at the crib scene, the boy telling the story of the escape of the Israelites from Egypt, are indeed exhilarated by the experience as are the other members of the family. The bonds of the community are strengthened by this experience. The child becomes conscious for the first time of these bonds and the adult becomes aware of them again, recalls his early bonding experiences, and feels the bonds being strengthened and renewed. While it does not follow that either child or parent thinks that the effervescence *is* God, it may well be that in the experience they become aware of the presence of a giver of good things.

I make no claim that these phenomena are self-conscious or explicit or that everyone experiences them with the same intensity. Moreover, I am prepared to admit that there are those who have no such experiences at all. Some may be only loosely tied to story-telling communities and others may belong to no such community—or feel they do not belong. Some may have lived childhoods that were innocent of religious ritual and festival. Some may have only unpleasant memories of those in which they were once forced to participate. Some may react with hostility and anger at what they think were the superstition and falsehood of such rituals. As I have said repeatedly (in response to the insistently agnostic sociology voice I hear) I make no claim that religion happens to everyone. What I have described in the previous paragraphs is a model that is part of a larger model, a Weberian "ideal type," variations around which are a legitimate subject of inquiry. The story-telling, ritual-enacting community is a context in which only some lives are lead and even among those lives there are variations in the intensity of the impact of the rituals and the stories. The confirmation experience (or the Bar Mitzvah) for two boys, perhaps cousins, may seem the same externally but for one it may be a major turning point, a critical rite of passage, in his life while for the other it may be merely a social occasion in which one collects gifts and is the center of attention at the party.

My point is modest: for some people some kind of story-telling and ritual-enacting community does exist and for those, to some extent, the community, its stories, and its rituals are an important part of their quest for meaning because the community and its festivities become an arena in which their hope renewal experiences may be safely recounted, reinforced, and confirmed.

I have deliberately chosen for my examples "small-screen" rituals—the visit to the crib and the Seder meal—because they are at the other end of a continuum of effervescence from Durkheim's exuberant festivals among the Australian aborigines. To be effective, rituals need not take place in a church or in large public gatherings. They can exercise their proper function—reenacting the central stories of the heritage and redefining the nature of the community in which the heritage is embodied—in small, quiet, almost private ceremonies. Often sociologists seem to want to limit the ritual to the great public ceremony, the "collective re-presentation" that Durkheim describes. But in fact, most rituals, religious and nonreligious, are much less grandiose. At an anniversary dinner enjoyed each year at the same restaurant or during a weekend spent occasionally at the same hotel, a married couple may re-present to one another the experience of their marriage and their early love and thus renew their hope in the relationship and renew its vitality (a renewal that may or may not also be religious, depending on the couple). Or a visit to a cemetery may keep alive a memory that is also a hope. A fiftieth reunion of a grammar school graduation class may recall youth and perhaps promise that youth is never totally lost. While none of these private rituals are explicitly religious they can easily become religious. Just as the small-screen, private, nonreligious (but potentially religious) ritual is often deeply moving, so the small-screen and explicitly religious ritual is surely more common and perhaps more effective than the solemn high liturgy, though both have their place in re-presenting the story that binds the community together.

In the Catholic and Jewish traditions, rituals tied to the seasons of the year keep alive the nature of religious rituals of sacred times. Christmas and Passover experiences, which I have described previously, are feasts of sacred time, interludes in the cycle of seasons in which grace is likely to be encountered, hope especially likely to be renewed. These festivals are still important to Jews and Catholics as Ellen Eider (1992) demonstrated in her research on elderly people: Catholics and Jews (but not Protestants) "delay" their deaths until after the celebration of festivals. Catholics, and Jews (to some extent), also have their sacred places, locales in which hope renewal experiences are especially likely to occur. That Protestants are not affected by sacred time in Eider's research should not be surprising. In part the Reformation was a reaction to what was taken to be Catholic superstitions about sacred time and place.[27] In order to purify religion it was thought that it was necessary to desanctify nature, the cycle of the seasons, and to some extent the house of worship. But in the United States secular festivals of Protestant origin—Thanksgiving, Decoration (later Memorial) Day, Armistice Day, Mother's Day—all assume quasi-sacred status; Christmas has become part of the Protestant calendar; and the festival of St. Valentine (stricken from the Catholic calendar because there was no historical evidence for the saint's existence) has become for all Americans the feast of romantic love, though a feast with little of its sacred content left.[28] However, Eider's work suggests that the sacred calendar still means less to Protestants than it does to Catholics and Jews.

While some religions may be more conscious of the importance of ritual than others, ritual seems to be an essential part of the human religious condition. Ritual is a drama that reenacts the primal events that launched a religious heritage and give it meaning. Moreover, ritual not only recalls the primordial experience, makes it available once again, and correlates it with the personal experiences of the members of the community, it also may generate new experiences of grace in the community members, beginning the cycle of experience, symbol, story, and community all over again.

Two Additions to the Theory

There are two tools that have proven useful in the development and testing of my theory: the distinction between the popular tradition and the high tradition; and the comparison of the Analogical and Dialectical Imaginations.

A heritage contains many different versions of its story; it is convenient for my purposes to group them (or most of them) under the headings of the poetic and the prose traditions or the popular and the high traditions. The former is the tradition of experience and story, the latter the tradition of catechism and creed. The former may be relatively unreflective or may have been subjected to reflection between the first and the second naiveté. It is the tradition that shapes the worldview of ordinary people, has a logic and structure of its own, and at various times and places may have only a tenuous connection with the high tradition—often because only a tenuous connection is either possible or necessary (in the era, for example, when most Christians were illiterate peasants living in isolated villages).

The latter is the version of the story told by religious adepts, leaders, thinkers, teachers, philosophers, and theologians. It is systematic, rationalized (given its first principles), elaborate, detailed, reflective, precise, prosaic, and formal. It may often be boring but it is necessary and not merely a necessary evil, necessary because humans must reflect on their experiences and find (what seem to be) rational grounds for accepting them. It is also necessary so that some group of deputized decision makers within the community have final authority to determine whether a given version of the story is truly compatible with the heritage. To put the matter somewhat differently, the two traditions must critique one another; the popular tradition will critique the high tradition for what often seems its bloodlessness and arid rationality, and the high tradition will critique the popular tradition for its wildness, its unrestrained emotion, its transient and self-deceiving enthusiasm. Without the watchful guidance of the high tradition, the popular tradition may slip over the boundaries that separate religion from magic; in the absence of the energy and vitality of the popular tradition, the high tradition will find itself talking to empty churches or meeting houses.

The various titles which Catholic theologians attribute to the Mother of Jesus may mean something to them but rather little to the ordinary folk who have very clear memories of the May crownings of their youth. But without the theologians the May crownings could degenerate into superstition and without the May crowning (and similar devotions) the theses of the theologians would become arid and, to everyone else, dull.

While my emphasis in this book is on the poetry of the popular tradition, I am well aware of its limitations, as a next chapter on the religion of the Middle Ages will demonstrate.

I distinguish between the popular tradition and folk religion (and hence try to avoid the use of the confusing term "popular religion"). Folk religion is a mixture of the stories of a religious tradition with stories of pre-existing animistic or magical traditions, a blending of which the elaborately poetic traditions, like Catholicism or Hinduism, seem especially prone, but from which no tradition of any of the world religions is immune. In the absence of effective conversation between the high tradition and the popular tradition, folk religion is inevitable.

Moreover, it is one of the primal insights of the sociological tradition that Catholics are different—or at least were different at the times when Durkheim noted the lower Catholic suicide rates and Weber observed the lower advanced school attendance rates. Catholics seemed then to be more "communal" than Protestants who were more likely to emphasize individual freedom in religious matters. In fact, the more accurate way of putting the matter might have been that Protestants were different, since religious individualism was an innovation that the Reformation introduced into the human condition.

Whether these differences persist is a matter of some debate. Some sociologists see Catholics becoming "just like everyone else" (for example, Alwin 1986). Some Catholic leaders lament that American Catholics are indistinguishable from other Americans, meaning that their sexual values and behavior are not distinctively Catholic.[29] It remains to be seen, however, whether the different emphases reported at the beginning of this century by the founders of sociology have truly disappeared.

David Tracy (1981), in his study of the "classics" of the Protestant and Catholic heritages, has described differences in the Catholic and Protestant imaginations which I will use as auxiliary tools for my theory. Catholicism tends to be more mystical, Protestantism more prophetic; Catholicism tends to emphasize the manifestation of God's goodness, Protestantism tends to emphasize the proclamation of God's judgment. Catholicism tends to emphasize God's presence in the world, Protestantism tends to emphasize His absence from the world. Catholicism tends to use a liberal metaphor to describe God ("God is like…"), while Protestantism is wary of the abuse that metaphor can cause (God is *not* like…). Hence, Catholicism indulges in such religious artifacts as angels, saints, holy souls, Mary the Mother of Jesus, stained glass windows, statues, elaborate processions, ornate vestments, holy water, votive candles, and all the other devotions and practices that the classical Reformation theory abhorred as idolatry.

Tracy calls the Catholic imagination "Analogical" and the Protestant imagination "Dialectical" because the former says "God is like..." and the latter says "God is *not* like...." Neither style, he contends, is better than the other. Both are part of the Christian heritage and essential to it. Neither heritage has a monopoly on its own style. In individual members both styles may well be combined. But there is a different emphasis nonetheless on the way God, world, human nature, and human community are pictured in the two religious imaginations. In applying my theory of the poetry of religion I will keep open the possibility that Catholics may still have more vivid religious imagery and that the Catholic heritage may well be what has been called a rain forest of metaphors. Certainly Eider's research on the elderly suggests that the religious imaginations of Catholics and Protestants may still be different.

Specifications

In social research there is always a big jump from articulating a theory of the middle range (one that is designed to be tested by data) to specifying a hypothesis that will in fact test the theory and then finding or creating measures that will operationalize the hypotheses. In later chapters I will describe the admittedly imperfect measures so far developed to capture the quality of a respondent's religious imagination—imperfect indeed but nonetheless effective predictors.

If the theory of religion as poetry is correct, however, one would expect that the more benign a religious story (the more hopeful it is about purpose in human life and a purposeful cosmos), the more benign will be the other stories in a person's life. One would not expect someone with gracious images of God, for example, to be a racist or a bigot. One would expect such a person to be more tolerant of the imperfections of others whether it be the intimate other (a spouse or a child) or a distant other (a condemned criminal or an AIDS victim, for example). Further, one would not expect someone with a benign religious story to be repressive in attitudes toward those who are different and one would expect a benign religious story to correlate with social concern for the poor and the oppressed. One would not expect someone who relates to a gracious God to be harsh and self-righteous in moral judgments and one would expect such a person to be supportive of human sexual love.

These expectations do not predict strong correlations; in sociology high correlations are rare. One merely expects statistically significant correlations and/or differences to make some difference in human attitudes and behaviors.[30]

Minimally, I would expect religious stories to be stronger predictors of attitudes and behaviors than other religious measures such as religious affiliation or church attendance.[31]

Conclusion

The basic premise of my theory is that religion is the story[32] (of God) we tell to ourselves and others to explain what our life means. The basic expectation of my theory is that religious stories will be predictive of other stories. Our relationship to the Other will be predictive of our relationships to others, both intimate and distant. Our religious stories will correlate with and be filtered through our familial, political, social, artistic, and common sense stories. The correlations will not be large because in social science no correlations are all that big and because other events and stories will intervene between religion and the rest of life. But if religion is to be a useful predictor variable in social research, the best way to measure it will be to measure religious stories and not doctrinal convictions or church attendance.

Modestly I ask little more of my fellow sociologists than that when they think about religion they keep the poetic dimension of religion, the religious imagination, in mind. I ask the same thing of theologians and teachers of religion.[33] Because that is precisely all that useful theory does. It provides certain perspectives that ought not to be overlooked by the sensible investigator. My request of colleagues may not be all that modest, as I will observe in my final chapter.

I intend to demonstrate in later chapters the kind of research questions one might ask and insights one might obtain from research analysis if one keeps the poetic dimension of religion in mind. Before that, however, I must turn to the "secularization" hypothesis, which stands over the sociology of religion like a brooding and, in my judgment, evil giant who forecloses serious discussion of the poetry of religion before it can begin.

Notes

1. Thus, it would appear that in response to the question of whether Jesus was the "Messias" the answer is that he was, but in none of the senses of the word that Second Temple Jews had used before the emergence of the Jesus movement; rather he was the Messias in the sense of the word that the Jesus movement developed out of their experience at Easter. That the word has a different meaning for the two heritages means that any discussion on the subject between the two is almost certain to collapse If the Jesus question is to be resolved between Jews and Christians, the use of this word should perhaps be bracketed and some other focus found.
2. Here I am alluding to Paul Ricoeur's "meaning in front of the text."
3. Hope is often dismissed by hard-headed unbelievers as "wish fulfillment," a will to believe that there are grounds for hope when in fact there are none. But the fact that we would be much happier if there were grounds for hope neither proves that such grounds exist nor that they do not exist. The data remain inclonclusive.
4. Can hope be completely extirpated from human consciousness by those who believe that there are absolutely no reasons for hope? Perhaps. Once again, however, I am not making a case for the universality of hope, only its commonality.
5. By choosing an "ordinary" religious experience, I wish to exclude but not slight the importance of mystical and shamanistic experiences. I am not persuaded as some scholars (Ginzburg for example) that shamanism accounts for the origin of religions. The shaman or the mystic obviously has every reason to believe. But I fail to see how he could sell his faith to others unless they also had lesser but sufficient religious experiences.
6. Formed from, among other things, paintings, sculptures, songs, festivals, devotions, liturgical celebrations, hymns, and stories—to bring all the other elements of my theory into play.
7. I find Fawcett's description of the experience a useful one. But it is not essential to my theory. A reader who knows a phenomenology that seems more satisfactory is welcome to use it.
8. The novelist George Bernanos ends his *Diary of a Country Priest* with the observation from the priest that everything is grace. The Catholic theologian Karl Rahner said that in order for some events and objects to be Sacraments (metaphors that occasion grace) everything must be a sacrament. Even those objects, events, and persons that seem especially sacramental—water, fire, light, darkness, food and drink, the body of the beloved, spring, autumn, birth, death— can become the occasions of hope renewal only when they combine with an existential need and awareness of that need for a transformation of the linguistic structures of one's perceptions. Grace, in other words, is not of much use to a given person unless she/he encounters it at just the right time.
9. There are of course other kinds of limit experiences—encounters with scientific order and with moral imperatives, for example. Tracy discusses them at great length. For the purposes of this study, however, it is enough to illustrate what I take to be the most common of such experiences.
10. Note that the terms "horizon," "limit," and "wall" are all metaphorical.
11. The sociological voice equates religion with institution and with God, and, generally, perhaps for very good reason in its own life story, doesn't like either.
12. "Meaning" and "explanation" in this paragraph do not stand (yet) for propositional articulation of meaning but of the imagery which is the raw material of meaning.

13. Sociology, to repeat myself perhaps, has nothing to say about whether there is a reality that corresponds to the God image. It must be content to note that for large numbers of people the God image does serve as a privileged symbol of the collection of metaphors which explain their lives to them. As I often note facetiously NORC (National Opinion Research Center) interviewers have tried repeatedly to interview Her, and She's never been home for us.

14. Gods come in many shapes and kinds and some are notably less gracious than others. Indeed as I shall argue subsequently it is precisely the graciousness of your God that provides me with a good hint of other stories in your life.

15. I leave open here the issue of whether angels, should they exist, are necessarily incorporeal. For the first thousand years of Christianity, theologians believed that angels had bodies, if ethereal ones, because only God was pure spirit. I address this problem at some length in my novel *Angel Fire,* which is about the angel Gabriella, Gabriel in the tradition often being depicted as a womanly angel. Social scientists who are not Marxists will perhaps not be offended to learn that Gabriella is a high status angel, a seraph in fact.

16. Or a similar plot in which the gender of the protagonist is changed.

17. Whose work I follow in this part of my efforts at theory construction.

18. Schank (1992) is true to his principles. In a more recent book he tells stories about his pursuit of good food and good wine to illustrate how the mind works.

19. The difficulty that inhabitants of the world of prosaic nonfiction have in grasping the distinction between literal and historical truth on the one hand and existential and religious Truth on the other was driven home to me when in the usual disclaimer at the beginning of one of my novels, I wrote, "The story is nonetheless True." An officious copy editor corrected the last word to read "true" and thus provided grist for the mills of reviewers who wanted to claim (falsely) that the story was autobiographical. I should have known better.

20. If, for example, the child hears the story in which the babe of Bethlehem beats up on a little shepherd boy, or worse, a little shepherd girl.

21. If there is a wise woman among the wise men who come to Bethlehem or if Jesus is old enough to thank politely the wise men for their gifts.

22. An eighteenth-century Lutheran word which Catholic bishops have adopted for themselves, apparently unaware of its origins.

23. To satisfy the sociological voice, I note here that I make no claim that everyone has a story-telling community, merely that most people do.

24. Hence, the Mother of Jesus is experienced not as someone who endorses and supports young love and the life-giving possibilities in such love (at whatever age in life) but rather as a person who expects one to sing "Mother Beloved" at the end of a high school prom so that one is reminded that passion must be restrained after the prom is over. The problem here is not that passion need not be restrained, but that such restraint is only part of the story and the lesser part at that.

25. Perhaps installed under the tree for the first time in anticipation of telling the story to a child who is now old enough, though just barely, to want to hear it.

26. One of the reasons for using the mother-and-child experience, image, and story as the running example in this chapter is that it is common to many if not quite all religions. Catholic Christianity has no monopoly on it. Rather, the image is almost universal because the experience of life renewed in the birth and nourishment of a child is inevitable in the human condition. However, the story is not

one, despite Joseph Campbell, of a heroine with a thousand faces. As Wendy Doniger has pointed out, the skeleton of all the stories may be the same, but it is the flesh and bones of the story (the shape of the face and figure in the present context) that make it interesting. The flesh and bones differ from story to story. There are a thousand spring heroines, if one wishes, all of them with similar yet very different stories to tell. All the stories are of life restored and renewed, of superabundant fertility. But the life that is restored, the method of restoration, the source of the fertility, and the response demanded from the one who hears the story all differ from story to story. The Mother of Jesus is not Astartre or Nut or Venus or Aphrodite or even Brigid in her pagan manifestation and their stories are not her stories, even though like them she is a lovely young woman who invites us to love of life in spring. Not for nothing, as the poet Hopkins sang, is May Mary's month, a month in his song of abundant fertility.

27. The Puritan feast of Thanksgiving was introduced in New England as a sober and godly substitute for the popish superstitions of Christmas. Till the end of the last century in Boston the latter was a work day and the public schools remained open.

28. Many Catholic parishes in the United States now have ceremonies in which marriage vows are renewed and then "romantic" dinner dances are held after the church ceremony.

29. In this assertion the Catholic leaders are, as I shall demonstrate in a later chapter, quite wrong. It is not clear, however, that they would approve of the difference that I will report.

30. After thirty years of sociology, my rule of thumb is that a 6 percentage point margin is worth writing about.

31. Ideally, theories are refined by being tested: sometimes they work and sometimes they don't work. There have not yet been—and there may not ever be, given the indifference of sociologists to religion—enough tests to permit much refining of my theory. However, at this writing I'm inclined to think that the theory works especially well when the dependent variable specifies a person and less so when it specifies an ideology.

32. The religious story is a model that humans impose on the cosmos to make sense and purpose out of their lives. Most scientists and most social scientists would probably contend that the models are nothing more than constructs, which, while they may be necessary for humans, do not correspond to any reality (not to say Reality) that actually can be found in a senseless and purposeless cosmos. However, such a determination goes beyond the boundaries of science and becomes a matter of faith. One could just as well commit oneself in an equal leap of faith to the conviction that religious stories resonate in deep metaphor to processes at work in the cosmos itself. Some scientists now insist that the cosmos itself is a story or at least has a story. Swimme (1988) contends that at the most basic level the universe is not so much matter or energy or information but story. While it does not follow that the universe story correlates with religious story, that correlation is at least a possibility.

33. Although few sophisticated theologians would dispute in the contemporary academic climate the importance of religious imagery, they show little disposition to take it into account in their work. Thus, in the outpouring of books on the one hundredth anniversary of Pope Leo XIII's encyclical "On the Condition of Labor" (*Rerum Novarum*) none of the writers considered the possibility that papal

4

The Faith We Have Lost

*"Everyone has an idea of the Middle Ages and
most of the ideas are corrupt."*
— Umberto Eco

*"Not only are the English more religious than they
think they are; they are more religious than they
have ever been."*
— Rodney Stark

The secularization theory in a crude form dominates thinking about religion in the world of great universities and, by contagion from them, the elite national media. That humans are not as religious as they used to be is so taken for granted as to be unquestioned and unquestionable. Sociologists who are sophisticated in their own fields will dismiss the necessity of including religious variables in their analysis on the grounds that "religion doesn't matter anymore." They listen impatiently to one's argument that it does still matter and then dismiss the subject from their consideration. A staff member of a funding agency will write requesting a book that will measure religious change in the last half century using survey data to measure and specify that such a book is to describe the decline of religion in America during the last five decades. He is not specifying a finding, he is simply repeating what everyone knows to be true, even though it is not true.

Sociologists of religion are somewhat more precise in their definition of secularization: Religion no longer has the influence on society that it once did—often without specifying when "once" was. Or, to use a slightly different and more Continental European version: Modernization, Urbanization, Individualization, and Rationalization have produced Secularization.[1]

If the argument means that religion does not have so much direct control over society as the Church did in the Middle Ages, then it be-

57

comes no more than a truism, though how specifically religious this control was might be open to question. Moreover, one could ask whether Richard the Lion-Hearted was more influenced in his political behavior by his religious faith than is, let us say, Mario Cuomo (governor of New York).

But when one says, as did Thomas Luckmann did at a conference at the University of Chicago, that religion can no longer support a major political movement in the Western world, one runs the risk of being asked to account for the Civil Rights movement in the United States or Solidarity in Poland.

However, the basic question that must be addressed to this form of the "secularization" model is whether religion (as distinct from religious institutions), deprived of some forms of direct influence, also loses all indirect influence on human social behavior. There is considerable variety in statements of the "secularization" hypothesis by sociologists of religion, though Tschannen (1991) has compared all the recent ones and found that they come virtually to the same conclusion.

A nasty twist to the secularization theory, which gives it an unfair advantage in serious discussion, is that in addition to being descriptive, it often is implicitly normative. Not only has religion become less important, it *ought* to be less important. Not only is it declining in importance, it *ought* to be declining. Thus, those who propound it are able to assume the position of being hard-headed and objective social scientists as well as supporters of rationality and enlightenment while its critics can be dismissed as not only special pleaders, but reactionaries as well. Even if the so-called hard-headed social scientists have no data to support their position.

If, therefore, someone wishes to introduce a new theory of the sociology of religion, he will be faced with some version of the secularization theory as indisputable proof that he ought not to be wasting his time on a subject that is no longer important. He had better be prepared to strike a mighty blow against the notion that religion is in decline if only to defend the possibility of his own theory (other than asking a pointed question about the Fundamentalists' movements in, for example, the Islamic world). It is just such a mighty blow I intend to strike in this and the next chapter before I go on to test my theory of religion as poetry. I shall assault "secularization" from both the *terminus a quo* and the *terminus ad quem*. In this chapter I shall summarize the (mostly recent) lit-

erature on the social history of religion in the Middle Ages. That literature, as all those who work in that field understand, does not know an
"Age of Faith." In the next chapter I will report on recent research in
fourteen countries which demonstrates continuity rather than change in
human religious behavior and a resurgence of religion in countries where
socialism had attempted to destroy it.

An Age of Faith

Surely Rodney Stark must be wrong in the epigraph quoted at the
beginning of this chapter. Was not England once called Mary's Dowry?
Before the Reformation were not the English people deeply Catholic? Is
not the present religious situation in England the result of centuries of
de-Christianization?

The answer to all these questions, I think, must be in the negative.
The mass of English people were never orthodox and devout Christians
in the sense we would tend to define both words today. Neither was
anyone else. Keith Thomas went too far, as Eammon Duffy (1992) has
recently shown, when he said of medieval England, "it is problematical
as to whether certain sections of the population of this time had any
religion at all." The actual situation seems to have been rather the opposite. Far from not believing in anything, the peasantry of England (and
of the rest of Europe) believed in everything; their religion was a blend
of Christianity and animism, Christianized animism and animistic Christianity. By our modern standards it was neither an orthodox nor an especially devout religion.

> James Obelkevich (1979) says it better than Thomas: Modern research reveals that
> there never was an "age of faith." In every period the majority resisted as well as
> accepted the elite religion: the discovery of deviant folk beliefs and practices, of
> lukewarmness verging on indifference, not to mention anticlericalism, has alarmed
> clerical reformers since the advent of Christianity. The church accomplished great
> things in western Europe: but it never fully Christianized it.

The histories of the British churches in the nineteenth century are
filled with quotes deploring the lack of devotion among the people. Even
allowing for the clerical propensity to view-with-alarm it seems clear
that the industrial urban working class was not devout at the beginning
of the nineteenth century. In E. R. Wickham's study of Sheffield, there
is a glimpse through the mists of that city at the beginning of the eigh-

teenth century and there is little evidence of religious devotion. Was England "burned out" religiously because of the religious wars of the seventeenth century? Or was there, even when the Puritans were fighting the King's Men, just beneath the surface of events, little propensity to religious devotion. In any case, the portrait of the Church of England in the nineteenth century's most perceptive "sociological" novelist, Anthony Trollop, hardly would lead one to believe that congregants were pushing each other to obtain admission to churches and chapels on Sunday morning.

Nor were the low levels of religious devotion merely to be found in Protestant England. The French social historians and historical demographers describe a similar situation in France as far back as their data go—to the fifteenth and the fourteenth centuries. Studies of Spanish religious behavior fit the same pattern.

Roger Finke and Rodney Stark (1992) note that most medieval rural churches were far too small to provide room for all the people in their regions. They cite an Oxford Diocese Visitation in 1738 as evidence that thirty parishes reported only a combined total of 911 communicants as an average on the four great festivals: Christmas, Easter, Whitsun, and Ascension. They cite Peter Laslett as evidence that only 125 of 400 adults in a particular English village received Easter Communion in the late eighteenth century (which Laslett considers a high level of religious devotion!). They calculate British church membership in 1800 as 11.5 percent of the population, in 1850 as 16.7 percent, in 1900 as 18.6 percent. The data that Finke and Stark quote extend back into the beginning of the modern era (a time covered by David Gentilcore, Michael Carroll, and William Christian). But as they peer back into the mists before this time, few scholars find any evidence of more intense orthodox religious devotion—religion, oh yes, lots of it, but not what we would consider acceptable today.

It is hard to find any evidence that there was an age of intensely orthodox Christian peasant life in the years between the sixth and the sixteenth centuries and every reason to think there could not have been. There was so much tragedy and death in the years from 1300 to 1600 in Western Europe that, if anything, men and women would have been drawn to greater religious intensity than their ancestors. Plague and famine devoured populations. In France, for example, population fell between 1350 and 1450 from 20 million to 10 million (and rebounded to

20 million again in the next hundred years). The Black Death and the Little Ice Age (which destroyed crops just as completely as did the potato blight in the nineteenth century, and for much longer periods of time) were apocalyptic events for the European peasantry, events that aborted an early attempt to leap into modernity. Yet there is no evidence of an intensification of religious behavior. If devotion was not very intense in times of plague and famine how could it have been intense in the centuries immediately before? In so far as we have evidence it would seem that the threat of the plague (and in Spain the threat of the Moors) led to more superstition and more hatred for witches and Jews but not to more attendance at Mass and certainly not more reception of Holy Communion.

Moreover, two Catholic conciliar decrees suggest that the peasantry was anything but devout in the previous centuries; the obligation of weekly mass attendance (Council of Agde in 506) and yearly reception of Holy Communion (First Lateran in 1215) would not have been imposed if frequent Church attendance and reception of Communion were typical behavior. Nor is there any evidence that these requirements were effectively enforced in the peasant parishes of Europe during, let us say, from the ninth to the twelfth century.

What about the earlier years? Since the evidence is so limited one is forced to make an a priori case: it was impossible for the Church to have thoroughly Christianized the peasant masses in the Dark Ages. Invaders, war lords, and bandits pillaged Europe for centuries. Transportation was difficult and dangerous and at times impossible. Communication was slow and problematic. Plagues and famines repeatedly devastated populations (though perhaps not so badly as after 1350). The Church lacked the resources (in personnel and money) and perhaps the motivation to catechize (if that be the appropriate word for the time) the peasant masses, at least beyond the monastery lands. The people in the larger towns and cities (such as these might be) could be nudged toward deeper religious devotion, but the peasantry? What could you do for them or to them? They were Christian in their own way but it seemed an insurmountable task to make them better Christians.

I will propose to present in this chapter a tentative and speculative portrait of the religious life of the European peasantry before the modern era. This model will be useful if: (a) it leads to a search for evidence that supports or refutes it; and (b) it creates a healthy suspicion about the "ages of faith." I would persuade the reader to consider the possibility that "The Faith We Have Lost" (an allusion to Peter Laslett's book *The World We Have Lost* [1981]) is in fact a faith we never had and that "stories" of religious decline provide poor models with which to understand religion at any time in human history. My portrait covers a millennium and a continent. Obviously there could be and probably were enormous variations in time and place from the outlines of the model. I have assembled some of the bits and pieces of the model from passing references in the work of social and demographic historians (who, by and large, as I have noted, are not all that interested in religion). Hence, my portrait is to a very great extent a work of speculation and imagination, subject to improvement and refinement (and perhaps ultimate rejection) in response to data and observations from those who know more about the subject than I do. However, my model is quite similar to that of scholars who have written monographs on the subject—for example, Jean Delumeau (1977), David Gentilcore (1992), Jane Schneider (1990), Irene Flint (1992), Emmanuel LeRoy Ladurie (1974), Carlo Ginsburg (1983), John Bossy (1985), C. John Sommerville (1992), and Robert Whiting (1989). These authors, each in their own way, argue or imply that the Middle Ages were never Christian in any fully meaningful sense and that the idea of an Age of Faith is a myth. The peasants were spirit worshipers whose Christianity was swallowed up in folklore. Only the two Reformations created a semblance of a "Christian Europe," but not for very long. The religious struggles of the Reformation era were in fact a struggle between an educated elite and illiterate mass culture. Jane Schneider describes a medieval religion that was largely "animistic" in which humans bartered on a quid pro quo basis with the powers of the world to be protected from evil. She sees the Reformations as attempts to extirpate animism, and she sees the Witch Hunts as the same type of attempt pushed to its logical conclusion. Carlo Ginzburg even argues that in the witch trials the elite judges imposed on animistic practitioners the judges own pre-conceived explanations of the phenomenon of magic.

One would expect that as Europe reorganized itself and reduced the chaos, as the Church grew in power and wealth, there would be reform movements that would attempt to "catechize" or, to use a currently fashionable cliché word, "evangelize" the peasants. In particular the work of the mendicant orders (from the twelfth to the fourteenth century) and the Clerks Regular (from the fourteenth to the eighteenth century) can be seen as, in part, efforts to Christianize the peasantry. Moreover, the two Reformations (Protestant and Catholic) were also, in part, efforts in the same direction, thought not necessarily defined as such.

But what about all the saints and theologians, the monasteries and the cathedrals, the pilgrimages and the shrines, the heresies and the Councils, the kings and the bishops? Are not their stories the stories of a vital, if far from perfect, Catholicism?

Such stories describe life among a tiny elite, perhaps only 5 percent of the population, surely no more than 10 percent, and an elite that lived for the most part in the cities and the towns and the monasteries. The rest of the population of "Christendom" were peasants living in the countryside and wrestling their living from the land, the *"pagani,"* the *"paisani,"* the *"paysants,"* whose very name has come to mean the absence of Christianity. There is no reason to believe that the peasant masses of Europe were ever very devout Christians, not in the sense that we usually mean when we use these words. There could be no de-Christianization of Europe as the term is normally used because there was never any Christianization in the first place. Christian Europe never existed.

Before "Secularization"

A European theologian in a conversation with me about "secularization" some years ago offered what he thought was the decisive argument: "The peasants paused in the field to pray when the Angelus bell rang." Perhaps they did. But one would want to know how many peasants at what historical times did that and how much that was an indicator of their religious devotion. The issue is not whether the Church was a dominant force in the religious lives of the European peasantry for the thousand years after the end of the Roman Empire. It shaped the calendar of the day and the year. It set the festivals, Christmas, Carnival, Lent, Easter, St. John's Night, Twelfth Night, Lady Day in Harvest, and Halloween. It offered a panoply of intercessors to whom to pray and of evils from which to be protected. It presided over the key events of life: birth, marriage, and death. Its moral code and its canon law governed human behavior (how fully remains to be seen). It provided fundamental religious stories—Adam and Eve, Jesus and Mary, Peter and John—

around which men and women could organize and give meaning to their lives. Their imaginations were, up to a point, Catholic. If "secularization" means merely that this description is no longer applicable, then there would be no disagreement with it because it merely states the obvious. But all that is proven is that religion has changed, not that religious faith has declined.

The critical words in the last paragraph are "up to a point." And the question is where that point was. The fundamental issue is to what extent the European peasant masses brought into the Church from, let us say, the fifth to the tenth century were Christianized. They became Catholic when their rulers converted. They were baptized when their rulers were baptized. They were organized eventually into parishes founded by the diocese in which they happened to be located and presided over eventually by clergy appointed by the local bishop and then by the local lord, though the spread of a network of parishes throughout Western Europe was not completed before the eleventh century. The Catholic rituals and calendars were imposed upon them, and there is little evidence of resistance. But beyond the festivals and the stories, the rituals and the devotion, how deeply did Christianity affect their worldviews and their behavior? That they lived in a pervasive religious culture, a culture that has diminished if not vanished completely, is beyond question. But what remains open to question is whether that culture could fairly be called Christian.

This question divides into three separate questions:

1. To what extent did the peasant converts and their descendants have intellectual convictions in which to ground their popular faith?

2. To what extent was the popular faith mixed with superstition and belief in magic which pushed the peasant folk religious culture to and perhaps beyond the outer boundaries of a worldview that remains Christian?

3. To what extent did their folk religion move them to regular religious practices such as Church attendance and reception of Holy Communion?

The picture we obtain from the existing studies suggest that by the fourteenth century the answers were:

1. There were only the most rudimentary intellectual convictions among the peasantry because few were required since there was no serious religious competition and few were possible in an environment

in which the peasants were illiterate and their clergy often only semiliterate.

2. There was so much superstition (belief in witches, for example) and so much belief in magic among the peasantry that their folk religion was surely on the edge of the outer limits beyond which a worldview is no longer Christian.

3. The shrines were more important than the parish church, charms and spells more important than the Mass, amulets and apparitions more important than Holy Communion, Mary more important than Jesus or God—often not the Mary of mother love but the Mary, as Michael Carroll has pointed out, of enormous and dangerous spiritual power who could be especially punitive when she was offended.

Were they pagans or Christians, beyond the sense that the fact they lived in the country won them the name of *pagani?* That is a question I do not want to answer because any answer would patronize our ancestors by applying to them standards of our time, which are not relevant to their time. Patently they were a mixture of both as are we today. They surely thought they were Christians and some of them were doubtless better Christians in the essential meaning of the word (unselfish love of neighbor) than many of us are. The point here is that given the resources available to them and to the Church in that era, it was inevitable that their religious behavior would not be solidly grounded in intellectual conviction, would be mixed with superstition and magic, and would not move them to levels of devotion that moderns would think proper.

There is little reason to believe that the "old religions" survived as organized faiths. Animistic superstitions antedated Christianity—and the official religion of the Roman Empire, which Christianity supplanted. We know very little about the religion of European peasants before the fall of the empire and the coming of the tribes. Because Odin and Thor, Jupiter and Mars were the gods of the literature, the sagas, the epics of the time it does not follow that they were the gods of that 95 percent of the population who were not members of the literary elite or that these gods had the same roles in the lives of ordinary people that they played in the lives of those who recited and then wrote the sagas and the epics or, more precisely, those for whom they wrote. As Barstow (1986) suggests, the underbrush of European religion was more likely Celtic than Roman: "The focus on trees, poles, and boughs was inherited from Druidic customs, and the entire spring celebration of dancing, love-making, and healing came from ancient Celtic rites; like Celtic religion these folk practices were intensely local" (p. 5).

She also argues, correctly it seems to me, that Joan of Arc was very much a product of older Celtic customs; sacred trees, sacred wells, sacred high places figured importantly in her mystical and, according to Barstow, shamanistic experiences. Nor did Joan think the singing and dancing at such celebrations was wrong. She admitted to her judges that she had done both without any sense of shame or guilt.

However, Barstow seems to forget that this fascinating and enigmatic young woman was also by her own definition a devout and virtuous Catholic maiden, not only by the standards of her era but by the standards of our own, much more devout and virtuous then her judges. Devotion, virtue, and sanctity were not incompatible with a blend of folk practices and Catholic orthodoxy. The difficulty in judging the life of any person as well as that of a thousand years of history is determining where the balance was between orthodox (more or less) popular Catholicism and a folk religion that was shaped by magic and superstition. Even in Joan's time most young people her own age did not receive Communion even once a year.[2]

It is perhaps enough to say that the superstitions (holy wells in the Celtic lands, for example) were holdovers from the nature religions and leave the matter at that. The "folklore" religion of barely Christianized peasants was mixed with many practices that are best called "non-Christian animism" and indeed an animism that does not seem all that different from the animism that British anthropologists found among African nations in the first half of this century.

How deep was the Christian faith of European peasant folk religion? Deep enough to survive for a millennium. Not deep enough to survive changes in the religious affiliation of their political leaders during the Reformation, sometimes back and forth across denominational lines. Not deep enough in England to survive the ruthless destruction that Henry VIII began in 1529. Not deep enough to survive immigration to other environments—either European industrial cities or, in the case of pre-famine, Irish-speaking day laborers (the so-called "Bog Irish"), a generation without priests after their immigration to America.

The popular tradition without elements of the high tradition has two major flaws: (1) it does not have the durability or the depth to survive either outright attack or drastic change; and (2) it easily falls victim to folk religion, superstition, and magic.

Magic

Irene Flint writing about the beginning of the Middle Ages and David Gentilcore writing about the end agree that animistic magic was pervasive. They also agree that Catholicism "negotiated" with animism, condemning some of it, trying to convert some of it to Christian usage, and finding that some of it could be tolerated, a policy laid down in Gregory the Great's advice to Augustine of Canterbury to Christianize the pagan Anglo-Saxon shrines and festivals.[3] Whether the churchman be Gregory the Great, or Hincmar of Rheims in the early years, or the tolerant officials of the Roman Inquisition at the end of the Middle Ages, they understood the role of magic in responding to the anxieties of human life.[4] So casting lots could be replaced by random opening of the bible; astrology could be used to predict events in the heavens if not on earth; stories were told of Christian wonder workers who were more powerful than the animistic wonder workers; Christian angels would counteract the efforts of demons; Christian prayers could undo demonic curses and spells; Christian "amulets" such as the rosary or religious medals or especially the powerful relics of saints could protect those that wore them against bad luck.[5] Even the Eucharist, as Miri Rubin has pointed out, would become less a banquet than an adoration of a sacred object produced by the repetition of certain precise words, a theology far removed from that of the early Church.

Was there superstition in some or even most of this "Christianized" magic? To what extent , for example, was the rosary a reminder of the mysteries of the life of Jesus and to what extent was it a good luck charm? Was it not most likely a mixture of both? Might it not be that even today (including the rosaries that are supposed to turn to gold at certain Marian shrines)? Or the St. Christopher medal—is it a reminder today of God's presence with us so that we be courteous or careful on the road or is it a protection in and of itself from accidents? Or a mixture of both? It may be, as both Flint and Gentilcore suggest, that the nature of the human condition is such that some sort of tangible reassurance is needed against anxiety and random dangers, especially when life is very short and many illnesses seem incurable and love is hard to find because one loses so many lovers to death. (The midsummer novena to Saint Anne for unmarried women, part of the very recent Catholic past, probably owes its origins to devotion among the Celts to the goddess Ana who was the patroness of women seeking a husband, perhaps with more reason than devotion to the grandmother of Jesus who was indeed married.)

Consider with John Bossy three nature festivals: Christmas, a mostly Christianized[6] winter festival; May Day, a mostly depaganized Celtic spring festival; and Carnival, a mostly pagan beginning to Christian Lent. How does one sort out the components of the three celebrations, either in a culture or in an individual person? The Reformations tried to stamp out the paganism of such celebrations, with limited success at best.

Nor has animism disappeared: half of the people in Britain today believe in faith healers, two out of five in fortune tellers, one out of three in both good luck charms and astrology. In Britain the more likely one is to believe in God, the more likely one is also to believe in these animistic practices, while in Ireland (with a statistically significant lower score on the magic factor) the reverse is true.[7] The Reformations, the Enlightenment, the Industrial and Scientific Revolutions have not banished magic from the "civilized" world. *Plus c'a change...*

Whatever role magic may play today, it was, all authors agree, enormously important during the so-called ages of faith. Nor did those who practice it think of it as something distinct from Christianity. Religion was a "blooming, buzzing" smorgasbord. You took grace—the ability to survive in a dangerous world—wherever you could find it.

What was Peasant Religion Like?

If one wants to get a picture of peasant religiousness during the Middle Ages one should combine images from films—*The Return of Martin Guerre, The Seventh Seal*, and the dirt, the mud, the stench, the ugliness of the Monty Python recreations of that era. Or study the literature on pre-famine Ireland, a country in which medieval religion persisted into the last century and is better documented than earlier manifestations in other countries. The Irish church in the first half of the nineteenth century wrestled with three kinds of "pagan" practices: the holy wells, the wakes, and the "patterns." The last named were patronal feasts which were in fact excuses for commerce, marriage negotiations, drinking bouts, and fierce faction fights (with clubs) among rival gangs with numerous casualties and some fatalities, festivals that Flint describes as happening in other parts of Europe more than 900 years previously.

Or one could look at Christianity as it is practiced today in rural Mexico, Corsica, and Sardinia or urban Brazil, keeping in mind that life expectancy is much longer in all of these places than it was in the Middle Ages and that there is much more physical comfort for the middle class in Brazilian cities than there was even for kings and emperors in the medieval centuries.

How "Christian" were the pre-famine Irish? Religious certainly, oh yes, terribly religious, but hardly Christian enough to satisfy that Tridentine reformer par excellence, Cardinal Paul Cullen after the famine. How Christian are the peasants of Mexico or of the Mediterranean islands or the Maccumbe-practicing urban Brazilians? Do they represent an era of change whose high levels of orthodoxy and devotion can reasonably be called "secularization?"

What was religious life like in the medieval peasant villages? The village (in Western Europe, excluding perhaps Ireland which may not have had villages) was a handful of homes with a small population (no more than 200) clustered around a tiny church or near a manor house (whose inhabitants were in many respects not much different from the peasants). The fields in which they worked surrounded the village. During the planting, cultivating, and harvesting, season men and women worked from dawn to dusk. During winter there was time perhaps for singing and story telling and brew drinking, and worry about whether the food supply would last. Perhaps half of the produce of the fields would be confiscated by whatever local lord, major or petty, lay or cleric, had the immemorial rights to such a tax.

For the first half of the Middle Ages, forest, swamp, sea, and wilderness reclaimed much of Roman Europe whose population in the year 1000 is estimated to have been half of the 10 million at the height of Roman power.

There were almost always two social classes in the villages; in earlier years there were the *coloni* who were at the bottom of the social heap and the *servi* who were a bit above them, so much so, from the point of view of the times, that there were complicated laws regulating marriages across the line. In later years (the France of the sixteenth century, the Ireland of the nineteenth), the peasants were divided into the tenant farmers who, if they didn't exactly own their land, had some rights to it and the day laborers (called plowmen in England) who had only their work to rely on for their precarious living.

Life was short, very short indeed. Even those who survived child birth and infancy would be lucky to live till their thirty-fifth birthday. Marriages took place in the early and middle twenties and were broken by death within a decade, with remarriage occurring frequently between the survivors. Old age was rare and death a constant threat—from accident or disease or hunger or raids by enemies, native or foreign (though the peasants were relatively undisturbed by conflicts between lords and kings save in the impact these conflicts may have had on planting and harvesting the fields). In some places at some times a pregnancy meant one chance in six of the death for either the woman or the child or perhaps both.

Because death so often cost you a child or a wife or a husband it does not follow (as some writers, most notably French, have suggested) that humans did not love their spouses or their children, that young people did not fall in love, that they did not begin their marriages with hope. (We have to turn to the writings of higher levels of society for proof of this, but their death rates were not much lower than those of the peasants.)[8] Life was short and hard, if not necessarily brutish, and death lurked everywhere, but it would be the height of arrogance to suppose that the men and women of the peasant village did not love and hope and wonder what it all meant, much the way we do.

The lives of these farmers were local in a sense unimaginable to us. Few of them ever left the boundaries of their commune or manor. Their religion was tied to a specific place, its families, its landscape, its customs. The world beyond the boundaries of their lives existed for them only when it assaulted them with disease, famine, or the occasional invading army. The Church as an institution beyond the local village, whose priest was appointed either by the manor lord or some higher noble, interjected itself only rarely in their lives.

William Christian (1981) in his study of village religion in Spain in the early modern era was surely true *a fortiori* before then:

> there were two levels of Catholicism—that of the Church Universal based on the sacraments, the Roman liturgy, and the Roman calendar, and a local one based on particular sacred places, images and relics, locally chosen patron saints, idiosyncratic ceremonies and a unique calendar build up from the settlement's own sacred history.

Eamon Duffy in his monumental *The Stripping of the Altars* presents a different perspective on similar phenomena in England at roughly the same time. He argues that there was no or very little difference between the piety of the elites and the masses: "Religion was a single but multifaceted and resonant symbolic house, within which rich and poor, simple and sophisticate could kneel side by side, using the same prayers and sharing the same hopes...late medieval Catholicsm was a broad Church."

Duffy does not deny that late medieval Catholicism was shot through with quasi-magical practices, though he asserts that the magic existed in the context of devotion to the Eucharist and to Mary. He also asserts with very persuasive evidence that the synthesis was extraordinarily rich and vital and that those scholars like Keith Thomas who believe that there was no religion missed the point completely, because, though Duffy is too much of a gentleman to say it, for them any religion in which there were traces of animism was no religion at all, that is to say, not Reformation religion at all.

For our purposes it is enough to say that even among those peasants about whom Duffy writes, the standards of both orthodoxy and devotion to which we hold were not so much honored in the broad church of medieval Catholicism. It is clear from his work also that the English church of that time was engaged, however slowly, in an attempted reform of its own which was aborted by Reformation.

To return to William Christian, the oldest layer of devotion, he suggests, was composed of devotion to local saints in local shrines and their relics, only a step removed from pre-Christian rituals. The next layer was devotion to the Mother of Jesus (which perhaps began no earlier than the twelfth century). The subsequent overlay was devotion to more universal saints who were specialists in certain needs (such as young women looking for a husband). The final layer in the Spain of Philip II were devotions to Jesus, particularly the sufferings of Jesus (and of Mary) which were often joined with flagellant cults—of the sort which survived, as I noted in my prelude, in New Mexico into this century and perhaps even to the present. Such devotions of course admitted of orthodox interpretations but in practice they often appear to be little more than barely Christianized magic.

Babies were brought to the Church to be baptized. The dead were buried from Church. Marriages were another matter. Young men and women in many places would move in with one another, and only after the woman became pregnant would they formally "marry"—not always in Church by any means. Perhaps most peasant marriages during the early Middle Ages were "common law," which may be why the Church, for many centuries before the Council of Trent, required only the intention to consent for the validity of the marriage (no Church service being required). Menarche probably occurred in the middle or late teens, marriage several years later (depending on the relative prosperity of the particular era). A woman would produce four children before she died, though half of them (at least) would not live and she would have many more pregnancies. According to some contemporary scholars she would have virtually no menstrual cycles after her first pregnancy. Fornication was taken for granted, concubinage was accepted and commonplace, adultery was more or less frequent depending on time and place (moderately frequent in Leroy Ladurie's[9] *Montaillou* of the fourteenth century). Birth control measures were not normally required because people did not fear having too many children, but not having enough to take care of them in old age should they live that long—though Beatrice de Planissoles of Montaillou was persuaded by her priestly lover Pierre Clergue (as they made love in a bed he had arranged in his church!) that he had an amulet to prevent conception.[10] When population pressures increased for one reason or another, the most frequent form of control was abandoning the newborn in the field (with what one must assume was great regret if not guilt), though the secrets of contraception and abortion were not unknown.

Some men and women attended church services regularly. Others attended rarely and still others not at all (save in places in England and France in the early modern era where civil authority required such attendance). The homes did not contain religious images. Men and women prayed, however, especially at the shrines and the wells, especially to Mary and to patron saints;[11] they carried charms and amulets, and believed in curses and magical protections. If the demonic was present everywhere so was the wonderful and the miraculous. Apparitions of the saints and of Mary challenged them to reform their lives lest the plague or the Moors (or some other foreign invader) destroy them.[12] They feared witches and, in the later Middle Ages, Jews. They celebrated the great festivals with eating and drinking and singing and perhaps fighting and also perhaps churchgoing. They knew the basic stories of Christianity and believed them (with greater or lesser conviction). They also knew and believed in the magical and superstitious practices that they had inherited. They saw little difference between the two.

Bernard Hamilton (writing of towns and cities) notes that there were complaints in the later Middle Ages that apprentices played football on Sunday instead of going to Mass. Presumably the same problem existed in the villages with their small "box" churches, their incomprehensible ceremonies, and their semiliterate (at best until the later Middle Ages) clergy, especially since for the first 500 years after the fall of the Roman Empire much of peasant Europe seems to have lacked parish churches.

The parish priest worked in the field with the other men or perhaps at some special trade like toolmaker. He may have been literate (as the local lord might also have been literate), at least literate enough to struggle through the prayers in the ritual. At most times and places he also had a wife (or a concubine) and children of his own, if only because it would be very difficult for a single man to survive in such a world without someone to help him with his work. While the local bishop might disapprove of such women (and might just as well have one or more concubines himself),[13] rarely did he make a serious attempt to end the practice (at least before the Council of Trent). In many dioceses the matter was rationalized by charging a cleric a tax for his concubine and an additional tax for each child, a means of fund-raising that the contemporary Church might want to consider.

If the peasants in the Reformation countries so readily accepted a married clergy, the reason might well be that they already had one or could remember a time when their ancestors did.[14]

Eamon Duffy's work on very late medieval England suggests that the *Ignorantia Sacerdotum*—one of the first "primers" for clergy to emerge from the new printing press—offers evidence of the ignorance of the parish clergy on the most elementary aspects of religion: the nature and number of the sacraments, the proper manner of their administration, the basic truths of the faith, the sins that had to be confessed, and the proper way of hearing confession. He adds that the fact that the Church quickly used the printing press in an attempt to correct these problems, shows that it was aware of the problems and trying to do something about them.

The peasants took sexual love between man and woman for granted and—if they had marriage ceremonies—learned from the ritual that sexual love was indeed good and holy. James Brundage tells the story of a wandering preacher who tried to persuade the people of Anger that married sex was sinful (as the high tradition was teaching under the influence of Augustine); they were shocked at first and then dismissed him with laughter.

Hamilton argues that the greatest need the peasants felt for the Church was as intercessor for the dead. The laity could baptize in necessity, Mass and Communion were infrequent and unimportant, laity could (even according to Aquinas) hear confessions, marriage required only the consent of the two parties and sexual intercourse, but only the Church could formally intercede for the dead.

Periodic religious enthusiasms, stirred up by wandering preachers, would sweep the peasantry—the Hussites, the Lollards, the Cathari, the Waldensi. How many people, if any, in a given village would listen to an itinerant visionary seems problematic. Neither skepticism nor agnosticism (nor hypocrisy) are unique to contemporary humankind. But bizarre religious movements, like the flagellants in *The Seventh Seal,* enjoyed interludes of popularity. The phenomenon of the traveling religious enthusiast, in the later Middle Ages perhaps a Franciscan or Dominican friar, suggests that there was both a religious hunger among the peasants and a sense of an uncompleted task among churchmen. Catholicism was able to absorb the medieval attempts at reform. Later it was not strong enough to absorb the reforms begun by Martin Luther. However, if not always at the top of the agenda of reformers and Reformers, the Christianizing of the peasants was an important goal. In any case the theological issues that agitated the Reformers in the sixteenth century meant very little to the peasants.

How Effective a Reformation?

Did the various r(R)eformations work, in particular those of the sixteenth century? Were the peasants "converted" to deeper and richer Christianity? A simple answer which hides much complexity is that some were and some weren't. Martin Marty tells us that a third of the inhabitants of modern Iceland are descendants of the last Catholic archbishop. However, his successor, the first Lutheran Archbishop had, in addition to his wife, a harem of concubines just as did his Catholic predecessor. Richard Tomasson in his study of Iceland notes that Lutherans were no more successful in imposing Christian sexual ethics on Icelanders than were Catholics.

Periodic Protestant revivals in the nineteenth century, Methodism in Britain and Pietism on the continent and especially in Scandinavia, had considerable if somewhat short-lived impact. If the European peasants,

Catholic or Protestant, were believers in folk religion in the countryside who went to religious services rarely, they were virtually the same when they moved to the cities. They were not so much de-Christianized as inadequately Christianized (especially for such a migration) in the first place.

The Counter-Reformation seems to have had some modest success in countries where the decrees of the Council of Trent were promulgated and enforced: Michael Carroll presents a neat analysis of the differences in religion between northern Italy and the *mezzogiorno,* which can be explained in part by implementation of Trent in the north. In other countries the Tridentine spirit as reinforced by parish missions, preached especially by the Vincentians and the Jesuits, was particularly effective. French scholar Gabriel LeBras prepared two overlay maps: one of the regions in France where Vincent de Paul and his colleagues preached missions, and the other of the regions that are devoutly Catholic today. There is an almost perfect correspondence between the two. Emmet Larkin points out that Jesuit and Vincentian missions in Ireland were of critical importance in the mid-century devotional revolution.

In Ireland, as in Poland and Slovakia and Croatia, the work of the Counter-Reformation was also facilitated by the identification of religion with nationalist aspirations (which did not happen in Bohemia or Hungary). Moreover, as a number of scholars have argued recently in those countries where one church has not been "established" religion is much more likely to prosper than in countries where the official church need not compete to protect its position and prerogatives. Thus, pluralism, nationalism, and successful implementation of Counter-Reformation decrees—in varying mixes and blends—account in part for the success of Catholicism in converting to a deeper, more orthodox, and more devotionally active Christian the peasant masses and their descendants in some countries. Only in the United States and Northern Ireland and parts of Romania (and in its Latin American proselytizing)[15] has classical Protestantism had much durable success. Stephen Ozment (1992), no foe of the Reformation, cites with approval a "majority" conclusion that the Reformation was a rather minor episode in European history of the sixteenth century, a "conservative campaign on the part of elite Christian clergy to subdue a surrounding native culture that had always been and preferred to remain semipagan. What distinguished Protestant from Catholic clergy in the undertaking was only greater discipline and zeal." He adds with apparent approval the notion that the "Reformation was an attempt to impose on uneducated and reluctant men and women a Christian way of life utterly foreign to their own cultural experiences and very much against their own desires." He also accepts the idea that the Reformation, having undermined for many people traditional Catholic ritual and practice, unloosed far worse superstitions, especially concerning witchcraft, unleashing the horrors of "oral European culture."

In his study of the impact of the Reformation in Devon and Cornwall, Robert Whiting (1989) argues that it owed its success to "obligation to authority, xenophobia, the urge for social or sexual self-determination, the hope of material gain, the fair of material loss, the pressure of secular financial demands, the dread of social isolation, of corporal punishment or death." He adds,

> these factors were in themselves insufficient to create an intelligent commitment to the Protestant faith, and indeed must frequently have operated as deterrents against it. Together they help to explain why, for the average man and woman, the Reformation was less a transition from one form of religious commitment to another than a descent from a relatively high level of devotion into conformism, inactivity, and even disinterest.

One would suspect, however, that the "high level of devotion" could not have had much depth to it or remnants would have survived.

Be those judgments as they may, the critical point for this chapter is that none of these historians consider the pre-Reformation era to be an age of faith nor the Reformation to have been a particular success in winning the European peasants from animism to elite and orthodox Christianity.

C. John Sommerville summarizes the difference between the Middle Ages and modern times by saying that before the Reformation, England had a religious culture, and after the Reformation, religious faith. In the former era, religion, a mix of orthodoxy and animism, permeated all of life. In the latter era, in the absence of the support of a pervasive religious culture, intellectually grounded religious commitment and devotion became possible and necessary. Our standards for religious behavior require faith and devotion. These were not the standards that were required or for many even possible in an all encompassing religious culture.

Which is better? Since the eras are so different, comparison is hardly possible to respond to the question. But, as Sommerville points out, a really determined and powerful modern monarch like Henry VIII could stamp out a religious culture within thirty years.

One could add that the religious culture of France did not survive migration to the cities, and the religious culture of the bog Irish did not survive migration to the southern part of the United States in the first half of the last century. In times of change, religious culture turns out to be relatively weak if not supported by conviction and devotion as were the later Irish immigrants to the American north or the tenant farmers who remained in Ireland after Cardinal Cullen imposed Tridentine reforms.

The Church never did convert the baptized peasants to full Christianity despite efforts of greater or lesser determination over a thousand years. Then, quite suddenly, time ran out.

Reflections

Were the peasants of Europe finally converted to a Christianity which would be acceptable by modern standards and which could successfully resist the crises created when folk religion was no longer enough?

It seems to me that a balanced answer is that some were more so than others (Italy being an interesting case in which, according to Roberto Cipriani, a "diffuse" folk Catholicism has made an apparently successful transition to the modern world) but generally they were not so converted. If the Church could not fully and effectively incorporate the peasant masses who became Catholics when their leaders did, neither could it (and the other churches) incorporate them (for long) when the age-old agricultural society finally underwent a transformation and the Enlightenment and modernity began to ask questions that folk religion could not answer. Were they ever Christian in the first place? Their imaginations were to a greater or lesser extent suffused with Christian imagery and story (along with magical and superstitious imagery and story), but the popular tradition, the narrative tradition that is at the center of any religious heritage, I conclude, cannot survive dramatic change for long unless it is effectively linked with the high tradition and its reflective philosophical foundations. It does not follow that the ordinary folk needed or need to become (God forbid) theologians, but they do need a grasp of the intellectual foundations and reinforcements of their heritage, no matter how rich and vivid it may be, which will withstand change and assault.

As John Shea has put it, a metaphor (the Rosary, the Scapular medal, the Corpus Christi procession, the pilgrimage to Medjugorie) can be either a symbol or a talisman, a hint of what God is like and what life means or a magical instrument that attempts to force God to do what we want, to deal with us in a way that minimizes our anxiety. The issue is not so much when the metaphor is a symbol and when it is a talisman, as how much of the talisman is possible without the symbol being radically (in its roots) violated. Mary the Mother of Jesus is a metaphor for God's life-giving tenderness. She is surely a symbol of reassurance for troubled humans. But when she is presented as vindictive to those who do not honor her or as a guarantor of certain results (even the conversion of Russia) and of absolute reassurance if certain devotional requirements are met (wear the scapular and you will not die without a priest) then does not the talisman vitiate the symbol?

The question of how much traditional Christianity survives in the countries where historical circumstances did not favor "Christianization" of the peasantry (as occurred in the United States, Ireland, and Poland, for example) is an open one, subject to research investigation. My analysis in the next chapter persuades me that both faith and superstition survive and that indeed moderns may have a lot more in common with medieval peasants than they think. Moderns live longer than the Medievals did and have far better medical care available, but the Medievals were probably no more faithful than the Moderns are; and the Moderns may not be much less superstitious than the Medievals were. Perhaps the Age of Faith is yet to come. Or perhaps it is always present.

Michael Hout (in personal conversation) has propounded an interesting critique of the "secularization" theory of the sociology of religion. Where the advocates of that thesis went wrong, he suggests, was to think that religion would be routed in an age of "rationality." In fact religion could respond with tightly woven and internally consistent and coherent belief systems that were utterly rational so long as the systems' first premises were admitted. Magic is of necessity excluded from such systems. Professor Hout then is not surprised that there is less superstition in Catholic Ireland than in vaguely Anglican England. The starkly rational post-Tridentine Catholicism of Ireland (innocent of most emotion as its most perceptive reporter, James Joyce, realized) cannot tolerate animistic survivals. Thus, in support of Professor Hout's theory, among those who are not Catholic in Britain and Ireland (twenty-six counties) there are positive correlations between frequent prayer and strength of religious belief on the one hand and belief in magic on the other. Among Catholics in both countries, there are no such correlations and indeed a negative correlation between belief in magic and belief in God. Protestants in the north of Ireland, who also have a tightly woven and rational belief system (given their premises), are similar to Irish and English Catholics in this respect. The struggle of the two Reformations against animism was successful at least in Ireland.

Barbara Tuchman in her popular history of the fourteenth century exulted in our difference from the people about whom she wrote—and our superiority over them. As I read about the people of the millennium between the Fall of Rome and the Fall of Constantinople, I am impressed rather by how much they were like us, particularly the men and women of Montaillou who, with dignity and courage, told the story of their lives to the stern inquisitor Jacques Fournier (later Benedict XII). They seem to be the same kind of people with the same kinds of needs and hopes, fears and aspirations as the men and women I know. Beatrice de Planissoles, for all her falls from grace, is a woman whom it is difficult not to admire.[16]

As an alternative to the model of "Faith/Secularization" or "Christianization/de-Christianization/re-Christianization," one might propose a model in which most humans will always be somewhat religious (and somewhat superstitious) as long as, conscious of their own mortality, they need meaning for their lives and reassurance for their anxieties. Some will be very religious, some will have little interest in religion, most will be somewhere in between save at crisis times in their lives. Rationality, science, and modernization may diminish the number of phenomena that are attributed to the gods, but they do not and cannot (save perhaps for some people) respond to basic and elementary human existential needs. An evolutionary theory that sees such needs diminishing is at best improbable.

Notes

1. All the words beginning with capital letters in this sentence are presented often as one-directional, one-dimensional social energies that are virtually irresistible, despite the fact that the social scientists who have studied such phenomena empirically in African and Asian countries present far more cautious and nuanced views of the processes of so-called "modernization." For sociologists of religion

the terms are often little more than a reifying of a correlation so that instead of the term denoting the actual correlation it becomes a label for a vast and powerful social energy.

2. Barstow, a militant feminist, is much more interested in her task of "retrieving" Joan for contemporary feminism, than in understanding the world in which she lived. Hence, she is much less sympathetic to the problems the Church faced than are either Flint or Gentilcore.

3. Hence, the Christian Passover is called by the name of the Anglo-Saxon goddess of the dawn and of spring, whose three familiars were eggs, rabbits, and lilies.

4. And thus made a vehement reaction like the Reformation eventually inevitable.

5. As far back as early Carolingian times, trade in relics from Rome north was a thriving practice, often involving the "translation" of allegedly apostolic bodies (such as that of St. Stephen) north from Rome to the new Frankish empire.

6. Does "A Child's Christmas in Wales," marvelous poem that it is, tell us anything about the birth of Jesus? Christmas was not nearly Christian enough for Puritan New England, which dismissed it as "Popish superstition" and tried to replace it with the American feast of Thanksgiving. At the end of the last century Christmas was still a work day in Boston.

7. Thus, despite the English stereotype of the Irish as superstitious peasants, celebrated again last November in the attack of a *Daily Telegraph* columnist on EC commissioner Ray MacShary, the Irish are more than simply less superstitious (on these measures) than the British and the Germans (East as well as West).

8. Such conditions are almost unimaginable to contemporary Americans or Western Europeans, yet one must remember that in England at the beginning of this century a woman of twenty could expect to live to the age of forty-five and would spend fifteen years of her life in childbearing while at the present time a twenty year old women can expect to live to eighty and spend two years in childbearing. In 1930 in the United States one out of every hundred births led to the death of the mother. Currently the rate is one in several hundred thousand. The world we know is very recent indeed.

9. While *Montaillou* is an eminently readable book it suffers from many methodological weaknesses, which have been sarcastically skewered by, among others, the Dominican Leonard Boyle. However, these weaknesses do not prevent the book from providing rich data about peasant religion in the Middle Ages.

10. It is not clear how they used the amulet, but Beatrice (who would later bear four daughters) did not conceive. Pierre was a rake and a rogue but he apparently owed his success to tenderness and sensitivity. His various mistresses retained a fond affection for him after the affairs ended and apparently he for them. Beatrice, for her part, preferred priests as lovers to laymen because the former were more tender.

11. Including, as Michael Carroll tells us, patrons for prostitutes and for those who practiced cunnilingus.

12. William Christian describes apparitions of Mary in very early modern Spain in which both the phenomenon and the message are strikingly similar to those of the nineteenth- and twentieth-century Marian manifestations, different only in the punishing agency with which the faithless peasants were threatened unless they reformed their lives. The Spanish Inquisition disapproved of such revelations and stamped them out quickly, usually with a hundred lashes on the back of the visionary. Yet two centuries later the tradition of such apparitions was revived and continues until the present.

13. The Council of Basel was attended by a thousand men, of whom most were clerics. The demand for prostitutes was so great that the civil authorities had to import 500 "guest prostitutes" to respond to the needs of the Council fathers.
14. Emmet Larkin, in agreement with my suspicion that Ireland of the late eighteenth and early nineteenth century is a late example of what pre-Trent Europe was like, tells me that clerical concubinage was not unknown in the Ireland of those times, especially among the peasant priests who worked in the fields with their fellow peasants during the penal years—perhaps like the married underground priests and bishops in Communist Czechoslovakia.
15. Only 70 percent of "Hispanics" in the United States are Catholics, most of the others being either Southern Baptists or Pentecostals. A quarter of these Hispanic Protestants are second-generation Protestants.
16. Her first priestly lover, Pierre Clergue, died in jail. The second whom she took after both her husbands died, like Beatrice herself, was sentenced to jail. Bishop Fournier released both of them a year later. She had to wear on her cloak for the rest of her life the two yellow crosses (the original "double cross") that indicated a heretic. He did not.

5

The Persistence of Religion

If the past was not an age of religious faith, is the present an era of unbelief? Social scientists, journalists, and religious leaders, each for reasons of their own, have reported and either lamented or celebrated the decline of religion or the decline of its influence.[1] The available evidence (Greeley 1989a) indicates no major change in American religious belief and behavior for as long as surveys have been taken, save for some changes in Catholic behavior in the wake of the birth control encyclical of 1968. But European sociologists have often argued that while such a description may be accurate for the United States, it is not an accurate description of Europe. This chapter[2] is based on data from the 1991 International Social Survey Program study of religion and examines religious values and behaviors in sixteen countries (Greeley 1993d). While past measures on these matters are available on some items, the picture that emerges from this exploration is one that suggests that it is too early to write an obituary notice for religion. Although levels of belief and practice vary greatly among countries, only East Germany[3] appears to be an unreligious country and only the Netherlands a country in which rapid secularization is at work. In East Germany, however, as in three other former socialist countries, there are signs of a revival of religious belief, and in Russia there is evidence of a dramatic revival. The churches have better images in one-time socialist societies than in other societies, though in all the societies the churches score better in their public imagery than either the parliamentary or civil service sectors of society. Moreover, religion is not irrelevant to the ordinary concerns of life: as we shall demonstrate, frequent prayer[4] and belief in life after death correlate with attitudes on crucial problems which face the societies being studied. The picture then is mixed, as is the human condition: some decline, some growth, some stability—

the last especially on once crucial measure for which there is long-run trend data.

In some countries, most notably Ireland (or, if one wishes, the Irelands),[5] Poland, and the United States, religious devotion is high, arguably higher than it has ever been in human history. In other countries, while no case could be made that, on the average, people are particularly devout, the data collected by ISSP provide no confirmation for the position that the majorities are without religious conviction or that religion is totally unimportant in their lives. Finally, there seems to be occurring in Russia one of the great religious revivals of human history.

The Persistence of Faith

With the exception of East Germany and the Netherlands substantial majorities in all countries believe in God, with the proportions being nine out of ten in the United States and Ireland, eight out of ten in Italy and Austria, and more than two out of three in Israel, Britain, and New Zealand (table 5.1).

Moreover, with the exception of East Germany and Slovenia—both formerly socialist countries—the proportion who flatly reject the existence of God is generally less than one out of five. Finally the majority in eleven countries believe in life after death, the exceptions being East Germany (12 percent), Slovenia (33 percent), Russia (40 percent), Hungary (26%) and Israel (42 percent); and majorities in the Irelands, the United States, Italy, Poland, Britain, and New Zealand believe in heaven.

The majority attend church services regularly (two or three times a month) in Ireland and Poland, more than two out of five do so in both the United States and Italy and 21 percent in the Netherlands, 20 percent in New Zealand, 19 percent in Hungary, 17 percent in Britain, and 15 percent in West Germany. (There are no church attendance data from Slovenia or Israel.) Two out of every five Catholics (who are under special obligation in Church law to attend Church every week) in the sample attend services regularly: 84 percent in Northern Ireland, 79 percent in Ireland, 67 percent in Poland, 52 percent in Italy, 48 percent in the United States, 38 percent in Britain and New Zealand, 30 percent in East Germany, 27 percent in Germany, 21 percent in Hungary. Majorities pray every day in Ireland and Poland, a near majority in the United States and Northern Ireland, and substantial minorities pray weekly in

TABLE 5.1
Religious Beliefs and Practices in Twelve Countries

	Atheist	Theist[1]	After Life[2]	Heaven	Hell	Regularly Attend[3]	Pray Weekly	Pray Daily	No affiliation
West Germany	13%	67%	53%	43%	26%	15%	38%	21%	10%
East Germany	61%	26%	12%	19%	7%	4%	12%	7%	64%
Britain	12%	70%	51%	54%	29%	17%	34%	17%	33%
USA	2%	94%	78%	86%	71%	44%	65%	44%	6%
Netherlands	22%	50%	53%	40%	18%	21%	34%	27%	55%
Hungary	19%	64%	26%	27%	16%	19%	39%	27%	5%
Italy	4%	85%	66%	58%	48%	49%	60%	37%	6%
Ireland	2%	92%	80%	87%	53%	76%	82%	57%	2%
N. Ireland	2%	94%	78%	90%	74%	57%	70%	43%	9%
Poland	12%	88%	61%	64%	57%	67%	71%	51%	3%
Norway	16%	59%	60%	47%	25%	11%	28%	18%	6%
Israel	18%	71%	42%	43%	39%	—	16%	9%	—
Slovenia	27%	61%	33%	32%	28%	26%	26%	11%	11%
N. Zealand	8%	70%	70%	59%	34%	20%	40%	22%	29%
Austria	6%	82%	60%	40%	38%	26%	38%	22%	10%
Russia	25%	60%	40%	33%	30%	8%	12%	9%	70%

1. 100% minus the sum of columns 1 and 2 equals those who are not certain. The question of the existence of God is asked in three different fashions in the ISSP. The data reported here are taken from the "NEARGOD" and "GODCHNGE" variables. For a discussion of the different response patterns see Greeley 1992a.
2. "Certainly True" or "Probably True"—as in subsequent columns.
3. Two or three times a month or more.

Italy, Britain, Hungary, New Zealand, Norway, Austria, and West Germany. Fifty-seven percent of the Irish, 44 percent of the Americans, 43 percent of the Northern Irish, 37 percent of the Italians, and 27 percent of the Hungarians pray every day, as do approximately one in five of the West Germans, the British, the New Zealanders, and the Norwegians.

Finally, in all countries except East Germany, Russia, and the Netherlands,[6] large majorities retain religious affiliation. Seven out of ten Russians, a third of Britons, 29 percent of the New Zealanders, 11 percent of the Slovenes, and 10 percent of the Austrians and the Germans report no religious affiliation. For the rest of the countries, those with no affiliation are in single digit percentages.

These figures surely do not represent an ideal observance of either religious orthodoxy or religious practice. But they do not present a picture of countries in which religion has ceased to be important to most people. Whether in fact it might represent a deterioration (outside the Netherlands and the once socialist countries which are a special case) of religious practice from before, let us say, The Great War is difficult to estimate in the absence of comparable data. In six countries (Britain, West Germany, the United States, Ireland, Italy, and the Netherlands), where there are data for belief in God a decade ago there have been no statistically significant changes, save in the Netherlands where belief in God has fallen from 64 percent to 50 percent.

Most of the indicators in table 5.1 correlate positively with age, that is, older people are more religious than younger people. Some European scholars, especially those connected with the European Study of Values (EVSS), have argued that this correlation indicates that there is a sharp deterioration in religious faith and practice, especially in Europe. However, this analysis begs the question of whether the correlation is in fact a life-cycle phenomenon: Are the younger less religious because they represent social change or merely because they are younger? Are the older more religious because they represent a faith that has lost its grip on the younger or simply because they are older? Since there is ample evidence that youth is a time of search and experimentation in which men and women make decisions about job, career, spouse, and family, it might well be expected that it is a time when religious decisions are deferred, too. The issue then is whether any given cohort will become more religious as it grows older, whether those who are in their early twenties at T_1 will a quarter century later (T_2) be any less religious than those who were in their late forties at T_1. Research done in the United States in which cohorts were followed through the life cycle and measured both for their church attendance and their prayer does not support a notion of general religious decline. Church attendance in cohorts did not vary once age was taken into account and frequency of prayer actually increased (Hout and Greeley 1987, Hout 1993).

Fortunately there is one measure of religious faith that does not seem to vary either with age or time—belief in life after death (Greeley 1976), a belief which, be it noted, is at the center of the Christian belief system. Thus, such belief in life after death becomes an excellent indicator of whether there has been a recent deterioration of religion. Measures for the United States and Britain date back to the 1930s; Germany and Norway to the 1950s, and Ireland and the Netherlands to 1981. While the sample frames are different and the question wordings were probably

TABLE 5.2
Belief in Life After Death by Year and Country

	Britain	Germany	USA	Norway	Ireland	Netherlands
1936			64%			
1939	49%					
1944			76%			
1947	49%		68%	71%		
1958		47%		66%		
1961	51%	38%	74%			
1964		38%	74%			
1966				71%		
1968		42%	73%	56%		
1972			70%			
1981	57%	46%	76%		75%	50%
1991	56%	54%	78%	60%	74%	53%

Sources: Erskine 1965, Noelle-Neumann 1981, Gallup 1972, and ESV 1981

different, there is no evidence in table 5.2 to support the hypothesis of religious decline—and some evidence of a possible increase in religious faith in all the countries since the late 1960s, when it was confidently reported that God had died.

Norway, West Germany, Britain, and the United States have very different religious cultures, yet the fact that for substantial periods of time in this century there has been little variation in conviction about life after death (and what variations exist are positive rather than negative) strongly suggests that the massive deterioration of religion in the modern Western world, so dearly beloved by rationalist critics of religion and "viewers with alarm" in the religious institutions, may reveal more about those who think they are observing deterioration than about the actual religious situation.

In fact, while a conviction that humans do survive death is generally invariant, it does correlate negatively with age (figure 5.1), as do most other forms of religious behavior: as men and women become more mature (and thirty is the age when such maturity begins to be felt), they also become more religious. However, (figures 5.2 and 5.3) in eight countries that are part of the present analysis, there are statistically significant negative correlations with age in very different countries—East Germany, West Germany, Slovenia, Norway, Austria, Poland, Israel, and

FIGURE 5.1
Belief in Life After Death by Age and Country
(Normal Life Cycle Curve)

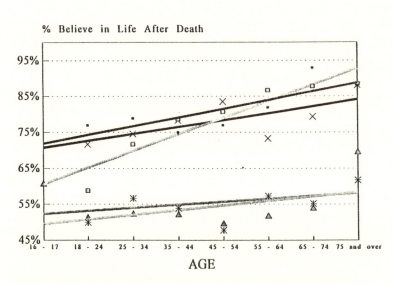

% Believe in Life After Death

AGE

➡Ireland ✳Britain ▫N.Irelnd ✳USA ▲Netherlands

Source: ISSP 1991

Russia (and for those with no religious affiliation in Hungary). Rates of belief in life after death in these countries are higher both among younger people and in general among older people than among middle-aged people. The U curve in figures 5.2 and 5.3 shows an alliance, if one may call it that, between grandparents and grandchildren against parents on the subject of the human survival of death. (The U curves were all judged significant in logistic regression equations.)

Then when the *theism* variable is entered into a logistic regression model (a belief that God is personally concerned about humans) the smile becomes a straight line: the age differences disappear.

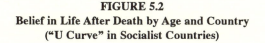

FIGURE 5.2
Belief in Life After Death by Age and Country
("U Curve" in Socialist Countries)

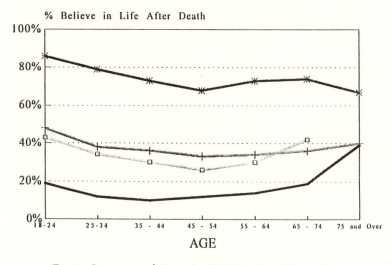

Source: ISSP 1991

Thus, belief in life after death has increased among the younger generation in the eight countries (four of them formerly socialist and the other four capitalist in one way or another) for the same reason that it declined among those same countries in the middle years of life. The latter had trouble believing in a God who cared about them personally and the former have, if no trouble at all (who has no trouble at all in such a belief?), at least less trouble than their parents and no more than their grandparents or their great grandparents.

The change, moreover, is not the result of a "post-modern, new-age" religious consciousness but rather in the partial revival of a traditional

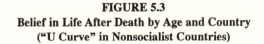

FIGURE 5.3
Belief in Life After Death by Age and Country
("U Curve" in Nonsocialist Countries)

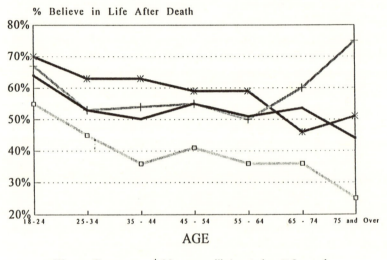

% Believe in Life After Death

← West Germany + Norway * Austria ▫ Israel

Source: ISSP 1991

image of a God who is concerned about humans, an image that was first introduced into the world religions (as opposed to the animist nature religions) by the Hebrew prophets and particularly the author of the second section of Isaiah.

Perhaps neither socialism nor Zionism are strong enough faiths for a new generation to live by. But how explain the apparent resurgence of belief in life after death in West Germany, Austria, and Norway? Perhaps material abundance in its social democratic form is not a strong enough explanation for what life is about either. But why then do not similar changes appear in the Netherlands? Perhaps because the collapse of the old religion-based pillarized social structure (*Verzuling*) in the Netherlands has yet to run its course.

In summary, Ireland, Poland, and the United States are the most religious countries, East Germany, Slovenia, and the Netherlands the least religious. Hungary is complicated, devout in some respects, less devout in other respects. Italy is somewhere in the middle, perhaps fitting the model of "diffuse Catholicism" suggested by Roberto Cipriani. Britain, New Zealand, and West Germany are less devout but scarcely unreligious. Israeli belief in an afterlife is higher than one might expect and is perhaps increasing. There is no persuasive evidence of long-term religious decline save in the Netherlands and in the former socialist countries and especially East Germany.

Finally, "pure" secularists, those who believe in neither God nor the animistic powers, are few and far between except in East Germany where a fifth of the population believe in nothing at all. The proportions are 8 percent in Britain, 6 percent in Slovenia, 5 percent in West Germany, and 1 percent in Ireland. "Secular man" is not alive and well, save perhaps on university campuses and possibly in the Netherlands. Moreover, there are statistically significant declines in the number of secularists among younger people in East Germany, Britain, and Slovenia.

Religion, in its many subtle and diffuse manifestations, continues to persist even among those who do not believe in God or at least in a "personal God." Thus, 14 percent of the atheists in Britain believe in miracles, 8 percent pray every week, 27 percent believe in faith healers, 35 percent in fortune tellers, 17 percent in good-luck charms, and 23 percent in astrology. Almost two out of five of the British atheists support prayers in the schools. Thirty percent of the East German atheists believe in miracles, 35 percent in faith healers, and 19 percent in astrology. Forty percent of the Irish atheists pray every week as do 20 percent of the Americans, 18 percent of the Northern Irish, 15 percent of the Italians, and 12 percent of the West Germans (To whom do they pray? Perhaps "to whom it may concern!") Thirty-eight percent of the Slovenian atheists believe in astrology as do 32 percent of the West Germans and 19 percent of the East Germans. Pure secularism seems to be hard to maintain even in the most secular environments, except in the Netherlands where atheists, usually of the first generation, seem consistent in their unbelief.

The Presence of Charity: Does Religion Matter?

That religion persists even the most resolute defender of the "secularization" theory might admit, but she/he would promptly raise the question of whether it matters. What difference does religion make in human life?

Is it true as Marx and Freud and many contemporary theologians like Paul Tillich have argued that belief in life after death is a selfish escape from responsibilities in this life? In fact, just the opposite seems to be the case. Belief in life after death (table 5.3) also often correlates positively with opposition to the death penalty, support for government intervention in the service of the poor, opposition to cheating the government, and personal happiness in thirty-seven of the sixty-four cells in the table. Only in two cells—for Israel opposition to capital punishment and opposition to cheating—are the relationships negative. The second column in the table is especially interesting. One might have expected that those who believe in life after death would be less concerned about the death penalty for condemned murderers. Are not they merely going to heaven a little before they would go there anyway? But in fact in twelve countries—Britain, Northern Ireland, Norway, and Russia being the exceptions—the influence of belief in life after death on support of the death penalty goes in the opposite direction. Those who believe in life after death are *more* likely to oppose the death penalty.

Thus, religion, both as doctrine and as devotion (prayer as we shall see in a later chapter), is important in shaping attitudes on crucial issues. Religion does matter.

The Resurgence of Hope: Socialism's End?

One of the most fascinating questions that can be addressed with the data from ISSP 91 is the question of what impact socialism has had on religion, both in its dominance for almost a half century and in its dramatic demise. The data for ISSP 91 were collected after the collapse of the Berlin Wall and for some countries before the August revolution in what was then the Soviet Union in 1991, a time of dramatic change for

TABLE 5.3
Belief in Life After Death
Personal Happiness, Opposition to Capital Punishment, Support for
Government Intervention, and Opposition to Cheating by Country

	Correlations (r)			
	Personal Happiness	Oppose Capital Punishment	Oppose Cheating Government[1]	Support for Government Intervention[2]
West Germany	.06	.12	.03*	.02*
East Germany	.04*	.07	.02*	.02*
Britain	.03*	.01*	.07	.05
USA	.07	.05	.08	.03*
Netherlands	.07	.08	.03*	.02*
Hungary	.00*	.06	.00*	.02*
Italy	.07	.07	.01*	.01*
Ireland	.06	.05	.06	.02*
N. Ireland	.09	.03*	.09	.05
Poland	.10	.09	.01*	.02*
Norway	.04*	.04*	.00*	.12
Israel	.01*	-.07	-.12	.06
Slovenia	.08	.07	.07	.09
New Zealand	.03*	.07	.06	.08
Austria	.05	.20	.07	.03
Russia	.03*	.02*	.00*	.05

*Correlation Not Statistically Significant (.05).
1. Condemn cheating on tax and on applications for money.
2. Favor Government intervention to provide jobs and to promote equality.

Europe and for the socialist countries. Clearly, from the first part of this chapter, religion seems to have suffered in three socialist countries in the study—East Germany, Slovenia, and Hungary, though hardly at all in Poland (save in distrust of the institutional Church). In Slovenia half of those who have no religious affiliation were children of those (mothers) who had no religious affiliation while in the other two countries one quarter of those without affiliation were second-generation unaffiliated. Will these countries recover from the impact of the opposition to religion due to socialism or will socialism's religious impact continue long after it lost power in the halls of government? East Germany is the most interesting case to study because West Germany is available for comparison. Why did religion decline so precipitously in East Germany (as it appears in comparison with West Germany) and far more sharply than it seems to have done either in Slovenia or Hungary? In Slovenia only 11 percent have no religious affiliation and in Hungary only 5 percent have no religious affiliation while in East Germany 65 percent have no religious affiliation. Granted that the regimes in Belgrade and Budapest may have been somewhat more benign toward religion than was the one in East Berlin, were there special structural problems in East Germany that may have made religion's plight more serious? Surely East Germany had nothing like the strong Catholic church in Poland with which to contend, since most East Germany Christians were "Evangelical" (Lutheran) rather than Catholic.

Moreover, Protestants in Germany are less likely to be devout than Catholics; and the East Germans who remained Protestants are less likely to be devout than West German Protestants. Thus, the decline of religion in East Germany can be accounted for in part by the fact that East Germans were more likely to be Protestants originally and Protestants were more likely to leave their Church than were Catholics and those Protestants who remained were not only less devout than Catholics but also less devout than West German Protestants. Finally, those who had no religious affiliation in the East are even less religious than those with no affiliation in the West.

However, the Church has a better "image" in the East than in the West. Within all three denomination groupings (Protestant, Catholic, and none), East Germans are more likely to have confidence in religious leaders and less likely to think of them as having too much power (perhaps because in fact they did not have much power at all for forty-five years). Moreover, in both East and West Germany there is a "smile" curve in belief in life after death; young people and older people are more likely to believe in life after death than middle-aged people. We shall return to this interesting phenomenon shortly.

In Hungary there has been a dramatic increase in religious behavior since ISSP 86 provided benchmark data about church attendance. In 1986 only a little more than a quarter of Hungarians admitted attending church *ever*. However, in 1991 two-thirds claimed to attend church services. In 1986, 6 percent reported regular church going (several times a month or more). In 1991 this rate had more than tripled to 19 percent. Moreover, this increase is evenly distributed through the whole population regardless of age. Indeed the Hungarians now are in a virtual tie with New Zealanders for regular attendance and trail only the Irish, the Polish, the Americans, and the Italians. Moreover, the Church's image flourishes in Hungary; Hungarians are the least likely of all the respondents to say the Church has too much power and the most likely to report high levels of confidence in Church leaders. An article by Tomka (1992) confirms the decline and then the resurgence of religion in Hungary. There can be no doubt that church attendance has increased dramatically though some of the change between 1986 and 1991 may be the result of a decline in reluctance to admit that one was attending church services.

Russia: Karl Marx versus St. Vladimir

Atheistic communism thought of itself as pushing forward the inevitable process of secularization in which religion would disappear from the face of the earth, a process which, in perhaps a milder form, is an article of faith to many dogmatic social scientists.

What impact do seven decades of state atheism have on a religious tradition? What is there left to be revived when state socialism finally collapses? A few symbolic appearances by Russian Orthodox clergy in their flowing robes? A few babushkas praying in empty churches? An occasional nod by shrewd politicians to the small number of believers that might still be around?

Russia is the most interesting test case of all in which to examine the issue of whether a long period of enforced secularization will either destroy religion or leave it so enfeebled that it has little resiliency once the weight of oppression is lifted. Were the followers of Karl Marx able to crush or at least fatally weaken a millennium-long heritage which dates back to St. Vladimir of Kiev? Or to more narrowly define the issue, will religion in *fin de siècle* Russia be more like that of Hungary or that of East Germany?[7]

Despite seventy years of socialism God seems to be alive and well and living in all Russia and not just Moscow (though a little more perhaps in Moscow than in the Far East). Between a half and three-quarters of Russians believe in God, depending on how the question is worded. Two out of five Russians believe in life after death, half of them believe that God is personally concerned with each human. Approximately a third believe in heaven and hell, more than a quarter report that they

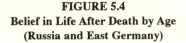

FIGURE 5.4
Belief in Life After Death by Age
(Russia and East Germany)

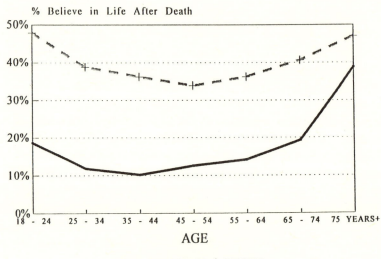

Source: ISSP 1991; N=(East Germany) 1,486 (Russia) 2,964

personally feel very close to God and two out of five believe in religious miracles. On all these items, Russians not only score higher than East Germans at levels of statistical significance (except in the matter of belief in miracles),[8] but the differences are considerable: they are more than twice as likely for example to believe in both a caring God and in life after death.

Figure 5.4 focuses in on the U curves in belief in life after death for both Russians and East Germans. Both curves are statistically signifi-

TABLE 5.4
Attitudes towards the Existence of God

	East Germany	Russia
Never Believed	51%	50%
Believed, but Now Don't	25%	3%
Didn't but Do Now	5%	22%
Always Believed	20%	25%

cant (using logistic regression analysis) but the Russian curve is both higher and steeper.

Moreover, on two measures that enable us to simulate time-series analysis there is striking religious growth in Russia and religious decline in East German (as of 1991). Only 5 percent of respondents in the latter country (table 5.4) say that they did not used to believe in God but now do while in Russia 22 percent have become believers. In East Germany a quarter of the population are former theists who have become atheists, while in Russia only 3 percent fall into that category. Thus, theists have suffered a 20 percentage point loss in East Germany while they have gained a 19 percentage point increase in Russia. Approximately a third of those who were once atheists (by their own admissions) have become theists.

The proportion of Russians who have abandoned atheism for theism is twice as high as the closest competition in the ISSP data—two times larger than in New Zealand and three times larger than in Hungary. It should be observed that this is a personal religious report on the part of each Russian respondent and not merely a global shift in proportions like the church attendance increase in Hungary previously discussed. The Russian respondent admits (perhaps the word "claims" should be used) that she/he used to be an atheist and is one no longer. No claim seems inherent in the wording of the question that the respondent pretended to be an atheist but was in fact a secret believer.

Moreover, only 11 percent of the Russian respondents said that their religion was Orthodoxy when they were growing up but two and a half times that many (28 percent) claimed Orthodox affiliations at the present. One out of six Russians (17 percent) are "converts" to the religion of their heritage. These numbers and those showing the emergence of New Believers (as I will call the atheists turned theist) would seem at least at first glance to demonstrate, after the most serious attempt to obliterate religion in human history, the most dramatic religious revival in human history. Perhaps St. Vladimir may have triumphed over Karl Marx after all. In East Germany, however, affiliation with the Evangelical church has decreased by 19 percentage points from 48 percent to 29 percent. (The comparison with East Germany seemed appropriate because it is the socialist country on which we have data that was most strongly opposed to religion after the Soviet Union).

Thirty percent of the East Germans pray as do a quarter of the Russians, but one out of ten Russians prays everyday compared to 7 percent of the East Germans. Two out of five East Germans attend church services and one out of three Russians; 7 percent of the former go at least once a month as opposed to 8 percent of the latter. But the 8 percent of Russians who attend regularly must be compared with the 27 percent who attended at all when they were young; and the 7 percent of East Germans must be compared with the 63 percent who attended when they were young. By those standards Russian church attendance seems to represent a dynamism which is going up, and the East German, one that is going down.

Thus, to the summary question of whether God survived atheism in Russia, the answer must be that She did and is experiencing a wave of popularity seldom seen in the modern world. Moreover, the Orthodox church is also flourishing having more than doubled its adherents and apparently enjoying more popularity than any religious institution in the ISSP countries. God is not only alive and well in Moscow, but He might be found, it would seem, even in the churches.

The change from atheism to theism of about a fifth of all Russians (a third of those who were once atheists) reported in the last section is especially likely to happen among younger Russians as figure 5.5 demonstrates. The dark portion of the chart represents those who have always believed while the shaded portion those who have switched to belief. The proportion who always believed has declined with age, but this effect has been canceled out by the increase of the switchers among the younger generation so that all age groups under sixty-five are equally likely to believe in God.

When, one might wonder, does the change occur? Some 30 percent of Russians under twenty-five, 25 percent of those between twenty-five

FIGURE 5.5
Belief in God in Russia by Age

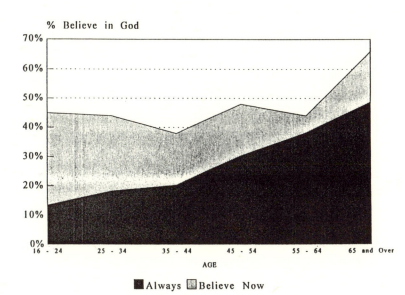

% Believe in God

■ Always □ Believe Now

Source: ISSP 1991; N=2,964

and thirty-four, and 20 percent of those between thirty-five and forty-four report that they have switched from atheism to theism. For those under twenty-five the change must have been rather recent, within perhaps the last five years. Did it occur at the same time among the older Russians? Was there a period of time before 1991 when a massive number of Russians who had not previously believed in God decided that they now believed in God? It would not be a difficult question to research. One could merely add to the "change" question, a question about how long ago it happened.

FIGURE 5.6
Religious Experience for New Theists by Age and Gender

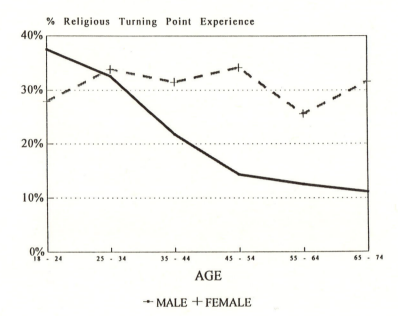

% Religious Turning Point Experience

AGE

-- MALE + FEMALE

That the conversion to theism is in part driven by religious experience, especially for young men, is demonstrated by figure 5.6. For women the proportion of the New Believers who report a turning point which made them immediately religious is a little under a third and does not vary significantly through the course of the life cycle. But there is a sharp increase among young men, two-fifths of whom report such an experience. For many Russians, whether men or women, young or old, however, the conversion from atheism to theism is associated with and perhaps driven by a presumably powerful religious experience. Students of religious experience would doubtless be very interested in the nature of that experience.

FIGURE 5.7
Denomination and Age in Russia

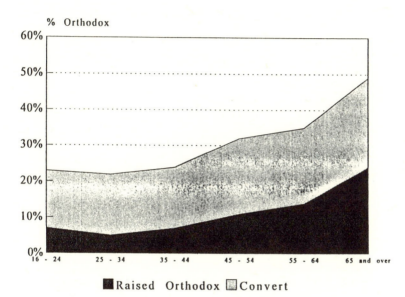

% Orthodox

Raised Orthodox Convert

Source: ISSP 1991; N=2,964

To state the finding in terms of all Russians and not just the New Believers, more than one out of ten Russian men under twenty-five report a "turning point" experience that made them instantly religious (as opposed to one out of twenty Russian men over twenty-five). For Russian women the rate is one out of ten at all age levels.

The pattern is somewhat different for the conversion to the Orthodox church (figure 5.7). The change has been greater among those over forty-five and in that respect builds on an already existing base of Orthodox affiliations with the result that identification with Orthodoxy correlates positively with age, from a high of almost 50 percent for those over

FIGURE 5.8
Religious Experience for Converts by Age and Gender
(Converts to Orthodoxy)

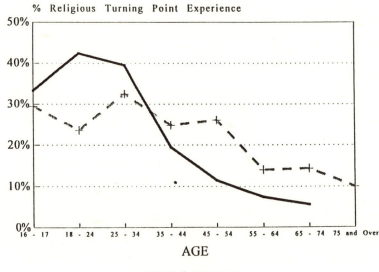

% Religious Turning Point Experience

AGE

-•- MALE + FEMALE

sixty to a low of a little more than a fifth for those under twenty-five. Nonetheless, Orthodox converts under thirty-five are twice as numerous as "cradle" Orthodox. For those under twenty-five the conversion must have been rather recent.

Both younger men and younger women are more likely to report a religious experience in connection with their turn to Orthodoxy; two out of five young men and one out of three of the young women (figure 5.8).

Was there a time, one must wonder, during the middle years of the Gorbachev era when large numbers of Russians rediscovered religion

FIGURE 5.9
Religious Orientations of Russians
(1991)

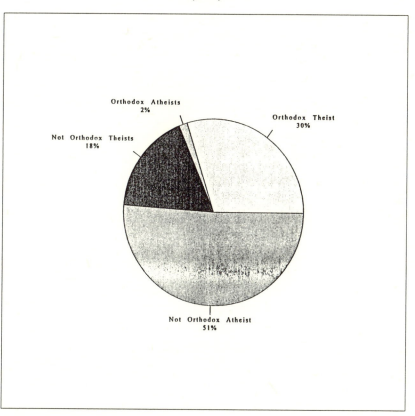

Source: ISSP 1991; N=2,964

or their religious heritage or God and invited Her back to Moscow and everywhere else?

The result in 1991 was a Russia in which atheists and theists were both approximately half the population and Orthodox affiliates a third of the population (figure 5.9). From the point of view of the sociology of religion and in particularly of the sociology of "de-secularization" it would be enormously important to know the "when" of the Big Change, its "why," and what has happened since 1991.

The scope of the change can be pictured by comparing figure 5.9 with figure 5.10. The latter is a simulation of what the religious distribution of the Russian people was like before any of the changes occurred. The biggest migration is across the line separating Orthodox theists from non-Orthodox atheists. The latter category has declined approximately 20 percentage points (losing thus two-sevenths of its members) and the former has increased its membership by approximately a factor of three, from 9 percent to 30 percent.[9] One out of every five Russians has moved from rejection of God and religion to acceptance of both. Since the mass conversions of the early Middle Ages, has there ever been such a widespread and rapid change in religion? Is this remarkable religious growth limited to certain demographic segments (besides age and gender) of the population or is it relatively invariant?

Some Russian regions are more likely than others to register such change. The average in the whole country for New Believers is 30 percent. In the north central region it is 37 percent, in the Urals 36 percent, and in Moscow 28 percent, while in the Far East and Kamerovo it is 15 percent.

There are also correlations, though not very large, with occupation, education, and party affiliation. Managerial and professional workers and skilled workers (perhaps social classes that have more of a vested interest in the socialist regime) are less likely than white-collar workers, unskilled workers, and those not in the labor force to be New Believers. A similar pattern holds for conversion to Orthodoxy except that there is a change among the skilled and unskilled workers with the latter being less likely than the former to affiliate with the Church, perhaps because of a feeling that they might not be at home there. Those with a tertiary education are less likely to become New Believers as are those with a secondary and a tertiary education to become converts, though there are no significant differences in the younger age groups across educational lines. Finally, voters who lean toward the various Communist parties are less likely than those who opt for the opposition parties to change from atheism to theism (save among the younger cohorts) while no such difference seems to affect conversion to Orthodoxy. Both Communists and non-Communists are equally likely to have switched from nonaffiliation to affiliation. Thus, the structural variables of education, occupation, region, and political affiliation have at best only a modest impact on the Russian religious revival.

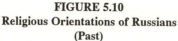

FIGURE 5.10
Religious Orientations of Russians
(Past)

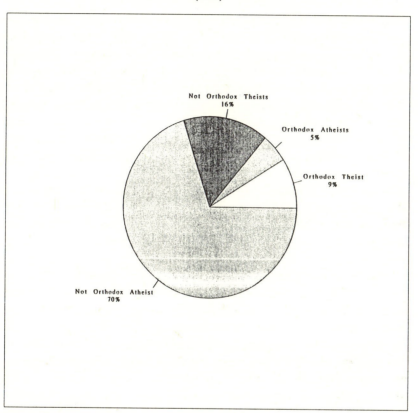

Source: ISSP 1991; N=2,964

Why is there a religious revival in Russia and not one in East Germany? Perhaps because Orthodoxy is twice as old as Lutheranism and has deeper roots in Russian culture than Lutheranism has in East German culture. Perhaps because Orthodoxy has resources of art (icons), music, liturgy, monasticism, and mysticism which Lutheranism lacks. Perhaps because after the collapse of socialism, Orthodoxy seemed to be the only bearer of Russian culture.

At the center of the Russian religious revival lurks the image of a God who cares, doubtless an old image in Russian culture and one which, for whatever reasons, seems to have been rediscovered. Arguably God is alive and well in Moscow (and elsewhere) because She never left.

That fact may raise certain problems and perhaps certain fears about the impact of resurgent religion on the Russian society, polity, and economy. Might it portend an outburst of extreme nationalism, Pan-Slavism, anti-Semitism, and imperialism as a reborn "Holy Russia" resumes its messianic fervor and seeks once more to dominate the Eurasian land mass with its powerful heritages and traditions?

One would have to be blind to history to deny that such strains have been characteristic of Russian religion in the past, though they are by no means the only or even the most important strains in that religion. The Orthodox church, unlike the Catholic church in Poland, has been generally circumspect in its political involvement. Pamyiat and similar organizations seemed to have little appeal to anyone in our data. Faith and affiliation have yet to generate high levels of religious devotion (or they had not done so in the spring of 1991). While God has survived in the Moscow underground for seventy years, it does not follow inevitably that She will be seen with quite the same face that she appeared to display in other centuries of Russian history. Perhaps at present one would have to say that it is too early to know what mixture of the benign and malign may emerge from the reappearance of God in Russia. There is however solid reason for studying its developments carefully.

A powerful religious revival, therefore, seemed to be underway in Russia in the months before the traditional Russian flag replaced the hammer and sickle above the White House. A fifth of the Russian people had moved from atheism to theism and from nonaffiliation to Orthodoxy. This change was particularly strong among the young men, though women were still far more religious than men. Much of the change, including an increase in belief in life after death, follows a U curve pattern with the younger being more like their grandparents than their parents. The change seemed to emerge from a complex mixture of fatalism, religious experience, and a belief in a God who was concerned about individuals. It may also have emerged as recently as the late 1980s. It is too early to say how this remarkable development, unlike anything we know in human history, will play itself out. However, it is not too

early to say that antireligious socialism failed completely to crush out
the Russian religious heritage, as it failed in most of its other efforts.
The Liturgy is being celebrated again in the Cathedral of the Dormition
in the Kremlin and Lenin's body has been ejected from Red Square. St.
Vladimir has routed Karl Marx.

Is there then a religious revival in the former socialist countries?[10]
Surely there is not a massive "return to religion," nor a change that is
immediately observable, except in Hungary and Russia. Yet the change
is, as social changes go, both dramatic and unexpected, especially in
Russia. It is reverse of everything the theories of "secularization" and
"religious decline" would have led us to anticipate, a religious rebound
that has not been observed, as far as we know, in any other data set
concerned with religion.

Conclusion

What then have we learned from consideration of the data in the ISSP
1991 study of religion?

1. The critical religious variable of belief in life after death does not
seem to have changed over time in those countries where we have time-
series data: the United States, Great Britain, Norway, Germany, and
Ireland, and the Netherlands.

2. This variable influences attitudes on a range of social policy issues, especially concern for the poor, honesty in dealing with the government, and sympathy for the condemned criminal. The "story" of trust
in God's power to sustain life after death correlates with the story of
concern for the poor and the criminal.

3. In eight countries, four formerly socialist and four "capitalist," belief
in life after death actually increases (against the religious life cycle paradigm) among younger people so that the older and the younger are more
likely to believe in this crucial religious truth than those in the middle
years of life.

4. This increase can be accounted for by a parallel U curve in belief in
a God who personally cares for us as individuals. Thus, the "story" of a
caring God relates to the "story" of humans believing that they survive
death and to the "story" of humans caring about other humans.

5. In Russia there seems to be a notable surge in religion, both in
affiliation with the Orthodox church and in conversion from atheism to

theism, the latter driven in part by religious experience, especially among the young.

6. In some countries, therefore, religious belief and devotions are high (Ireland, Poland, the United States) and in some they are low (East Germany and Slovenia) and in some they are in between (West Germany and Britain); in some they are going down (Netherlands) and in some they are going up (Russia).

The picture is far more complex, and more interesting, than any simple-minded (I use the word advisedly) model of a general decline of religion and religious influence. As usual reality is far more intricate and varie-gated than theories driven by ideology want it to be.

Thus, both *termini* of the "secularization" thesis seem dubious at best. Sociologists who resist ideological constraints on their work should therefore be open to the possibility that other theories might be fruitful for the sociological study of religion.

In the next chapter I turn to data which support my religion as poetry thesis.

Notes

1. Many sociologists will contend that there are different secularization theories. However, Tschannen (1991) argues that all the major theories can be reduced to similar basic concepts: "differentiation, rationalization, and worldliness." He adds other concepts which are often if not always present in the theory: "autonomatization, privatization, and pluralization." Note that these "-ization" concepts assume an inevitable and one-directional social evolutionary process; many if not most American sociologists who work with empirical data are pro-foundly skeptical about the existence of this process. Indeed some European so-ciologists come dangerously close to a circular argument when they use a social evolutionary assumption to prove a social evolutionary fact.
2. The International Social Survey Program, founded in 1985 with participants from seven countries, is now a consortium of twenty-one research centers. Only three major conditions are placed on institutions that want to participate: (1) they must use probability samples in their data collection; (2) they must draw samples of at least a thousand respondents; and (3) they must not "pass up" two annual projects in a row.
3. Despite German unification, the ZUMA institute in Mannheim, the German par-ticipant in the ISSP, continues to interview full samples in both of the former divisions of Germany.
4. The effect of frequent prayer on these problems will be reported in a subsequent chapter.
5. The use of this term throughout the chapter merely acknowledges that separate surveys were conducted in the twenty-six counties governed in Dublin and in the six counties (of the nine in historic Ulster) governed in London, the former by

SSRC at University College Dublin and the latter by SCPR in London. No implication is contained in the language used about Ireland in this chapter about the author's opinion concerning the division of the island into two states.

6. The "secularization" theory seems to fit Holland. Protestants and Catholics alike have suffered a 50 percent loss when father's religion is compared to respondent's religion. The two religions together account for only two-fifths of the population of the country. The fact that the losses are equal for Protestants as well as Catholics would suggest that the propensity of conservative Catholics to explain the decline in the Netherlands as a result of the Second Vatican Council is mistaken. Perhaps the collapse of the religious "pilarization" of Dutch society along religious lines accounts for the decline.

7. There are 2,964 respondents in the Russian ISSP, selected from the Russian-speaking population of the Russian Federation.

8. In East Germany more people believe in religious miracles than believe in God, a paradox if not a contradiction.

9. There is a strong correlation between conversion and new belief, .60. But not everyone who is in one category of change is automatically in the other.

10. An Israeli colleague of Michael Hout suggests that in Israel, Zionism might be the equivalent of socialism in the other countries, not so much a god who failed as a god who is inadequate to respond to the ultimate questions of life. But then how to explain West Germany? Perhaps capitalism is also a god who has failed in that country.

6

Testing the Links

Having done my best to break through the "Iron Curtain" of the "Secularization" dogma, I will now try to persuade the reader in this and subsequent chapters that my "Religion as Poetry" model is a useful way for sociologists of religion to explore data.

It would be useful if I could construct an empirical general linear model of the five variables in my theory with a sixth added to represent a story of life affected by the religious story. But such a model would require more cases and more precise measures than those currently available. It would have to be a very elaborate model to test all the possible interaction effects that might occur. In the present state of the data and the technology, I must be content with two and three variable models which test some of the links that are postulated by my theory. The first issue to be addressed in this chapter is whether hope is as widespread as my theory assumes that it is.

The Presence of Hope

In a study of American religion carried out in 1972 in which the theory of religion as poetry existed in an early form, my colleagues and I administered three vignettes that dealt with tragedy: birth of a handicapped child, long illness, and fatal illness, all natural disasters. Four-fifths of the respondents replied with answers that could be considered hopeful or optimistic. Moreover, closeness to parents when one was growing up and parents whose religious style was defined as hopeful correlated strongly with such positive responses to tragedy (McCready and Greeley 1976).

In a subsequent survey of young adults (Greeley 1981), half said that they had experiences of being in touch with the sacred and half said that they had experienced order and purpose in their lives; a third reported ecstatic encounters. Seven out of ten had at least once such encounter, two out of ten reported one or the other such experiences several times, and one out of ten reported them often.

So both hope and religious experiences of one sort or another are widespread in contemporary America. As we shall see shortly, so too are hope renewal experiences in the strict sense of the word, those which the person involved says explicitly renew religious faith.

Religious Images

The most difficult aspect of trying to operationalize the theory that religion is poetry is to find survey questionnaire items that are themselves sufficiently poetic. After many years of experimentation (see Greeley 1984 for an account of how the items evolved), I decided to use two scales, one more symbolic than the other, to measure a respondent's religious story, both of which have been used in the General Social Survey since 1984.

The first set of items is as follows:

> There are many different ways of picturing God. We'd like to know the kinds of images you are most likely to associate with God. Here is a card with a set of contrasting images on a scale of 1-7. Where would you place your image of God between the two contrasting images—Mother/ Father; Master/Spouse; Judge/Lover; Friend/King?

Only approximately 1 percent of the respondents were unable to answer the questions. The items clustered into what I call the *grace* scale.

The second set of items is as follows:

> People have different images of the world and human nature. We'd like to know the kinds of images you have. Here is a card with sets of contrasting images. On a scale of 1-7 where would you place your image of the world and human nature between the two contrasting images? "The world is basically filled with evil and sin/ There is much goodness in the world which hints at God's goodness." And "Human nature is basically good/ Human nature is fundamentally perverse and corrupt."

These items clustered into a *Tracy* scale, named after David Tracy who suggested that they operationalize his theory of the two imaginations.

My expectations were that Catholics would score toward the more "graceful" end of the first scale and the more benign views of creation and human nature. In fact on three of the four items Catholics were significantly more likely than Protestants to picture God as a friend, a lover, and a spouse. The differences were statistically significant but not large (on the average 5 percentage points). Moreover, the four items clustered on one factor on which Catholics differed significantly from Protestants and, when Protestants were divided into categories, also significantly from both Fundamentalist and moderate Protestants (more from the former than from the latter, as might be expected) but not from liberal Protestants (or Jews). As will be evident subsequently, this (grace) scale interacts with being Catholic in its impact on dependent variables.

Catholics were also more likely to score higher on the *Tracy* scale, that is, more likely to think of both creation and human nature as good and religion as a manifestation of that good instead of prophetic denunciation of evil. Figures 6.1 and 6.2 show that in two countries, Ireland and the United States, Catholics have higher scores on the Tracy scale than do members of other religious denominations.

Both scales then establish that Professor Tracy's theories about different religious images seem to admit of becoming theoretical sociological hypotheses. It remains to be seen what effects they will have on dependent variables.

Hope Renewal Experiences

A "limit" or "horizon" or a "grace" experience, as I have said previously, is an experience that points toward a limit or a horizon of life and hints that there may be something beyond the horizon. Such experiences might be considered "low intensity" religious experiences when compared with the ecstatic experiences described by William James (1961) and others. The questions in this section are: (1) whether such experiences are frequent in American society; (2) whether they correlate with increased religious faith and devotion; and (3) whether they seem to relate also to crises in personal life.

The data are taken from the special religion module in the 1988 General Social Survey, an annual study conducted by the National Opinion Research Center. The 1,479 respondents are a random probability sample of the American population.

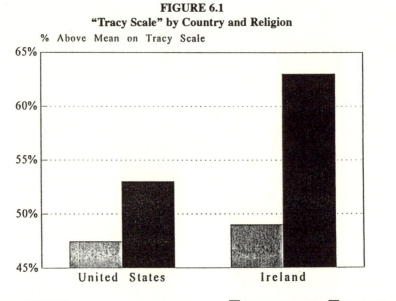

FIGURE 6.1
"Tracy Scale" by Country and Religion

% Above Mean on Tracy Scale

Source: ISSP 1981

Not Catholic   Catholic

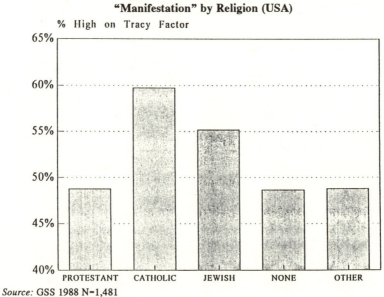

FIGURE 6.2
"Manifestation" by Religion (USA)

% High on Tracy Factor

Source: GSS 1988 N=1,481

They were asked:

How often have these events strengthened your religious faith—often, sometimes, never?
1) Death in the family
2) Birth of a child
3) Marriage
4) Intense sexual pleasure.

Twenty-nine percent responded that a death in the family had often strengthened their religious faith and 40 percent more said that it sometimes had. Forty-nine percent said that the birth of a child had often strengthened their faith and 29 percent more reported that it sometimes had. Thirty-six percent reported that marriage had often strengthened their faith and 34 percent more said that it sometimes had. Finally, 11 percent said that intense sexual pleasure had often strengthened their faith and 23 percent more said that it sometimes had.

Only 11 percent of the population reported that they had none of these faith-strengthening experiences. Twenty-nine percent said that they had all four of them and another 36 percent said they had three out of four. Thus, two-thirds of Americans had at least three varieties of limit experiences (as these questions define them). Forty percent of Americans say that they've had at least two of these experiences often. In retrospect then, most Americans invest some of the commonplace events of their lives with religious significance and only one out of ten find no religious significance in any of them.

Ninety-one percent of those who report three or four varieties of experiences believe in God, while 70 percent of those who have had fewer than three experiences believe in God.[1] Fifty-one percent of the former attend church at least several times a month, while only 29 percent of the latter attend. (Forty-two percent of those who have had none of these experiences believe in God and 20 percent of them go to church regularly.)

The relationship between experiences on the one hand and faith and devotion on the other is obviously complex. Surely those who have a strong faith are more open to limit experiences than are those who do not. Just as surely, however, the experiences have strengthened faith, by the respondents' own admission. The survey analysis technique used here tells us very little about the nature of the experience. One would like to know in much greater detail what the experience was like. Nonetheless, the analysis does establish that most Americans have faith-strengthening experiences at crucial times in their life cycle, that these experiences correlated with higher levels of faith in God and religious devotion, and that they seem responsive to doubt experiences. Thus, Fawcett's thesis is sustained by empirical evidence.

As the theory of hope renewal experiences would lead us to expect, the number of these experiences correlates positively with the number of doubts. Those who have fewer doubts about their faith also have fewer faith-strengthening experiences. NORC asked four questions about doubts in the 1988 survey:

> How often have these problems caused doubts about your religions faith, often, sometimes, never:
> 1) Evil in the world
> 2) Personal suffering
> 3) Conflict of faith and science
> 4) Feeling that life has no meaning.

Those who have had no doubts have on the average 2.3 limit experiences often or sometimes, while those who have had four doubt experiences report an average of 3.2 such experiences. The correlation is sharper for Catholics (.29) than it is for Protestants (.17), perhaps because Catholicism is more likely to emphasize rituals that accompany life, death, and marriage. Catholics are no more likely to have limit experiences at such times, but their limit experiences at these times are more likely to correlate with and perhaps be responsive to their doubts precisely because Catholic rituals force Catholics to ask more questions of themselves at times of death, birth, and marriage.

Similarly the number of limit experiences one has correlates for Catholics with the image of God as a lover and not a judge (figure 6.3) but not for Protestants, again perhaps because of the ritual and sacramental element in Catholicism. Figures 6.4 and 6.5 present three variable models that demonstrate links among three of the variables in my paradigm. In figure 6.4 it is to be noted that the proportion of those who say that intense sexual pleasure renews their faith (experience) increases both with frequency of prayer (ritual) and image of God (image/story). More than half of those who picture God as a spouse and pray once a day or more report that experiences of intense sexual pleasure have often or sometimes strengthened their religious faith, as opposed to only a quarter of the entire sample.

FIGURE 6.3
God as Lover by Limit Experiences by Religion

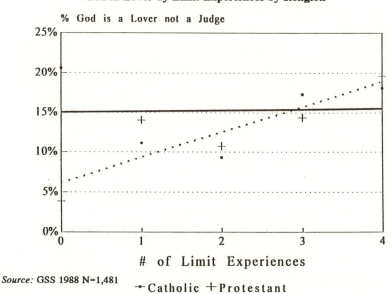

% God is a Lover not a Judge

Source: GSS 1988 N=1,481

⊶Catholic +Protestant

FIGURE 6.4
Sex and Faith by Frequency of Prayer and Image of God

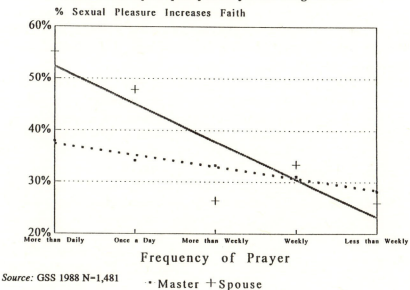

% Sexual Pleasure Increases Faith

Source: GSS 1988 N=1,481

•Master +Spouse

FIGURE 6.5
Sex and Faith by Church Attendance and Image of God

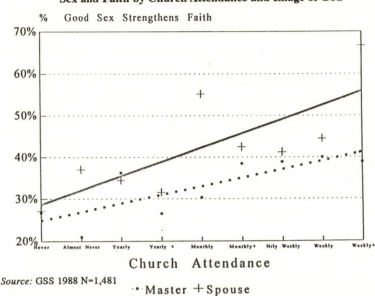

Source: GSS 1988 N=1,481

Figure 6.5 shows that the same phenomenon is at work when the ritual is public: both frequent church attendance and the image of God as a spouse increase the probability that an experience of intense sexual pleasure will strengthen faith. As in the previous figure, it should be noted that the two variables have independent effects: they are not merely surrogates for one another.

Finally, when community is substituted for ritual, the same effect results: a combination of a larger number of friends belonging to the same congregation and a spousal image of God produces the highest proportion reporting that intense sexual experiences strengthened their religious faith.

These graphs involve all the variables in my theory (since the image of God as a spouse[2] is both a symbol and a narrative). They relate to one another as the theory says they should. Moreover, it is improbable (though obviously not impossible) that, in the absence of the theory to prod in this direction, anyone would have asked whether there is a relationship between friends in the same congregation and image of God on the one hand, and intense sex as a religious experience on the other.

To complete this examination of the links among the variables in my paradigm I had to find a story in the world beyond religion which can be linked to a religious story, preferably a three-variable model. I discovered two such models. In the first I correlated a Catholic (high) score on the grace scale and the number of close Catholic friends with the proportion who were strong Democrats. For those low (below the mean) on the grace scale, the number of Catholic friends had no effect on the proportion who describe themselves as strong Democrats. But for those high on the grace scale, the number of Catholic friends correlated significantly with the proportion strongly affiliating with the Democratic party. Being integrated into the Catholic community produced a payoff for the Democratic party only among those who tended to have high scores on the Analogical Imagination.

Exactly the opposite was the case for Protestant affiliation with the Grand Old Party. The number of close friends Protestant produced a payoff for strong affiliation with the Republican party only for those who had low (or Protestant) scores on the grace scale (God as Father, King, Judge, and Master). Just as the Analogical Imagination and community integration led Catholics to be strong Democrats, so did the Dialectical Imagination lead Protestants to be strong Republicans.

Thus, grace experiences are common in modern America; they do correlate with stronger faith and religious devotion; they do seem to be responsive to personal religious crises, their effect is correlated with image, ritual, and community. And the variables in my theory, in combination with the story of God, do effect other ongoing stories in human life.

Quality of Family Life

If the story of political affiliation represents an "output" variable in my theoretical model, the story of the family in which one grew up can represent an "input" variable. I had assumed that relations with mother and father and between mother and father would affect one's own religious story. In the 1981 European Values Study (EVSS)[3] questions were asked about these three relationships. A scale from zero to three was composed with the highest score on each relationship counting for one point. This scale correlated with many religious variables, church attendance, prayer, belief in life after death.

It also correlated with two items that might give some hint of a person's "story of God":

How often, if at all, do you have the feeling that life is meaningless?

And how important is God in your life? Please use this card to indicate; 10 means very important and 1 means not at all important.

The two items constitute a factor that correlates with the family life scale at .20 for Catholics and .11 for Protestants[4]—one of many examples we will see in this book where correlations for Catholics with religious poetry variables is stronger than for Protestants. Moreover, there is a correlation of .07 between agreeable family life in the family of origin and agreement with spouse (on social, moral, religious, sexual, and political matters) in the family of procreation.[5] When one interjects the Importance of God/meaning factor between these two variables in a regression equation on the premise that it is a religious story that connects the first family story with the second family story, that correlation falls to .035—still significant because of the large number of cases. However, the fact that the original relationship is diminished does establish that the religious story, the importance of God in a respondent's life, does mediate at least partially between the two family stories.

Moreover, in the same study there is a question about drinking behavior, in the response to which Catholics are more likely to be total abstainers than are others (even in Ireland!). The correlation between Catholic and abstinence is .09. It falls to .06 when quality of family of origin is taken into account. Then, when an interaction between being Catholic and satisfactory memories of family of origin is added[6] to the regression equation, the relationship between abstinence and family relationships falls to .00. Thus, the religious story appears to mediate between the story of the family in which one grew up and one's present story of one's own life, a pleasant family of origin and a lower propensity to drink.

The poetry of religion seems to relate in the predicted way to both input variables (memories of growing up) and output variables (political affiliation).

Conclusion

This chapter has been a search for "probable cause" that would justify further examination of the theory of religion as poetry. It would seem that probable cause has indeed been found. Most Americans do indeed hope. Grace experiences of one kind or another do abound, especially, as would be predicted among those who are more prone to religious crises. The variables within the model—ritual, private or public, story, experience, and community—do relate, one to another, in ways that would be surprising without the theory but are predictable (and were predicted) in light of the theory. The model itself also relates in the expected fashion both to output and input, to party affiliation and present family agreement and drinking behavior. Stories of grace are affected by the family in which one grew up and affect both the family in which one lives and one's drinking behavior.

As expected, Catholics are different; their memories of family life are more positive and that affects their religious images more strongly and their religious images have a stronger effect on the quantity of their religious experiences.

Notes

1. The question:

    > Please look at this card and tell me which statements comes closest to expressing what you believe about God—
    > I don't believe in God.
    > I don't know whether there is a God and I don't believe there is a way to find out.
    > I don't believe in a personal God but I do believe in a higher power of some kind.
    > I find myself believing in God some of the time but not at others.
    > While I have doubts I feel that I do believe in God.
    > I know that God exists and I have no doubts about it.

    Sixty-four percent of Americans checked the last item and 19 percent selected the second to last item. These two items are combined in the analysis. Only 5 percent of the respondents checked the first two items.
2. I have found that when analyzing the impact of religious imagery on sexual behavior it makes more sense and is more convenient to use only the master/spouse imagery.
3. In this analysis data from England, the countries that are used are Ireland, Northern Ireland, Italy, France, Spain, Germany, Denmark, Belgium, and the Netherlands . The EVSS is a very weak project. There seems to be no theoretical orientation behind it other than an assumption that religion and virtue are everywhere in decline. The questionnaire construction is often crude: no items on the role of women, a clumsy political party affiliation item, and a stupid question about prayer, for example. The various analytic reports are usually content with asserting religious decline based on age correlation (without considering the possibility that such a phenomenon is a life-cycle relationship). The archives from

7

Different Poetry for Different People

In this chapter,[1] having established some plausibility for my model, I will inquire about the apparent denominational differences in religious stories between Catholics and Protestants and whether these might be related to traditional sociological notions about the communitarian ethos of Catholics and the individualist ethos of Protestants. Are there different "ethics"— Protestant and Catholic—because there are different underlying stories? Do Tracy's two imaginations account for differences in "ethics" between Protestant and Catholic?

As I have remarked earlier in this book, modern sociology emerged in substantial part from a discussion of the differences between Catholics and Protestants. Weber (1958) thought that the "communitarian" ethic of the former seemed to impede educational and economic achievement while the "inner-worldly asceticism" of the latter with its emphasis on individual achievement facilitated the success of the latter. Durkheim (1961) believed, on the other hand, that the "individualism" of Protestants induced higher suicide rates among them while the "communitarian" control available to Catholics tended to reduce suicide rates.

The theories of these two giants certainly fit the pattern of religious emphasis of the two denominational traditions. For Protestantism the tendency has always been to emphasize the relationship of the individual with God, while for Catholicism the tendency has always been to emphasize the individual relating to God as a member of a community. Suicide rates and educational achievement rates would be two manifestations (and perhaps not the most important) of fundamental orientations that permeate the two traditions.

Quite apart from achievement[2] and suicide rates, then, the question remains whether at the end of the century, which began with *The Protes-*

tant Ethic and the Spirit of Capitalism and *Suicide*, the distinctive orientations of the two heritages persist.

Progress made in the theory of the sociology of religion since the publication of these two works makes it possible to describe more precisely the nature of these two orientations. Religion, it has been argued in this book, may be conceived as a set of symbols that provide answers to issues of the ultimate meaning of life, stories that explain imaginatively what the world is about and provide templates for shaping human response to the world and thus the shape of the world in which humans live. Religion is an imaginative "cultural system"—a collection of directing "pictures" through which humans organize and give meaning to the phenomena that impinge on their consciousness, especially in so far as these phenomena require some explanation of the ultimate purpose of life.

While these "pictures" may produce theological and ethical codes, they are prepropositional and metaphorical. The codes are derivative, the superstructure, if one wishes, built on an imaginative and preconscious infrastructure. The fundamental differences between Catholicism and Protestantism, then, are not doctrinal or ethical. The different propositional codes of the two heritages are but manifestations, tips of the iceberg, of more fundamental differing sets of symbols. The Catholic ethic is "communitarian" and the Protestant "individualistic" because the preconscious "organizing" pictures of the two traditions, which shape meaning and respond to life for members of the respective heritages, are different. Catholics and Protestants "see" the world differently (or "saw" it differently). These preconscious "worldviews" are not, of course, totally different, but only somewhat different, different enough to produce different doctrinal and ethical codes, different Church structures and different behavior traits (or to have once produced different traits).

The central religious symbol is God. One's "picture" of God is in fact a metaphorical narrative of God's relationship with the world and the self as part of the world. Tracy (1982) has studied the "classics" of the two traditions to discover the underlying imagery that shapes these crucial works. On the basis of his study, he suggests that the Catholic imagination is "Analogical" and the Protestant imagination is "Dialectical." The Catholic "classics" assume a God who is present in the world, disclosing Himself in and through creation. The world and all its events, objects, and people tend to be somewhat like God. The Protestant classics, on the other hand, assume a God who is radically absent from the world and who discloses Himself only on rare occasions (especially in Jesus Christ and Him Crucified). The world and all its events, objects, and people tend to be radically different from God.

The word "tend" in the previous paragraph is used advisedly. Zero-sum relationships do not exist in the world of the preconscious. The Analogical and the Dialectical Imaginations exist side by side in the personalities of the authors of the classics, opposing one another but also complementing one another. Rarely does one encounter a religious imagination that is purely Analogical or purely Dialectical.

Tracy contends that two approaches to human society of the respective traditions are shaped by these imaginative pictures. The Catholic tends to see society as a "sacrament" of God, a set of ordered relationships, governed by both justice and love, which reveal, however imperfectly, the presence of God. Society is "natural" and "good" therefore for humans and their "natural" response to God is social. The Protestant on the other hand tends to see human society as "God-forsaken" and therefore unnatural and oppressive. The individual stands over and against society, and not integrated into it. The human becomes fully human only when he is able to break away from social oppression and relate to the absent God as a completely free individual.

Tracy's analysis complements and adds to the earlier insights of Durkheim and Weber. One may continue to speak of a "Protestant" ethic, but now one must understand the ethic as a set of fundamental world-explaining and world-shaping interpretative pictures. In this sense, ethos, as Geertz (1957) has observed, is the flip side of mythos. Formal ethical codes are derivatives of interpretative pictures. The higher suicide rates and the higher achievement rates of Protestants in turn-of-the-century Europe are the result ultimately of different symbol systems, or, if one may say it, different—though not totally different—stories of God.

In this perspective the more "conservative" Catholic stands on morality and doctrine are not so much the starting point of the Catholic tradition as rather the results of images of society and religion that are latent beneath the formal teaching of the tradition. Because communities are pictured by Catholics as sacramental, threats to communities must be resisted both by a reassertion of the values, which seem to protect the communities, and by support for doctrinal notions on which the communities appear to have been based. The Protestant heritage, freed from such powerful concern about the internal dynamics of traditional communities because it imagines the communities to be sin-filled and God-forsaken, can perhaps afford to be more flexible in matters of morality and doctrine and human relationships

Tracy's work provides useful background for reconsidering the insights of the Weber and Durkheim, but the issue that remains is whether the two different imaginations still persist in an urbanized, industrialized, ecumenized world of the end of the century. Do Catholics still see the world somewhat more analogically than Protestants? Do Protestants still see the world somewhat more dialectically than Catholics? Do Protestants therefore still tend to emphasize individual values? Do Catholics still tend to emphasize communal values? Does the Catholic value orientation still reflect an image of God as present in creation? Does the Protestant value orientation still reflect an image of a largely godless creation?

To put the issue bluntly: since the Reformation ethic can fairly be assumed, at some high level of generality, to have shaped the spirit of modern capitalism, is the dominant social trend away from communal ethic and toward individual ethic? Do the combined forces of modernization, urbanization, industrialization, ecumenization, and religious homogenization threaten the Analogical Imagination with extinction? Has the Catholic imagination already become, or is it in the process of becoming, a casualty of the modern world?

If one wishes (with a wary eye on the data available) to formulate expectations of how the different imaginations would shape values, one might very tentatively expressing the following "predictions":

1. Catholics will be more likely to value social relationships than Protestants because they see not sin but sacramentality, however flawed, in such relationships. The Analogical Imagination, which pictures humans as integrated into social networks—networks that in fact reveal God—will stress those values and behaviors that contribute to the building up and strengthening of those networks. The Dialectical Imagination, which pictures the individual as struggling for his personal freedom over against the sinful oppression of social networks, will stress those values and behaviors that contribute to the strengthening of personal freedom and independence from group control.

2. Catholics will be more likely to value equality over freedom than Protestants because equality makes for smoother social relationships. Moreover, because social complexity and diversity will also be seen as

sacramental, Catholics will be more tolerant than Protestants of diversity in their communities; Catholicism, as James Joyce remarked, means "here comes everyone."

3. Because Catholics view society as a community of communities they will be more likely than Protestants to advocate decentralization of control to the smaller communities; hence, the famed Catholic principle of "subsidiarity"—nothing should be done by a larger and higher organization that can be done as well by a smaller and lower organization— is a philosophical articulation of the Catholic "image" of society.

4. Protestants will value in their children the virtues of initiative, integrity, industry, and thrift more than Catholics while Catholics will value loyalty, obedience, and patience. Protestants will be especially likely to deplore vices that diminish personal integrity, honesty, and sense of duty. Catholics will be especially likely to be offended by actions that seem to violate relationship networks—adultery, prostitution, suicide. Catholics will stress the importance of common background in the choice of marriage partners; Protestants will stress compatibility of individual interests and personal fulfillment. Catholics will emphasize more than Protestants institutional religion, religious devotion, and doctrinal orthodoxy. Catholics will be less likely to feel lonely and constrained by social relations than Protestants (which Catholics do not take to be oppressive). Since Protestants are more likely to emphasize personal responsibility (Weber's "worldly asceticism") than Catholics they will also be more likely to emphasize a "work ethic" than Catholics, who will be more likely to work because they have to than because they want to.

5. Finally, because Catholics picture God as revealing Herself in society, however flawed the revelation might be, they will be more likely to advocate social change so that the disclosure of God will be improved. Protestants on the other hand will be more likely to despair of society ever being anything but God-forsaken and sin-ridden and hence will be less optimistic about and less supportive of social change.

In describing these expectations of a communal ethic against an individualist ethic, an Analogical Imagination against a Dialectical Imagination, a religious vision that pictures God in society against one that pictures God as radically "other" from society, one is not predicting anything more than differences in emphases and tendencies. To predict (as I will shortly) that Catholics are more likely to be willing to accept heavy drinkers in their neighborhoods than Protestants are is not necessarily to say that the majority of Catholics will tolerate drunks and the majority of Protestants will not. Rather it would be altogether possible for the majority of both groups to reject such deviants but the Catholic majority, according to the prediction, would be smaller than the Protestant majority.

To state the problem in terms of null hypotheses:

1. Denominational affiliation will be found to have no significant relationship to values.

2. To the extent that one might discover significant relationships between denomination and values, there will be no pattern in such relationships that corresponds to expectations based on the work of Weber, Durkheim, and Tracy.

3. To the extent that there still seems to be a Protestant ethic and a Catholic ethic, a Dialectical and an Analogical Imagination, the differences will be seen as diminishing over time, more likely to exist among an older generation than among a younger generation and among the those with lower levels of educational attainment than among those with higher levels of attainment.

Or in Tracy's terms, the null hypothesis could be stated as follows: If it is not already extinct, the Analogical Imagination is well on its way to extinction.

This analysis will proceed in three phases: the first will consider data from many nations to investigate the possibility of significant denominational differences in values. The second will attempt a replication of the first analysis with a different set of data, also from many countries. The third will concentrate on one nation to see if denominational value differences can be accounted for by differences in religious imagination.

Data and Hypotheses: Phase One

I propose to test the expectations described in previous paragraphs against data collected in the European Values Study (EVSS).[3] Similar (though often not identical) survey instruments were administered to national probability samples in various countries. The present analysis is limited to five English-speaking countries: Australia (n=1,228), Canada (n=1,254), Great Britain (n=1,231), Ireland (n=1,529),[4] and the United States. Each of these countries has sufficient numbers of Protestants and Catholics to examine the possibility that denominational subcultures might cross national lines. On the other hand, because they share a common language[5] and a common heritage (in varying degrees of completeness) they represent a congeries in which there is enough unity to facilitate a reasonable examination of diversity. At the conclusion of this phase of our analysis it will be asked whether predictions can be made on the basis of the findings in the five English-speaking nations, which will accurately anticipate findings in the two Continental European nations (Holland n=1,221; and Germany n=1,230), which have enough Protestants and Catholics to make comparisons possible.

Comparisons were made in the analysis between Catholics and Protestants only. There were not enough cases and not enough similarity in coding systems to make comparisons among Protestant denominations. Those with Anglican affiliation (19 percent of the sample) were excluded because it was impossible to sort out those with Catholic (High Church) and those with Protestant (Low Church) leanings and because in Great Britain "C of E" (Church of England) is often a residual category, albeit one which encompasses three quarters of the population. Similarly, Jews and those with other or no religious affiliation were excluded from the analysis both because they do not fit the Protestant/Catholic paradigm on which this project is based and because these groups are not large enough to be suitable for the research strategy that is being used. The sample sizes for those included in the final sample are:

	Catholics	Protestants
Australia	312	276
Canada	543	387
Germany (F.R.G.)	522	640
Great Britain	143	179
Ireland	1,231	138
Holland	387	312
United States	696	1,304
Total	3,834	3,236

The questionnaire items were designed to measure moral, social, political, familial, and religious values. Factor analyses (Principal Component with varimax rotation) were performed on value clusters, which either were asked as part of the same question or which seemed to have some logical coherence. Thirty-six variables emerged from this phase of data preparation.

Equality versus Freedom Factor

This variable is composed of responses to two questions: The first question asks about a choice between freedom and equality.[6] The second question asks about changing society. I expected that Catholics would emphasize equality more than Protestants and would be more likely to endorse change.

Fairness Factor

Three variables that measure "fairness" in the work world were found to constitute a single factor measuring attitudes toward pay scales, control of business firms, and the right of workers to understand before obeying. In line with their egalitarianism and their convictions about decentralization, Catholics can be expected to score higher on this factor than Protestants.

Social Change Factors

Three factors measured the respondent's opinion about desirable social changes:

1. Loadings on this factor stressed changes which would improve respect for authority and family life.

2. Loadings on this factor stressed changes in emphasis on money, work, and lifestyle.

3. Loadings on this factor stressed changes in more respect for the individual and less reliance on technology.

My expectations were that there would be higher scores for Catholics on the first and second factor and for Protestants on the third.

Confidence in Social Institutions Factors

Two factors measured confidence in social institutions: army, police, Church, legislature, and the civil service on the first factor; unions, press, the legal system, and education on the second factor. Since Catholics are less likely to see society as evil, my expectations were that they would score higher on both factors.

Work Factors

To measure the "work ethic," respondents were asked how they would spend their free time if their work week was reduced to three eight-hour days with the same pay they now receive for five days of work. Three factors emerged from an analysis of the responses:
1. Emphasis on family, hobby, relaxation, study.
2. Emphasis on community service and small business of one's own.
3. Emphasis on avoiding boredom and finding another job.

On the basis of Max Weber's theory, I predicted that Catholics would score high on the first scale and Protestants on the third. Catholics would also presumably score high on the second scale with its emphasis on community involvement.

Tolerance Factors

1. Highest loadings on rejection of immigrants, unwed mothers, members of sects, students, large families, and students as neighbors.
2. Highest loadings on rejection of political deviants of the left and the right.
3. Highest loadings on rejection of heavy drinkers, criminals, and emotionally disturbed neighbors.

Hypothesis based on the theoretical expectations described in previous paragraphs led me to predict that Catholics would be more likely to accept deviant neighbors than Protestants and hence score higher on all three scales.

Morality Factors

1. Highest loadings on disapproval of homosexuality, prostitution, abortion, divorce, suicide, mercy killing, adultery, premarital sex, and drug usage. This variable might be called a "life ethic" factor.
2. Highest loadings on disapproval of lies, bribes, cheating on tax, welfare, transportation fare, and buying of stolen property. This variable might be called a "personal ethic" factor.
3. Highest loadings on disapproval of strike breakers, political assassins, joy riding, fighting with police, not reporting an auto accident. This variable might be called a "social ethic" factor.

4. Disapproval of killing in self-defense. This variable might be called a pacifist factor.

My expectations lead me to hypothesize that Catholics would score high on factors 1 and 3 and Protestants would score high on factor 2. There is no reason to expect either group to score high on factor 4.

Spouse and Parent Factors

These two factors measure what commonalities respondents reported between parents and children and husband and wife. In both factor analyses to produce these variables only one factor emerged: the scales are in effect a count of the number of commonalties a respondent reports. It is expected therefore that, since Catholics are more concerned about community relations, they will be more likely to score high on both factors.

Marital Success Factors

Four factors emerged in response to a question about the qualities required for a successful marriage:

1. Highest loadings on similarity of background, religion, politics, taste, children, sharing of chores, and adequate income.
2. Highest loadings on tolerance and respect.
3. Highest loadings on satisfactory sex and living apart from in-laws.
4. Loading on faithfulness.

My expectations were that Catholics would score high on the first factor and Protestants on the second and the third. There is not basis for making a prediction on the fourth factor.

Divorce Factors

Two factors emerged in an analysis of responses to a question about when divorce was justified.

1. High loadings were on drinking, violence, unfaithfulness, absence of love, unsatisfactory sex, and personality conflict.
2. High loadings were on sickness, dislike of each other's relatives, and financial problems.

Very hesitantly I expected higher Catholic scores on the first factor and higher Protestant scores on the second.

Child-Rearing Factors

Six factors emerged from a question about the traits a respondent wished that a child would learn at home.

1. Displayed high positive loadings on independence, determination, leadership, and imagination and high negative loadings on manners.

2. Revealed high positive loadings on politeness, work and thrift, and high negative loadings on respect.

3. Loaded positively on obedience and unselfishness.

4. Loaded positively on religion.

5. Loaded positively on self control and patience.

6. Loaded positively on loyalty and duty.

The first two factors seem to be appropriate for the Protestant ethic, the last four for the Catholic ethic.

Family Revolution Factors

A factor analysis of six variables that measured attitudes toward sex and family life produced two scales.

1. Emphasis on sexual traditionalism.

2. Emphasis on traditional relations between parents and children.

Because of their emphasis on communities and the desirability of sustaining them, Catholics can be expected to score higher than Protestants on both these scales.

Religious Factors

Scales were constructed from three sets of questions about religion, each scale the result of a factor analysis that produced a single factor.

Church: measures satisfaction with the Church's response to human needs.

Devotion: measures religious behavior.

Doctrine: measures acceptance of traditional religious beliefs.

Since formal religion is more important to a religion of community than to a religion of the individual, we may expect Catholics to have higher scores on both doctrine and devotion. However, precisely because Catholics are more likely to expect leadership from their Church, they are also more likely to be disappointed, while Protestants, expecting less because the Church is less necessary, are less likely to be disappointed.

A final two variables were added to the list to be analyzed. In deference to Max Weber, "post-secondary" education was examined with the expectation, based on Weber, that Catholics would be less likely to seek post-secondary education than Protestants. In deference to Emile Durkheim I hypothesized that Protestants would be more likely to be lonely than Catholics.

Of the thirty-eight variables described in previous paragraphs, it was possible to make predictions about thirty-six from the perspective of the "ethic/imagination" theory postulated in this essay. Whether the Analogical Imagination is becoming extinct depends on whether significant relationships are absent between denomination and some of these thirty-six variables.

Analysis: Phase One

Four important analytic questions must be answered for this enterprise to be successful, for a decision to be made about the null hypotheses:

1. Are there significant relationships in the English-speaking nations, net of country, between denomination and values?

2. Do these relationships persist across national lines or are they the result of deviant behavior in one or two countries?

3. Are these relationships diminishing with time? Since there are no longitudinal data available, one is forced to ask if the differences diminish among younger respondents, conscious that if this phenomenon occurs it might be a life cycle and not a trend phenomenon. On the other hand, if there is little difference between younger and older respondents, then there is no evidence to sustain a hypothesis of a trend toward convergence of values.

4. Do the relationships that exist in the English-speaking countries enable us to make predictions about the two non-English-speaking countries in the present analysis?

Analysis of Variance (ANOVA) with the Multiple Classification Analysis option (MCA) appeared to be the appropriate technique to answer these questions. Table 7.1 presents a summary of the findings which resulted from the application of this technique to the thirty-six variables about which predictions were made.

TABLE 7.1
Values by Denomination by Country (English-Speaking)

	USA	GB	IRL	CAN	AUS	β^1	β^2	β^3
Equality	09[4]	13	48	14		.13	.07	.08
Fairness	34	27	30	31		.13	.11	.10
Change1	06	-04	10	29		.08	.08	.07
Work2	17	-03	06	-08	01	.06	.04	.04
Toler2	12	37	20	36	04	.03	.11	.09
Toler3	10	07	15	09	-12	.19	.05	.02*
Moral1	00	03	30	07	32	.24	.07	.07
Moral2	16	26	44	10	48	.11	.22	.20
Moral3	-10	42	16	10	34	.09	.09	.08
Spouse	16	36	29	25		.09	.10	.06
Parent	21	20	16	12		.11	.09	.11
Marry1	13	37	04	12		.11	.06	.06
Marry3	09	10	12	21		.21	.06	.06
Child2	06	10	17	11		.09	.05	.03*
Child4	05	12	19	01		.23	.05	.05
Child6	13	07	-33	30		.16	.05	.09
Family1	06	24	-32	37		.07	.08	.08
Family2	13	18	06	24		.19	.08	.13
Devotion	06	32	39	17		.19	.10	.03*
Doctrine	11	34	00	19	43	.28	.06	.11
Church	13	18	06	24		.19	.08	.13

*Not significant
1. For country.
2. For denomination.
3. For denomination under forty years old.
4. Difference in standardized points (Z score) in direction of the hypothesis.

The seventh column in the table reports the beta (standardized eta) between denomination and variable, net of country. Only those variables that related significantly to denomination are listed in the table. All the relationships are significant at a level of .01 or greater; all but four at the level of .001 or greater. Twenty of the thirty-six variables, then, relate at levels of considerable statistical confidence with denomination, all of them in the predicted direction. Only in the divorce and confidence in social institution categories was there not at least one statistically significant relationship. There were no significant correlations in the opposite of the predicted direction.

It is worth noting that neither on the work ethic measure nor on the post-secondary education variable was support found for specific hypotheses drawn directly from Weber. (Only in the Federal Republic was a statistically significant relationship observed between Protestant and post-secondary education: in that narrow sense, then, the original Weber finding was replicated. In the ISSP data to be analyzed subsequently, in which a much better educational code is available, there is no significant difference between Catholics and Protestants in educational achievement, even in Germany.)

Moreover, there was also no significant relationship found in the sample, net of country, between being Protestant and being lonely. Durkheim's finding is not replicated in most countries; only in the Federal Republic and Canada are Protestants significantly more likely to be lonely than Catholics. The two theories of the Founders seem to apply together only in Germany.

The first five columns of the table report the differences in the predicted direction between Protestants and Catholics (in Z score points) in each of the countries. A minus sign indicates that in a particular country and on the given variable, the direction of the finding runs in the opposite of the predicted direction. Minus signs appear only once in the United States, Canada, and Australia[7] and twice in Great Britain and Ireland, in seven of the eighty-eight relationships. Thus, the beta in the seventh column indicates not only a significant relationship when country is held constant but also a relationship that exists, to a greater or lesser extent, in all the countries being studied.

Moreover, when the analysis is repeated with the population under forty (the last column in the table), the relationships continue to be statistically significant on eighteen of the twenty-one variables, with the only exceptions being religious devotion, tolerance for those with drinking and emotional problems as neighbors, and polite and thrifty children. Since religious devotion is closely related to age (independent of cohort) the change on the first of the three variables may be illusory. Moreover, the magnitude of the betas between denomination and value are not notably altered when the analysis is limited to those under forty. Thus, the Catholic ethic Analogical Imagination and, conversely, the Protestant ethic Dialectical Imagination, are not withering away. David Tracy was right not only about the Classics of the past but, without realizing it at the time, about survey respondents in the present.

Thus, in all countries Catholics are more likely to emphasize "fairness" and "equality" while Protestants are more likely to emphasize "freedom" and "individualism" in the workplace. With the exception of Great Britain, Catholics are also more likely to advocate strengthening of authority and of the family. And in the United States and Ireland they are also more likely to say that if they didn't have to work five days a week they would devote themselves to the community and to a small business of their own.

In all five countries Catholics are more willing than Protestants to accept political extremists of either the left or the right into their neighborhoods. With the exception of Australia they are also more likely to accept those with drinking and emotional problems.

In Ireland and Australia and to some extent in Canada (though not in the United States and Britain) Catholics are more likely than Protestants to have strong positions on issues of "life ethics" (abortion, extramarital sex, euthanasia, suicide, etc.). In all five countries, Protestants are more likely than Catholics to emphasize issues of "personal ethics": lying, cheating, stealing, bribing. In all the countries but the United States Catholics are more likely than Protestants to disapprove of "socially disruptive" behavior such as joy riding, union busting, fighting with police, and failure to report damage to another's car.

In all countries Catholics are more likely than Protestants to report agreement on crucial issues with parents and spouses and to emphasize the importance of shared backgrounds (religion, politics, tastes) as conditions for successful marriage. Protestants, however, are more likely than Catholics to insist on the importance of sexual fulfillment and on living apart from parents and in-laws as conditions for a successful marriage.

In all countries Protestants were more likely to value industry and thrift in their children and Catholics more likely to value religious faith and a sense of loyalty and duty (with the exception of Ireland where Protestants rate loyalty and duty higher than do Catholics). These findings are not necessarily inconsistent with those reported by Alwin (1986) who found a convergence between Catholic and Protestant child-rearing values in the United States. The difference between Protestants and Catholics on the importance of thrift and industry are modest in the United States.

Moreover, that variable is one of the two in which there is no statistically significant relationship with denomination for those under forty

TABLE 7.2
Values by Denomination by Country (English-Speaking and Continental)

	English (F.R.G)	Germany	Holland
	(Z Scores)[1]		
Equality	26	01	05
Fairness	33	-24	08
Change1	15	-18	02
Work2	60	01	02
Toler2	21	-03	03
Toler3	24	-11	06
Moral1	16	29	-07
Moral2	41	07	29
Moral3*			
Spouse	26	02	-02
Parent	24	03	05
Marry1	09	03	20
Marry3	28	-19	02
Child2	02	16	01
Child4*			
Child6	12	03	22
Family1	13	29	-11
Family2	12	29	-11
Church	35	-37	50
Devotion	14	-44	20
Doctrine	20	-57	66

*Not significant
1. Difference between Protestant and Catholic in direction of hypothesis.

years old. Finally, Alwin is working with time series data from the General Social Survey and can therefore write with much more confidence about converging child-rearing values.

In all the countries Catholics are more likely than Protestants to emphasize traditional family values; and in all countries but Ireland Protestants are more likely than Catholics to be tolerant of "sexual revolution" behavior. In Ireland Protestants disapprove of such behavior even more strongly than Catholics, which is strong disapproval indeed.

Finally, as predicted, Catholics are more likely to be devout and to be doctrinally orthodox while Protestants are more likely than Catholics to be satisfied with the response to their needs provided by their churches.

In general differences between Protestants and Catholics, as measured by the scales available to this analysis, are more modest in the United States than in the other four countries. Perhaps "ethnic differences" account for the greater diversity in Ireland, Canada, and Great Britain—Northern Ireland versus Southern Ireland, French versus British Canada, Irish immigrant versus host culture in Britain. However, such an explanation would not account for the considerable differences between Protestants and Catholics in Australia on the morality scales, on the average the largest differences on these scales in any of the five countries.

Can we apply the predictions that were so successful in studying English-speaking respondents to Continental respondents? The data summarized in table 7.2 suggests that, while the English-speaking findings are useful in predicting differences between Catholics and Protestants in Germany and Holland, the theoretical orientation of this chapter is much less successful in the Continental countries. In eight of the twenty-one variables the differences between Catholics and Protestants in the Federal Republic run in the opposite of the hypothesized direction. In several other variables the differences between Protestants and Catholics are slight. However, on issues of family values, "life ethics," and "personal ethic" morality questions, the differences between Protestants and Catholics are larger than in the English-speaking world.

The first four variables in the table might be described as measures of the Catholic ethic, which are the opposite of the Protestant ethic in Max Weber's classic sense of the term. Interestingly enough, therefore, the Protestant ethic is less likely to be found in Germany than in the English-speaking countries, even if German Catholics seem less likely to seek post-secondary education.

In Holland there are only four variables in which the findings go in the opposite direction from the predictions; on two of these variables (family values) the differences between Dutch Protestants and Catholics are exactly the opposite of the differences among their West German neighbors. Similarly, the Dutch respondents provide strong support of our religious predictions, again just the opposite of the Germans where Catholics are more satisfied with their Church than Protestants but less devout and doctrinally orthodox than Protestants. Finally, while the Dutch sample provides confirmation for some predictions about moral values and child-rearing values, the confirmation occurs precisely on scales where there is either no or little support in the German sample and not on the scales where confirmation can be found in the German sample.

The English-speaking findings then provide a useful road map for a tour of the Continent, but part of the map applies in Holland and a different part applies in the Federal Republic. Presumably such differences can be accounted for by variation in the history, geography, and political and social structures of the two countries. Attempting to explain them in detail is beyond the purposes of this chapter and probably beyond the capacity of the EVSS data set to provide the raw material for explanations.

Data and Hypotheses: Phase Two

The previous analysis involved data from five English-speaking countries—Great Britain, Ireland, Canada, the United States, and Australia—and two continental countries—West Germany and the Netherlands. By turning to the International Social Survey Project data for 1985 and 1986 one may attempt to replicate the previous findings with different samples and completely different questions.[8] The ISSP surveyed four of those countries (Great Britain n= 1,530; the United States n=677; Australia n=1,528; and Germany n=1,048)and two others (Austria n=987 and Italy n=1,580) in 1985. Moreover, the next phase of the ISSP in 1986 involved seven countries (Great Britain n=1,416; United States n=1,470; Australia n=1,250; Hungary n=1,747; Germany n=2,808 Austria n=1,027; and Italy n=1,027). The 1985 ISSP study focused on attitudes toward government and the 1986 study attempted to measure social support networks. The ISSP data also provided an occasion to test the possibility that education can diminish the differences between the Protestant and Catholic imagination.

It should be noted that there is no significant correlation, net of country, between Catholics and Protestants[9] either in education or in self-perceived social class; thus, whatever differences may emerge cannot be accounted for by educational or social class variables.

Twenty-four variables that seemed appropriate for study were created by factor analysis:

1. A factor based on measures of respect for laws and contractual responsibilities. It seemed reasonable to expect that Catholics would score lower than Protestants on this variable.

2. Two factors were constructed from variables concerning social protest. The first with high loadings on the first four items represented protests that did not involve violence, the second factor with high loads on the fifth and sixth protests represented protests that involved violence. Despite their respect for society, and possibly because of it, Catholics, I hypothesized, would be more likely to approve of resistance to oppressive government. (In an old and long forgotten debate of the Reformation days, Catholic theologians argued for the possible legitimacy of tyrannicide, Protestants against it.) In the EVSS data, Catholic willingness to resist oppression was indeed stronger than Protestant.

3. Two factors were computed from responses to questions about civil liberties. The first seemed to measure respect for freedom of speech, the latter for freedom of publication. The Catholic church has often opposed both sets of liberties and Protestantism has always emphasized freedom of conscience. On the other hand, the Catholic imagination is more open to diversity and the Protestant imagination more likely to respect law. Because imagination is more powerful than institution, the tentative hypothesis is that Catholics will be more likely to advocate civil liberties, just as they will be more likely to approve revolutionary action. Two other factors measured responses to feminism, the first emphasized the fact of injustice against women, the second the state's obligation to provide extra support for women. Other research (Greeley 1988, 1989) indicates that Catholics are more likely to imagine God as a woman and to support feminist positions.

4. However, Protestants would, I suspect, be less likely than Catholics to approve of tight police supervision and restraint of criminals and suspects. The Catholic might support the revolutionary against an oppressive government but she/he would not support the criminal who threatens the networks of ordinary life, which for the Catholic are sacramental. Thus, I expect higher Protestant scores on the two factors that indicate opposition to police power against both suspects and criminals. The first factor reflects opposition to trailing and intercepting the mail and the phone calls of suspects and criminals, the second opposition to holding them over night.

5. Two factors emerged from an analysis of responses to questions about political efficacy. The first had high loadings on responses concerning despair about dealing with government. The second emphasizes

participation in government. One would expect higher scores from Protestants than from Catholics on feelings of oppression and lower scores on participation in government.

6. Three variables constitute a single variable of support for aid to students. Catholics, more inclined to support welfare and government intervention in support of social goals, might be expected to score higher on this factor than Protestants.

7. Three factors were extracted from a series of questions about government intervention in the economy. The first measures attitudes toward jobs and hours, the second attitudes toward wages and prices, and the third opposition to government regulation. Catholics might reasonably be expected to score higher than Protestants on the first two factors, Protestants more likely to score higher than Catholics on the third.

8. Two factors record reactions to government-spending programs; the first emphasizes spending on social problems, the second spending on police and the military. Catholics are more likely to approve of government intervention than Protestants, so should score higher on both these factors. Another factor measured attitudes toward taxation, on which Catholics, because of their belief in government intervention and the fundamental goodness of society, would be expected to have higher scores.

9. A single factor based on the three variables concerning the power of business, labor, and government, measure a respondent's feeling that there is too much power concentrated in social institutions—a classic measure, it would seem, of the view that society is sinful and God-forsaken. Hence, Protestants might be expected to score higher on this measure than Catholics.

10. On the other hand, a single factor that measures support for government ownership of industry would also appear to be a measure of the classic Catholic propensity to support government intervention in economic life. Hence, Catholics will be more likely to have high scores on this scale than Protestants.

11. Yet another single factor measures attitudes toward government responsibility in economic life. Again one would expect Catholics, with their greater confidence in society, to favor these government interventions than Protestants.

12. A final factor was designed especially to measure the Catholic egalitarianism reported in the previous analysis. Hence, Catholics can be expected to score higher on this scale (Equality).

The "communitarian" emphasis of Catholicism and the "individual-ist" emphasis of Protestantism, it was suggested, is the behavioral re-sults of these different pictures of social reality. The Catholic propensity will be to see virtue as integration into social realities while the Protes-tant propensity will be to see virtue in the struggle for freedom from the constraints of social realities. Salvation, both religious and personal for the Dialectical Imagination, is an individual effort. For the Analogical Imagination it is a social effort.

13. Therefore, in particular with the data of ISSP 86 in mind, Catho-lics will form more intense family networks. They will live closer to and visit relatives more often than do Protestants.

Thus, the prediction is that, net of the influence of the various coun-tries, Catholics will be more likely to live close to and visit their mother, father, sister, brother, daughter, son, and other relatives than will other Christians.

Analysis: Phase Two

Table 7.3 presents results of an analysis of attitudes toward govern-ment intervention and the family network patterns of Protestants and Catholics. Twelve of the twenty-two attitudes toward government pre-dictions were supported at levels of statistical significance (all but two with a probability of error less than .001). None of the predictions were refuted by significant evidence in the opposite direction. Only in the categories of Spend and Aid was there no evidence to support the hypotheses.

Thus, Protestants are more likely than Catholics to support obedience to laws; Catholics are more likely than Protestants to approve violent protests and to support freedom of publication and to recognize unequal treatment of women; Protestants are more likely than Catholics to resist temporary arrest for suspects and criminals, to feel oppressed by the power structures of society and lack of power in dealing with govern-ment. They are also more likely than Catholics to think taxes are too high. Catholics are more likely than Protestants to support government intervention in the economy, government ownership of industry, and equalization of income.

The Catholic attitude toward the role of government may seem paradoxical—on the one hand, supportive of more intervention, and on

TABLE 7.3
Religion and attitudes towards government and family networks by education

	β net of country	
	All	**More than eleven years**
	Attitudes Toward Government	
Obey1	.06	.05
Prot2	.06	.06
Lib2	.05	.00*
Fem1	.04	.05
Crime2	.05	.06
Govt1	.04	.10
Pol1	.06	.04
Tax	.05	.04
Power	.07	.04
Ownership	.06	.06
Welfare	.07	.09
Equality	.05	.06
Average	.06	.06
	Visits	
Mother	.04	.21
Father	.04	.24
Sister	.04	.04
Brother	.06	.01
Son	.07	.04
Relative	.04	.11
	Distance	
Mother	.04	.18
Father	.03*	.18
Sister	.05	.19
Brother	.07	.18
Daughter	.05	.05
Son	.05	.03
Relative	.04	.04

*Not statistically significant

the other, more likely to approve of violent resistance. Perhaps the reason is that the Catholic imagination inclines people to expect the government to be good, modestly and imperfectly good perhaps, but still good. When the flaws in government become intolerable those who believe government can be a positive good are more likely to take to the streets than those who take it for granted that governmental power is always evil. Catholic theologians like Thomas Aquinas approved of tyrannicide in certain circumstances. Martin Luther disagreed.

To repeat a theme of the previous analysis, the "liberal/conservative" paradigm cannot cope with the Catholic propensity to support "liberal" policies of government intervention and egalitarianism and conservative policies on response to crime and criminals. However, a paradigm based on a theory of different "imaginations" (or "ethics") can easily account for and find consistency in the patterns reported in this chapter: under ordinary circumstances Catholics tend to picture society as supportive and not oppressive; Protestants tend to picture society as oppressive and not supportive.

The second and third sections of table 7.3 present the results of an analysis of the family network variables in the ISSP 86 study. Of the thirteen items analyzed in ANOVA equations, twelve correlate at levels of statistical significance with religion when the effect of different national cultures is removed. Catholics are more likely to visit parents, children, siblings, and other relatives than other Christians. They are also more likely to live close to everyone (but their fathers) than are other Christians. Net of national differences, then, Catholics do form more intense family networks than do other Christians, as the theory suggested they would. Moreover, the propensity to visit is additional to and independent of the propensity to live near relatives (except for brother and other relatives).[10]

The second column in table 7.3 presents the beta correlation in ANOVA analysis for country and religion for those respondents who have had twelve or more years of education to test the possibility that differences between Protestants and Catholics may diminish among those who have higher education. Differences in scores on the LIB disappears but there is an increase in differences on political efficacy and welfare. The average correlation is the same for those who have had advanced education as it is for the rest of the sample. Among those who have advanced education, Catholics are even more likely than Protestants to visit mother, father, and relative, and live closest to mother, father, sister, and brother in comparison with the general population. Perhaps the increased educational attainment provides the affluence required for such choices.

Thus, twenty-six of the thirty-six hypotheses fashioned for testing against the ISSP data are sustained. There is no evidence to support any of the contrary hypotheses. Analysis of ISSP data, then, neatly replicates the analysis of the EVSS data. In two separate samples, taken by different organizations and using different sets of questions, evidence is found to reject the null hypothesis that denominational differences do not effect attitudes and behavior. Moreover, since the theory of the Analogical Imagination enables one to make forty-seven out of seventy-two possible correct predictions about the direction of the differences (and in none of the others is the difference significant in the opposite direction) one must also reject the hypothesis that the differences between Protestants and Catholics cannot be accounted for by different ways of imagining the world and human society and communities.

Data and Hypotheses: Phase Three

There are no variables in the EVSS that enable us to ask whether the differences between Protestants and Catholics recorded in the first two tables of this chapter can be linked to differences between Analogical and Dialectical Imaginations. However, the special religion module of the 1988 General Social Survey does provide items that measure both values and the religious imagination.[11]

The null hypothesis for this third phase of analysis is that the correlations that exist between denomination and values in the United States cannot be attributed in whole or in part to differences in religious imaginations between members of the two denominations.

The following variables seemed appropriate for analysis.

Feminism

Factor analysis of five items measuring attitudes toward equality for women were found to constitute one scale. Because of Catholic acceptance of the goodness to be found in the complexity of human relationships, it is expected that Catholics will be more tolerant of multiple roles for women and hence score higher on this scale than Protestants.

Welfare

A single factor was discovered with loadings on four welfare items. It was expected that because of their communitarian orientation, Catholics would score higher on this scale than Protestants.

Capital Punishment

A single item measures respondents' attitudes toward capital punishment. It was expected that Catholics, with greater tolerance for the complexity of the human condition, would be more likely to oppose capital punishment than Protestants.

Presence of God

Because they are more likely to see God as an intimate other with whom one can disagree instead of a distant and absent God and because they believe that God, present in the world, is responsible for the world, Catholics are likely to score higher on a factor that measures anger toward God and doubts about Her.

Devotion

A factor emerged which emphasized being born again, reading the Bible, inviting someone else to accept Jesus as savior, and saying grace. Such devotions seemed clearly Protestant in their orientation.

Moral rigidity

Four items that stressed rigid moral decision making constituted a single factor that seemed to reflect a dialectical approach to reality. Hence, Protestants were expected to score higher on it than Catholics.

Doubts

Four questions were asked about events that created doubt about religious faith. These also clustered on one factor. Since Catholics, I have hypothesized, are more likely to doubt, it is expected that they will score higher than Protestants.

Faith

Four items were asked about phenomena that strengthened religious faith; they too clustered on a single scale. Since Catholics see the world and its events as revelatory, it was expected that they would score higher than Protestants on this scale.

Life Decisions

Two factors emerged in an analysis of four items about influences on life decision making: one with high loadings on the Bible and Church leaders, the second with loadings on self and others. It was expected that Protestants, with their emphasis on individual decisions and the Bible as road map would score higher than Catholics on both these factors.

Personal Goodness

Four questions were also asked about what constitutes the good person. All four clustered on the same factor. With the emphasis on following one's own conscience in this factor it was expected that it would also produce higher scores for Protestants.

Attitudes Toward Science

Two factors were developed from four questions about science, one emphasizing the positive aspects of science, the other the negative. Since Catholics are more likely to see the world as sacramental, they would be more likely to appreciate the scientific study of the world and score higher than Protestants on the positive scale and lower on the negative scale.

Analysis: Phase Three

There are thirteen variables to be tested for denominational difference. Once a difference is discovered, it must then be asked whether the

TABLE 7.4
Values, Denomination and the Religious Imagination

	r[1]	β[2]
Feminism	.10	.05*
Welfare	.10	.06*
Capital Punishment	.11	.06*
Presence of God	.12	.08
Devotion	.31	.26
Moral Rigidity	.15	.10
Good person	−.10	−.05*
Life Decisions1	.21	.16
Science1	.08	.03*
Doubts	.11	.09

*Not statistically significant
1. Correlation with denomination in the direction of the hypothesis.
2. Correlation with denomination net of religious imagination.

religious imagination items developed for the General Social Survey (Greeley 1988a, 1989a) can account for some of the differences. Catholics are more likely to see God as an intimate other—lover, friend, spouse, and mother—than Protestants and the world and human nature as basically good, as the theory of the Analogical Imagination predicted they would. Does this difference account for at least some of the denominational value differences that exist in the General Social Survey?

The first column in table 7.4 reports the significant differences between Protestants and Catholics in the GSS data. Only Science2, Faith, and Life Decision2 did not correlate significantly with denomination. The Good Person scale relates in the *opposite* of the predicted direction: Catholics are more likely than Protestants to emphasize all the characteristics of the good person.

The second column in the table presents the standardized correlations between denomination and the value scales when the religious imagination is taken into account. All the correlations decline, half of them into statistical insignificance.

Thus, Catholics are more likely than Protestants to support feminism and welfare. Protestants are more likely than Catholics to engage in certain devotional practices (such as reading the Bible and being born again), to support capital punishment and to disapprove of science. Catholics have lower scores than Protestants on moral rigidity and are less likely than Protestants to rely on the Bible and on authority for moral decisions. Protestants are less likely to have doubts and to be angry at God than Catholics. All these differences are reduced, some to the point of insignificance once one takes into account the differences in religious imagination between the two denominations.

The EVSS and ISSP data show denominational value differences in nine countries. The GSS data show that somewhat parallel differences in one country can be accounted for in part by differences between the Analogical and Dialectical Imaginations. The final null hypothesis must therefore be rejected.

Discussion

Granted that all but one of the differences reported in tables 7.1, 7.3 and 7.4 are in the hypothesized directions and that they are statistically significant, how important are they? Only seven of the standardized etas for denomination are higher than .1, only one higher than .2. Are not such differences trivial in the general order of human diversity? Granted that they exist, what difference do they make?

One notes, as sociologists always do when such an objection is raised, that most social variables, even those that everyone agrees are important such as gender, income, and education, explain rather little of the variance in human behavior precisely because humans are so variegated and complex.

One also adds that there ought not to have been any reasonable expectation of enormous differences between the two denominations. As was observed earlier, the two different "imaginations" represent tendencies and not zero sum views of reality. Moreover, both Protestant and Catholics are part of the Western cultural heritage, the North Atlantic tradition (which can for present purposes be extended to include Australia), and the "English-speaking World." One could not expect enormous differences between denominational communities, which in all but one of the countries continue to coexist more or less amicably with one another (and do so even in the Republic of Ireland, whatever may be happening in the six counties).

On a list of predictor variables, then, where might one rank denomination? How important is it relative to other variables? In table 7.1, with

TABLE 7.5
Differences between Protestants and Catholics (English-Speaking)

	Catholics	Protestants
Same Pay	34%	22%
Owners Run	53%	61%
Obey without Understanding	53%	66%
Reject		
Drinkers	49%	59%
Disturbed	29%	35%
Right extremists	23%	29%
Left extremists	29%	36%
Disapprove strongly[1]		
Bribe	80%	88%
Dole	75%	84%
Bus fare	67%	78%
Euthanasia	51%	41%

1. Ten and nine on a ten-point scale of approve/disapprove.

six exceptions, the beta between variable and country is larger than that between variable and denomination. The average beta for country is .16, the average for denomination is .09. However, the average beta for the relationship between gender and the twenty-one variables in table 7.1 is .045. How important then is denomination in predicting values (of the sort measured by EVSS)? Not as important on the average as nation but more important on the average than gender.

One leaves denomination out of design and analysis, then, with less reason than one would exclude gender. However, such a mechanical approach to the cross-national importance of denomination is artificial. In the real world one would want to know who the people were, where they were from, and what the relevant value was. If one was, for example, dealing with issues of tolerance of deviants in a neighborhood or of moral decision making or of the sexual aspects of family revolution or of the "fair" use of authority, one would want to be very sensitive to nuances of denominational difference because they would likely be as important as the differences in national background.

Thus, table 7.5, which replaces ANOVA with simple cross-tabulations on specific items, demonstrates that the differences between Protestants and Catholics on certain matters can be important to policymakers—and possibly dangerous for the policymakers who have persuaded themselves that in a modernized, urbanized, and industrialized society, differences in denomination ethic/imagination no longer matter.

Thus, in the work situation, Catholics are 13 percentage points less likely to accept orders they do not understand. They are 12 percentage points more likely to demand equal pay for equal work, regardless of the quality of the latter. They are 8 percentage points less likely to take for granted the right of owners to manage a firm. They are 7 percentage points more likely to choose equality over freedom. A factory manager or trade union leader with equal Catholic and Protestant proportions in his constituency would be ill advised to ignore such differences.

In neighborhood situations, Catholics are more likely to be willing to tolerate those with drinking problems and emotional disorders and political extremists of either hue, than are Protestants. A neighborhood leader, opting for increased diversity, should be aware of where he is likely to find allies and where adversaries.

Moreover, a political reformer should also understand that while the majority of Catholics are likely to oppose bribery, cheating on welfare, and on public transportation, their opposition is not as strong as is the opposition of Protestants. "Reform" historically has been a word with which Protestants are more comfortable than Catholics.

Finally, a college administrator would want to take into account that more than half of the Catholics with advanced education in the ISSP sample report that they had visited their mother and/or father at least several times a week as opposed to a third of the Protestants. An increase of free time for family visits might improve the morale of Catholic students more than the morale of Protestant students.

These four sets of differences, easily predictable from the theoretical orientation of this chapter, demonstrate how useless it is to try to pin the labels "liberal" or "conservative" on either denominational heritage. On issues of sexual morality and family life, Catholics are clearly more "conservative" (because of their imaginative predispositions, I have argued). But on issues of social justice and neighborhood community they are just as clearly more "liberal." And on matters of "corruption," whether they are more "tolerant" or more "corrupt" probably depends on which denominational heritage provides the observer's perspective.

Summary and Conclusion

In summary, the four null hypotheses can be safely rejected. There is no evidence in the data analyzed in this chapter that the Analogical Imagination is either extinct or becoming extinct. The Protestant ethic and the Catholic ethic are alive and well, though perhaps not in their original form in the land where the idea originated. Both ethics seem to result from preconscious narrative symbols.

Modern empirical social science emerged just at the time when change from an old order to a new order was everywhere (in Europe) to be observed, a change already far along according to the men who founded our tradition. The "mechanical" society was being replaced by the "organic" society, "*Gesellschaft*" was replacing "*Gemeinschaft*," "association" was replacing "community." The Protestant ethic, broadly defined as the "individualist" ethic, was replacing the Catholic ethic, broadly defined as the "communal ethic." Humankind (European and North Atlantic) was on pilgrimage from one end of what Talcott Parsons would later call his pattern variables to the other end.

Since the end of the Second World War, scholars have refined and nuanced that vision and concluded that, while change has occurred and continued to occur, it is far more complex, uneven, multidimensional, and multidirectional than appeared a hundred years ago.

Despite contemporary sophistication about the evolutionary changes, which the Founders noted, there still is often a moment of surprise when one finds that in yet another matter, the old, the archaic, the communal manages to survive, especially when that matter is religious. For example, virtually all the individual reports from the EVSS assume as a given, without time-series evidence, the disappearance of old-value structures; the possibility that denominational differences across national lines can persist despite the forces of modernization seems too absurd to consider.

Ought not the Catholic ethic, clearly a relic of earlier, more rural, less industrialized times, gradually erode in the face of the irresistible forces of individualism and social and geographic mobility? How does one explain the residual strength of this supposedly outmoded worldview?

How does a value orientation rooted in an agricultural and feudal experience manage to survive in an utterly different environment? Did not
even Weber himself predict that industrialism would eventually eliminate differences between Protestants and Catholics?

The answer seems to be that worldviews are not neatly written propositional paragraphs that can be explicated and critiqued in rational and
discursive fashion. Rather they are, in their origins and their raw, primal
power, tenacious and durable narrative symbols that take possession of
the imagination early in the socialization process and provide patterns
of meaning and response that shape the rest of life. The theory of different imaginations of society, encoded in different stories of God's relationship with the world, on which this chapter is based, can explain the
durability of separate worldviews among Protestants and Catholics. The
differences will disappear only when Protestants become more likely to
picture God as present in the world and/or Catholics more likely to picture Her as absent from the world.

Surely there are convergences as Alwin has established among American Protestants and Catholics in their child-rearing orientations. But how
central to the religious imagination are expectations about child rearing? Or to put the question at a more general level, what is essential to
an imaginative tradition and what is peripheral? What changes more or
less easily and what resists change, perhaps implacably? What values
flow almost inevitably from one's image of a god present in society or
absent from society?

At the present time there are no data to answer that question and
perhaps no theory to provide the questions to ask of a data set. The items
in the EVSS study were there to be used, but there is no reason to believe that of themselves they can do any more than force us to reject the
null hypotheses of the present chapter. They do not necessarily reflect
what is essential to the different religious imaginations, save perhaps in
remote and indirect ways.[12]

The GSS findings, limited to one country, give a hint that images of
God and world can indeed account for some of the value differences
between Protestant and Catholic, but such an exploration must remain
tentative until the technique for measuring religious imagery becomes
more sophisticated.

The Analogical Imagination may be alive and well, but there is much
work to be done before we begin to understand it and the Dialectical

Imagination, its counterpart and complement. In this chapter, however, I have been able to link the analyses of the Founders to that of David Tracy and thus show that doctrinal and ethical differences between Catholics and Protestants exist on an imaginative infrastructure. Moreover, I have demonstrated that such differences in imaginative substructure are remarkably durable and that Catholics continue to be different from Protestants in ways that are predictable if one understands how the Catholic religious stories differ from Protestant religious stories. In an era which some persist in calling postmodern, there might be more hesitancy than there was in the time of the Founders in deciding that, because the Catholic ethic (and the Catholic imagination that underpins it) is necessarily the inferior of the two ethics.

In chapter 13 I will contrast the Catholic imagination (Catholicism as poetry) with the imagination of members of the Southern Baptist Convention, the second largest American denomination and one that might be expected to weave quite different religious poetry.

Notes

1. The findings in this chapter were first reported in Greeley 1989a.
2. In the United States today Catholics score higher on achievement measures than do Protestants, and Jews higher than Catholics.
3. This project was inaugurated in 1981 by a consortium of research organizations under the loose direction of British Gallup and a committee of scholars assembled in Amsterdam (Abrams, Gerard, and Timms 1985; Calvaruso and Abbruzzese 1985; Fogerty, Ryan, and Lee 1984; Halman, Hennka, Moor, and Zanders 1987; Harding, Phillips, and Fogerty 1986; Kerkhofs and Rezohazy 1984; Noelle-Neuman, and Kocher 1987; Orizo 1983; Petterson 1987).
4. The Irish sample is of the thirty-two counties of historic Ireland.
5. Though both Ireland and Canada are legally bilingual.
6. A description of the wording of each question in a factor is available from the author at NORC, 1155 East 60th Street, Chicago Illinois, 60637.
7. Not all the questions administered to respondents in the North Atlantic countries were also administered in Australia. Hence, scores are presented on only seven variables for respondents from that nation.
8. Data and codebooks are available from the Zentralarchiv für Empirische Sozialforschung of the University of Cologne. Data were collected by RSSS in Australia, ZUMA in Germany, NORC in the USA, SCPR in Great Britain, IS in Austria, and Eurisco in Italy.
9. Even in Germany, where Max Weber found his data, Catholics report 10.0 years of education and Protestants 10.1, a difference that is not statistically significant.
10. In a multiple regression analysis not presented here.
11. The 1988 GSS contained 1,480 respondents. To control for race, black respondents were omitted from this analysis since there are not enough black Catholics

8

The Pragmatics of Prayer

Religious stories, like all stories, are about relationships. In the religious story the interaction partner is and has been for most people the Ultimate Other, a.k.a. God.[1] Thus far in this essay I have considered the religious story to be contained in the narrative images of God. But in addition to the image of the relevant other in a relationship, one must also take into account the telling of a story, the frequency of interaction with the other. I may have a benign image of the president of the University of Chicago, but since I interact with her rarely or never, that image is not important in the story I tell myself and others about the university. On the other hand, I have a positive image of the mayor of Chicago and interact with him frequently (because he is a neighbor), so he is an important part of the story I tell to myself and others about the "city that works."

So it would be with God. Relevant to the religious story I tell is both my image of Her and the frequency of my interaction with Her. Hence, prayer is at least arguably (before the data) an important component of religious stories.

Meissner (1990: 82) summarizes the importance of prayer,

> In this activity, the believer immerses himself [sic] in the religious experience in a more direct, immediate and personal way than in any other aspect of his religious involvement. Thus all the unconscious and preconscious as well as conscious and reflective elements in the individual's relationship to God and the characteristics of his god-representation come into play.

Since sociology can fairly be called the study of patterns of human relationships and the constraints these patterns impose, prayer is a legitimate subject for sociological inquiry. Prayer represents a human relationship, perhaps even an intimate human relationship, to the transcendent. As Heiler (1932: 358) puts it, *"Prayer is therefore a living communion of the religious man with God, conceived as personal and present in experience, a communion which reflects of the forms of social relations of humanity"* (italics in original). Whether there is in fact a transcendent to which to relate is a question for which sociology cannot provide an answer. However, to paraphrase W. I. Thomas the fact that a person considers a relationship to the transcendent to be real in itself is a reality that merits study, especially since that relationship, however nonexistent the interaction partner (or Partner if one wishes) in it may be, may impose constraints that affect behavior in other relationships. If relationship to the transcendent is considered real, it will be real at least in its consequences.

Why do humans engage in prayer, dialogue with a partner who is at best transcendent and at worst either nonexistent or uninterested? Is prayer a "rational" behavior? Does it provide a payoff in human happiness that is worth the effort? As will be noted subsequently, most Americans believe that prayers "are heard." Heiler (1932: 355) observes, "it is always a great longing for life, for a more potent, a purer, a more blessed life. 'When I seek thee, my God,' prays Augustine, 'I seek a blessed life.'"

The research question is whether there is any evidence that prayer does indeed provide a more "blessed life" for those who pray and for those to whom the praying person relates in one form or another. If it does, then prayer might not be written off as irrational behavior even by those who are convinced that no one is listening.

This investigation is based on my theory of the sociology of religion, which assumes that religion does not end in experience, image, story, ritual, and community but that it begins with such phenomena and takes its raw power from them. Reflected religion is derivative of experiential religion, prose religion is derivative of poetic religion. Not everyone need have a religion though in the course of human history, most people have had a set of narrative symbols which purport uniquely to explain the real and to respond to ultimate questions of suffering, injustice, and death.

One's religious images and the intensity of one's relationship to God in prayer may be considered as experiential religion. One's relationship to the transcendent (or if one wishes the Transcendent) is a template for other human relationships. Prayer is one of humankind's endeavors to communicate to the transcendent. I hypothesize that such a relationship, especially when combined with a benign image of God, will affect other human relationships, particularly the more intimate relationships, but also the more distant relationships, even with condemned criminals. As we relate to the Other, so we tend to relate to the other, whether it be the intimate other or the distant other. Prayer is a story of relationship to God and hence will influence the other stories with which humans make sense of their lives.

Moreover, since the theory argues that religion is experiential, metaphorical, and narrative before it becomes cognitive and doctrinal, there is reason to expect that it will be the actual fact and experience of praying and not formal doctrinal convictions about the existence of God which will produce the predicted correlations.

Finally, since the Catholic imagination is "analogical," that is, inclined to think of creation as a metaphor for God, it might be more open in some instances to being influenced by a prayer relationship with the Ultimate Other in its relationships with the contingent other. The persistent Catholic interaction may also occur when frequency of prayer has become the predictor variable.

This chapter is divided into three parts. The first will consider the phenomenon of prayer in contemporary American life. The second will consider religious poetry (using prayer as I used belief in life after death in a previous chapter) as a predictor variable. The third will attempt to replicate the American findings in other nations, just as we did in the last chapter.

To formulate expectations as hypotheses, I propose the following:

1. Intense and benign relations with the Transcendent Other, as measured by frequent prayer and benign images of God, will tend to correlate with benign relationships with the contingent intimate other—the self, the spouse, the family—and the distant other—the condemned criminal and the AIDS victim.

2. It will be the experience of prayer itself and not formal doctrinal position on the existence of God that will be decisive for the effect mentioned in the previous paragraph.

3. Because Catholicism is a religion that heavily emphasizes the objects, events, and persons of creation as metaphors for God, the effects predicted will tend to be especially strong for Catholics.

Or to formulate the expectations of this essay as a null hypothesis: prayer will have no effect on attitudes toward other humans.

Frequency of Prayer: United States

Beginning in 1983, NORC (Davis and Smith 1991) asked a question ("How often do you pray?") about frequency of prayer in its annual General Social Survey. Responses (n=8,683) to this question indicate rates of prayer that are alarmingly high (if one is a convinced supporter of the "secularization" theory): 57 percent of Americans pray every day, 78 percent pray at least once a week, only 1 percent never pray. Moreover, these rates of prayer represent a net increase of 4 percentage points in daily prayer over a NORC survey from 1972, a positive correlation (and statistically significant) between time and frequency of prayer. This increase can be accounted for by the slightly different prayer patterns of certain age cohorts. The cohort born between 1955 and 1970 (a "post-Vietnam" cohort if one wishes since this cohort came to maturity after the time of the war in Vietnam) began its prayer life cycle at a higher intercept than the previous cohorts, born between 1939 and 1954 (the "Vietnam" cohort). Forty-four percent of the "post-Vietnam" cohort prayed at least once a day in the late 1980s when they were between eighteen and thirty-three years old[2] while 37 percent of the "Vietnam" cohort prayed at least once a day in the early 1970s when they were between eighteen and thirty-three years old. Moreover the "Vietnam" cohort in the late 1980s (when it was between thirty-four and forty-nine years old) was 4 percentage points less likely to pray daily (50 percent) than was the pre-Vietnam cohort when it was the same age in the early 1970s (54 percent). Thus, the prayer behavior of the "Vietnam" cohort seems somewhat deviant, though the deviance diminishes with age (but does not disappear). The increase in prayer between the two time periods thus can be accounted for by the higher rates of prayer of the "Post-Vietnam" cohort relative to its predecessor.

It is possible to be more precise about the time of the change in prayer for those under thirty-three years old. If one groups the respondents under thirty-three years old at the time of inquiry into three-year age cohorts and considers the proportion praying daily in each of the cohorts (table 8.1), the upswing begins with those born between 1951 and 1953, 44 percent of whom pray at least daily as opposed to 38 percent of those born between 1948 and 1950. Among those born between 1954 and 1956, the proportion praying at least every day rises to 49 percent, 11 percentage points higher than the cohort six years older, a striking generational change and one *against* the perennial "secularization hypotheses."[3]

TABLE 8.1
Daily Prayer by Age and Cohort

Born	Under 33	34–49
35–38		58%
39–41	37%	54%
41–44	36%	53%
45–47	40%	50%
48–50	38%	49%
51–53	44%	
54–56	49%	

The second column in table 8.1 traces the subsequent history of the "Vietnam" generation into the middle years of life, between 34 and 50, and demonstrates that their divergence from patterns of prayers continues. The four cohorts born between 1939 and 1950 are notably less likely to pray daily than those who came before them. Assuming that they came of age roughly between 1960 and 1970, they represent in their middle years of life lower levels of prayer presumably because of the experiences of their formative years. The difference between them and those born in the middle and late 1930s is especially striking for the last two of the four cohorts who came of age in the late 1960s. They are 8 and 9 percentage points less likely respectively to pray daily than those born immediately before them.

The generational decline in prayer seems to have begun with those born in the early 1940s and to have ended with those born in the early 1950s. The former were less likely to pray than their successors when they were under thirty-three three years old and less likely to pray than their predecessors when they were between thirty-four and forty-nine years old.

This phenomenon suggests that prayer may continue to increase in the United States in the years to come. It also confirms the suggestion made by Wuthnow (1976) that the generational experiences of a given cohort may shape its religious behavior but that such behavior may not necessarily predict the behavior of subsequent cohorts. The "Vietnam" cohort seems to be marginally less religious than either its predecessors or successors and not the harbinger of long-term social change.

Three-fifths of "Fundamentalist"[4] Protestants in the General Social Survey Data pray daily, as do 55 percent of "moderate" Protestants and

49 percent of the "liberal" Protestants. Fifty-seven percent of Catholics pray everyday, as do 22 percent of the Jews, 14 percent of those with no religion, and 56 percent of those with an "other" religion. Sixty percent of those who believe in life after death pray daily, as do 38 percent of those who reject a belief in life after death and 41 percent of those who are not sure about life after death.

Seventy percent of those who believe in God pray everyday (as do one out of ten of those who do not believe in God); approximately one out of five of those who believe in a Higher Power or believe in God sometimes also pray daily as do a little less than two out of five of those who believe but doubt. Seventeen percent of those who are uncertain about the existence of God or reject it and do not believe in life after death pray at least once a day; 35 percent of this group pray at least once a week.[5]

How can one explain such frequent prayer, not only among those who believe in God and life after death but especially among those who do not believe in God or survival? Do they address their prayers "to whom it may concern"?

Obviously one needs to know more about the content, the occasion, and the expectations of such prayers. But it is possible that there are pragmatic reasons for prayer. In the 1972 NORC study 88 percent of Americans believed that prayers were heard, 56 percent were very sure that they were heard, 25 percent were pretty sure, and 6 percent not so sure. Thus, more than half of the population believed that prayer worked, and only 18 percent were either sure than it did not or "not so sure" that it did. Under such circumstances why not pray? What does one have to lose?

Moreover, the older one is the more likely one is to believe that prayers work. The correlation between age and prayer is .26. It is reduced to a standardized coefficient of .19 when the increased confidence that prayers is heard is taken into account, to .14 when an increased sense that one is near to God is entered in the equation and to .00 when an interaction between age and confidence that prayer is heard is added to the equation. Thus, not only does confidence that prayers are heard increase with age but the impact of that confidence on prayer becomes stronger (hence the interaction term). As one grows older, one is more confident that prayers are heard and that one is intimate with the one (or One) to whom the prayers are directed and hence more likely to pray.[6] Prayer is perceived as pragmatic behavior, something that works.

It does not follow that this pragmatic explanation of prayer is justified by the facts. It follows only that as Americans mature they are more likely to believe that there are solid grounds for prayer and that life has taught them that it is reasonable to pray.[7]

The Pragmatics of Prayer: United States

Prayer does seem to have, or at least relate to, payoffs that could confirm such pragmatism. Personal happiness (percent "very happy"), marital happiness (percent "very happy" in their marriage), and satis-

FIGURE 8.1
Life Satisfactions by Prayer

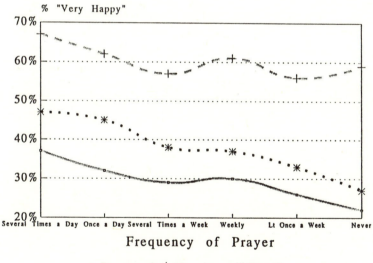

Frequency of Prayer

-- Personal + Marriage ✳ Family

Source: GSS 1984-91 N=12,203

faction with family (percent "greatly satisfied" with their family life) all increase with the frequency of prayer (figure 8.1) and all the correlations are statistically significant.

At least three possible explanations could be offered for these relationships: (1) prayer itself, as intimacy with God, may make life more satisfying; (2) prayer may reveal an underlying worldview with a more positive orientation toward life; and (3) prayer may be the result of a satisfying life and the need to be grateful for it. Thus, prayer could be a cause, an indicator, or a result—or, as may be more likely, a complex mixture of all three.

The image one has of God, which may be taken as a narrative symbol that expresses religious belief metaphorically, reinforces the impact of prayer on marital happiness. Those who imagine God as "Spouse" rather than "Master" (on a seven-point scale) are more likely to say that their marriage is very happy but the highest level of marital happiness is reported by those who pray everyday *and* picture God as a spouse (figure 8.2). The combination of an intimate picture of God and frequent intimacy in prayer correlates with high marital satisfaction. The happy marriage may reflect the imagery and the intimacy with God or cause it; or, more likely, both processes are at work. In any case, devotion, imagery, and marital satisfaction do indeed relate with one another.

Moreover, frequent prayer and frequent sex produce the highest level of marital happiness (72 percent who report both are also "very happy" in their marriages, as opposed to 52 percent who report neither). Daily prayer adds to the level of marital happiness for both those who have sex more often than once a week and for those who do not; indeed daily prayer without sex more than once a week produces the same level of reported marital satisfaction as does sex more than once a week in the absence of daily prayer; In some marriages frequent prayer seems to be a substitute for frequent sex. Thus, the pattern of one's putative relationship to the transcendent as specified by the image of that transcendent and by frequency of prayer to it (or, should one wish, It) correlates with the reported pattern of relationship with one's spouse and family.

But does it affect one's relationship with others beyond the family boundaries, criminals for example? Does prayer correlate with attitudes toward the death penalty for condemned murderers? One would expect that those who pray often might be religiously rigid and hence more likely to support the punishment of criminals by death. However, just

FIGURE 8.2
Happy Marriage by Prayer and Image

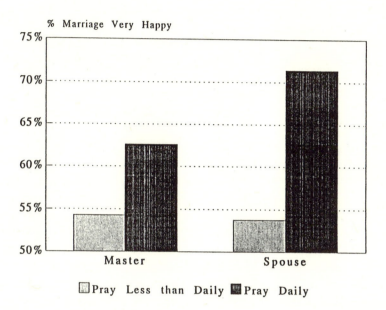

% Marriage Very Happy

Source: GSS 1984-91 N=12,203

the opposite seems to be the case (figure 8.3). Those who pray twice a day are twice as likely to oppose the death penalty as those who never pray (30 percent versus 15 percent). Moreover, this opposition to the death penalty is especially strong among those who pray more than once a day and score high on a grace scale. Those who pray more than once a day and have at least two "gracious" images of God (mother, lover, spouse, and friend as opposed to father, judge, master, and king) are twice as likely to oppose the death penalty as those who have less than two such images and do not pray more than once a day. Thus, both the

FIGURE 8.3
Death Penalty by Prayer and Image of God

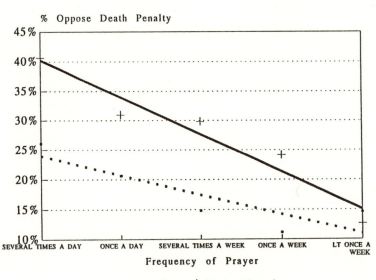

% Oppose Death Penalty

Frequency of Prayer

·· Less Gracious + More Gracious

Source: GSS 1984-91 N=12,203

frequency of prayer and the image of the one to whom prayer is directed create a template which has a considerable impact on relationships with others, even criminals.

In a previous chapter I established that the grace scale was correlated by the General Social Survey with attitudes toward AIDS victims. The theory on which this book is based would predict that frequency of prayer in combination with a high score on the grace scale would correlate with a willingness to endorse government funding of health costs for AIDS victims. However, no correlation emerged until denomination was held

FIGURE 8.4

Sympathy for AIDS Victims by Prayer, Image of God, and Religion

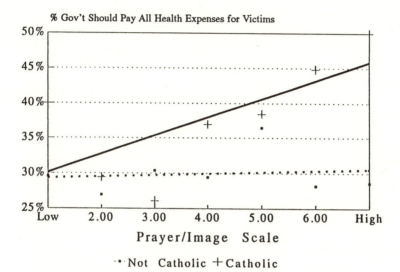

% Gov't Should Pay All Health Expenses for Victims

·· Not Catholic + Catholic

Source: GSS 1984–91 N=1,308

constant (figure 8.4). As our third hypothesis led us to suspect in some cases the effect of prayer would be especially strong among Catholics. Despite the relatively small size of the sample (N=190), there is a statistically significant correlation between frequency of prayer and sympathy for AIDS victims among Catholics, an effect that becomes even stronger when imagery of God is taken into account as in figure 8.4.

Frequent prayer therefore seems to be pragmatic not only for the one who prays but for those to whom the one who prays relates, if only atittudinally in the matter of the death penalty and AIDS victims. Prayer increases with maturity, relates to personal, marital, and familial happiness, and to orientations toward capital punishment and AIDS victims. It is especially potent in its impact on marital happiness, attitudes toward capital punishment, and help for AIDS victims if it is combined with benign images of God. The story of one's relationship with God, as contained in the frequency and object of prayer, shapes paradigms for the story of one's life (and presumably is shaped by the story of one's life).

Three Objections

Three objections might be leveled at these findings:

1. *A social desirability phenomenon may be at work. It is socially desirable to say both that you are happy and that you pray frequently. Therefore, the findings are an epiphenomenon and unimportant.*

The social desirability argument is an easy one to make about findings that a critic does not like and a difficult argument to refute. Opposition to the death penalty is surely not a socially desirable response in contemporary America nor is support for the government picking up all the expenses for the treatment of AIDS victims. Moreover, as we shall see shortly, the same relationships exist in countries where there is less prayer and no reason to think that the claim to frequent prayer would be a socially desirable response (most notably Norway). Finally, one must ask whether for those who do not believe in God or doubt Her existence, a claim to frequent prayer is in fact a socially desirable answer. Would it not just as likely or even more likely be a response of which one would be inclined to be ashamed because it represents a perhaps cowardly hedging of bets? Is the impact of prayer merely an indicator of the impact of religion as such on attitudes and values? What impact does prayer have on the attitudes of those who do not believe firmly in God?

The answer, it would appear, is that what counts is prayer and not certain belief in God. As figures 8.5 and 8.6 demonstrate, the correlation curve for those who are certain about God's existence and those who doubt or deny are almost exactly the same when the matter is personal happiness and opposition to the death penalty. Moreover, for Catholics, frequent prayer causes sympathy for AIDS victims to converge in the believers and the nonbelievers.

FIGURE 8.5
Marital Happiness by Prayer and Belief in God

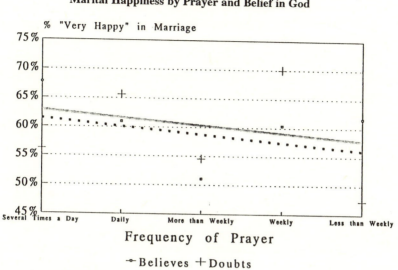

Source: GSS 1984-91 N=12,203

FIGURE 8.6
Opposition to Death Penalty by Prayer and Belief in God

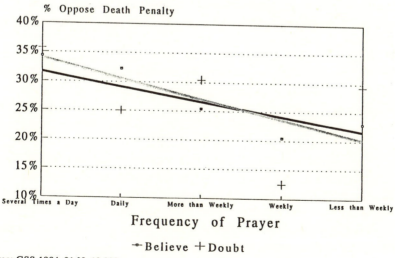

Source: GSS 1984-91 N=12,203

To restate this finding in percentages for two of the variables, 33 percent of those who prayed everyday opposed the death penalty as opposed to 24 percent who did not pray everyday and the proportions were the same for those who did not believe in God as for those who did.

Sixty-four percent of those who prayed everyday said their marriages were "very happy" as opposed to 56 percent of those who did not pray everyday. The proportions were unaffected by certainty about the existence of God.

Frequency of prayer affects even those at the agnostic and atheistic end of the belief continuum—those 13 percent of Americans who do not believe in God or say that there is no way to know if God exists or go no further than granting that there might be some "higher power." Frequency of prayer correlates with their opposition to the death penalty and conviction of a "very happy" marriage in the same way (same intercept, same slope) as it does for the more theistically oriented—those who believe sometimes, those who believe but doubt, and those who "know" that God exists.

Finally, if one looks at the tiny proportion (2 percent) of Americans who flatly reject the existence of God, the correlations between frequency of prayer on the one hand and opposition to the death penalty and happy marriage on the other persist at the same magnitude though they are no longer statistically significant because of the small number of cases.

Prayer "to whom it may concern" or to "if anyone is listening which I doubt" nonetheless correlates with one's attitudes and value; and magnitude of the correlation is the same as that which accompanies prayer to an interaction partner (or Partner) about whose existence one is certain.

This pattern would cast doubt on the notion that "prayer" and "very happy" marriage are part of a response syndrome. Why would atheists and agnostics want to claim that they pray? Would they not, on the contrary, be inclined to deny they pray? Yet prayer has the same impact on their responses as it does on that of theists.

2. *Prayer is only one of many religious variables that affects other attitudes. Granted that it is the one that the present theory predicts would be a useful predictor variable, it may well collapse into statistical insignificance when other religious measures are taken into account.*

Six such variables were entered into multiple regression equations with four dependent variables: personal happiness, marital happiness, opposition to capital punishment, and sympathy for AIDS victims (Catho-

TABLE 8.2
Standardized Correlations between Religious
Variables and Attitudes toward "Others"

| | β | | | |
	Capital Punishment	Personal Happiness	Marital Happiness	Sympathy for AIDS*
Church Attendance	.02	.00	.00	−.15
"Close to God"	.00	.06	.04	.09
Life After Death	.04	.02	.00	−.16
Bible	.03	.02	.02	−.05
Strength of Religious Affiliation	.06	.01	.03	.03
Prayer	.12**	.07**	.08**	.16***

 * Catholics only
 ** Significant at .01
 *** Significant at .08. When entered in a backward regression equation (POUT=.10), the beta for prayer rises to .22 signficant at .001.

lics only in the final equation). As the standardized coefficients in table 8.2 demonstrate, among the twenty-four predictor variables, frequency of prayer is the only statistically significant positive correlate of any of the dependent variables: .12 with opposition to the death penalty, .07 with personal happiness, .08 with marital happiness, and .16 (for Catholics)[8] in sympathy with AIDS victims. Frequency of prayer seems to be the religious predictor variable *par excellence.*[9]

3. *Granted that prayer is the most important predictor variable among other religious predictors, it cannot sustain such importance when compared with the standard demographic variables that are used in social research—age, education, income, region, and gender.*

However, when entered into multiple regression equations with these variables (table 8.3), prayer continues to be a statistically significant predictor, indeed the strongest for marital happiness and opposition to the death penalty (.11 and .13 respectively), tied for the strongest for AIDS sympathy (.15), and the second strongest for personal happiness (.09) after real income. One leaves frequency of prayer off a questionnaire at the same risk one would encounter in leaving off age or gender or education.

TABLE 8.3
Prayer and Demographic Correlations
(Standardized)

	β			
	Personal Happiness	Marital Happiness	Opposition to Capital Punishment	Sympathy with AIDS Victims (Catholics only)
South	−.03	.06	−.02	−.05
Age	.04	.00	.05	−.02
Gender (Male)	.00	.07	−.06	−.02
Real Income	.11	.05	−.09	−.11
Education	.08	.06	.08	−.15
Prayer	.09	.11	.13	.15*

* Entered into a backward regression equation, the prayer correlation becomes .16, significant at .001.

Frequency of prayer is not only the religious predictor variable *par excellence,* it is also as strong a predictor in its own right as are the standard demographic predictors.

Replication in Other Countries

The American sociologist of religion is often told that his findings are unique to American society, which for some dubious reason seems to be resisting the worldwide rush to secularization. Preliminary data from the International Social Survey Program's 1991 study of religion[10] in a score of countries make it possible to attempt a replication of the findings of the pragmatics of prayer in the United States in other countries (Greeley 1993d). Table 8.4 demonstrates that only Poland and the two Irelands[11] have rates of prayer that compare with the United States, with approximately three-fifths of the Poles and half of the Irish, orange or green, praying at least daily. Among other countries, daily prayer trails off from 37 percent in Italy to 27 percent in Hungary and the Netherlands, to approximately 20 percent in Britain, West Germany, and Norway, to 10 percent in Israel, Slovenia, and New Zealand, to 9 percent in Russia. Weekly prayer rates are more robust with a majority of the Italians praying once a week and solid minorities of the West Germans, the Britons, the Hungarians, and Norwegians praying every week.

TABLE 8.4
Prayer in Eleven Countries

	Daily	At Least Once a Week	Once a Week for Atheists
West Germany	21%	37%	12%
East Germany	7%	12%	3%
Britain	18%	34%	8%
Netherlands	27%	34%	6%
Hungary	27%	39%	9%
Italy	37%	60%	15%
Ireland	57%	82%	40%
N. Ireland	48%	71%	18%
Poland	61%	71%	31%
Norway	18%	28%	5%
Israel	10%	16%	2%
Slovenia	10%	26%	8%
New Zealand	10%	26%	6%

The critical issue is whether, whatever the rates of frequent prayer may be in a given country, frequency still predicts personal happiness and attitudes toward the death penalty (there was no question about marital happiness in the ISSP study). In the absence of a question about AIDS, two factors serve as a surrogates for concern about the distant other—one measuring attitudes toward cheating the government either in paying taxes or applying for funds, the other measuring attitudes toward government intervention in favor of the poor and the unemployed.

The data in table 8.5 show that the impact of prayer is not limited to the United States. Sixty-four correlation coefficients are presented which test the impact of frequent prayer on personal happiness, opposition to the death penalty, opposition to cheating the government, and support for government intervention in aid of the poor and the unemployed. Forty-three of the sixty-four coefficients were statistically significant.[12] In six countries—the United States, the Irelands, Norway, Austria, and New Zealand—all the correlations between prayer and the dependent variables are statistically significant while in Israel none of them are statistically significant and in Hungary only the relationship between frequency of prayer and support for government intervention is significant. In the remaining countries, frequency of prayer has an impact on

TABLE 8.5

Frequency of Prayer and Personal Happiness, Opposition to Capital
Punishment, Support for Government Intervention, and
Opposition to Cheating by Country (r)

	Personal Happiness	Oppose Capital Punishment	Oppose Cheating Government[1]	Support for Government Intervention
West Germany	.03*	.03*	.10	.07
East Germany	.00*	.06	.07	.01*
Britain	.11	.03*	.11	.03*
USA	.11	.08	.07	.08
Netherlands	.15	.07	.11	.03*
Hungary	.04*	.02*	.03*	.06
Italy	.00*	.01*	.07	.09
Ireland	.06	.05	.11	.14
N. Ireland	.10	.14	.18	.05
Poland	.05	-.02*	-.01*	.23
Norway	.07	.08	.11	.08
Israel	.00*	.03*	.03*	.03*
Slovenia	.03*	.05	.00*	.05
New Zealand	.08	.05	.13	.05
Austria	.05	.05	.07	.09
Russia	.04*	.07	.08	.06

* Correlation not statistically significant (.05).
[1] Condemn cheating on tax and on applications for money.
[2] Favor Government intervention to provide jobs and to promote equality.

three variables in the Netherlands, all but government intervention; in
West Germany and Italy on the government variables; in East Germany
on opposition to cheating and the death penalty; in Britain on personal
happiness and opposition to cheating; in Slovenia on opposition to the
death penalty and in favor of government intervention; and in Poland on
attitudes toward government intervention (the correlation here is the biggest in the table: .23) and on personal happiness.

There are, to look at the table from another perspective, nine correlations with personal happiness, ten with opposition to the death penalty,
twelve with opposition to cheating the government, and twelve with
support for government intervention in favor of the unemployed and the
poor. Prayer then affects human attitudes toward "others" in countries

besides America. The relevance of frequency of prayer as a predictor variable is not limited to the United States.[13]

Moreover, the combination of a religious image measure and frequent prayer produces even higher levels of religious effect on these attitude variables. As a substitute for my rejected grace scale measures I used the *theism* measure ("There is a God who concerns Himself with everyone personally"). As figure 8.7 shows, the impact of prayer on opposition to the death penalty is concentrated among those who believe in a God with personal concern, a relational God. In fact the impact of prayer on opposition to the death penalty is negative for those who do not believe in such a God. Because of the size of the ISSP sample even the latter relationship is statistically significant. However, in a number of the individual countries both the positive correlation between frequency of prayer and opposition to the death penalty for those whose story is of a personal relationship with God and the negative correlation for those who do not accept that story are statistically significant: both Germanys, the United States, Britain, Northern Ireland, Norway, Slovenia, and Poland.

In Europe, then, as in America, it is the story of a relationship with the transcendent Other that is told in a combination of frequent prayer and graceful religious imagery which produces a benign relationship with the human other, even the distant other—the condemned criminal and the unemployed person.

Discussion and Conclusion

The average American prays six times a week, three times more often than he has sexual intercourse. While sexual intercourse does not impose constraints that lead her to oppose capital punishment, prayer, particularly prayer to a transcendent that is imagined as benign, does produce such constraints. The importance of intimacy with God as a sociological phenomenon therefore stands as proven, and its worthiness for further investigation is demonstrated. It is indeed a much more significant measure of religion than church attendance because it represents private behavior, which is less likely to be subject to social pressures than church attendance. Frequency of attendance, as noted in the analysis of American data, does not correlate with any of the life satisfaction variables used in this analysis or with attitudes toward the death penalty

FIGURE 8.7
Opposition to Capital Punishment by Prayer and Image of God

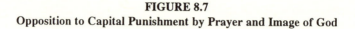
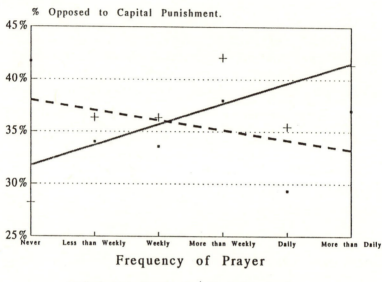

% Opposed to Capital Punishment.

Frequency of Prayer

-- God Not Involved + God Involved

Source: ISSP 1991 N=12,201

or AIDS victims. It may very well be that frequency of prayer (especially) when combined with benign images of God is an indicator of something else, a profound orientation toward the meaning of life, a worldview, an ultimate value system, a story which, above all others, truly matters. If we could find measures for that ultimate value system, the impact of prayer might be demonstrated to be spurious, though the possibility would remain that the very act of praying contributes to the development of such a value system.

The null hypothesis can safely be rejected. Prayer does relate to attitudes that are not specifically religious, especially when it is combined with benign imagery of God. It is the experience of praying rather than doctrinal belief that produces this correlation. In the case of AIDS victims, the impact is limited to Catholics. Prayer and religious imagery are the most powerful of the religious predictor variables. As did religious imagery, prayer compares favorably with the demographic predictor variables that are routinely used in survey research. Finally, prayer is probably an indicator of a general orientation toward life and creation; prayer and imagery constitute a "story" about the meaning of life and relationships. Prayer and imagery, in other words, *are* the religious story.

Notes

1. The analysis presented in this chapter was originally written in Greeley 1993c.
2. The cohorts are fifteen years long to match the fifteen-year difference between a 1972 NORC study (Greeley, McCready and McCourt 1974), in which questions were asked about the frequency of prayer, and the pooled responses from GSS 87–89.
3. One hopes that this finding cures sociologists of religion and particularly European sociologists of religion of the proclivity to confuse age correlations with social change.
4. The distinction is based on Smith 1986.
5. The question about the nature of one's belief in God was asked only in the special religion module in GSS 1988.
6. Or perhaps the increase in prayer creates both heightened confidence and sense of intimacy.
7. Social scientists cannot, with the tools available to them, determine whether anyone (or Anyone) hears prayers. But they can ask whether prayers "work." Thus, Byrd (1988) reports a "double blind" test in a hospital ward in San Francisco. Prayer groups prayed for a half of a sample of recovering cardiac patients, while no prayer groups prayed for the other half. Neither the patients nor the medical staff knew who was in which group. The former group recovered more quickly (Byrd 1988).
8. In a backward regression equation with POUT=.10, the result was .22.
9. These equations were tested for collinearity and the eigen values were all within tolerable limits.
10. As in all ISSP studies data were collected by research centers in each participating country with random probability samples of at least a thousand respondents.
11. As noted before this is a descriptive phrase and implies no judgment about the political division in Ireland.
12. Since most of the samples are the same size, one can note that in general correlations of .06 or higher are significant at the >=.02 level while correlations of .05 are significant at the .03 level.
13. Because the drafting committee of the ISSP would not include the grace scale items in the questionnaire (despite my data showing it was important), only a few countries asked these items.

9

Religious Stories and Political Stories

Since, in my theory of religion as poetry, religious stories provide ultimate meaning to human life, their shape ought to influence the shape of the other stories men and women tell to give more proximate meaning and direction to their lives. If therefore religious stories do not predict other stories, if there is not at least a modest correlation between the two levels of story telling, the theory of religion as poetry is threatened with collapse. In this chapter I explore the possibility that religious stories, as measured by the grace scale will have an impact on racial attitudes, civil liberties attitudes, and attitudes toward the role of women. In the next two chapters I will examine the relationship between religious stories and attitudes toward the environment and toward AIDS. If religious imagery (as measured by the grace scale) does correlate with these measures than it will follow that this measure of religion as a predictor variable cannot be ignored by those who do political research.

If therefore one can find some way to measure the quality of the religious imagery in an individual's organism, one will have access to his ultimate "culture system" and be able to make meaningful predictions about the way one will respond to the issues of life. Those whose religious imagination has a propensity to a warmer, affectionate, more intimate, more loving representation of ultimate reality will also be, I hypothesize, more gracious or more benign in their response to political and social issues.

Such a conclusion does not seem to be so extraordinary when stated that simply. Those who have a graceful image of God, it might be expected, will be more graceful in their relationships with their fellow human beings. Simple as the theoretical statement may be, however, no attempt has been made to test it. In this chapter it is hypothesized that even with appropriate measures of social and religious liberalism held

constant, those with the more gracious image of God will be more likely
to support racial integration, civil liberties, and the principles of feminism; more likely to oppose the death penalty, and less likely to vote for
a presidential candidate who is perceived as being less than gracious to
the poor and to minorities. The way you picture God, it is suggested,
will affect the way you vote, even when party affiliation and political
orientation are held constant.

The analysis in this chapter was based on the General Social Survey
conducted by NORC in the years between 1984 and 1991.[1] The sample
consisted of 12,220 respondents. The present analysis is limited to white
respondents because the patterns of correlations among blacks are different than the patterns to be reported in this chapter. The civil liberties
scale discussed in the chapter is based on a factor combining General
Social Survey responses to issues of the freedom of communists, social-
ists, militarists, and racists to teach, lecture, and to have books in librar-
ies. The feminism scale is based on a factor composed of General Social
Survey questions on workforce and political participation of women.

In the General Social Survey, as noted in a previous chapter, respondents are asked to locate themselves on a seven-point continuum between four forced choices of how they picture God: father/mother, master/
spouse, judge/lover, king/friend. These items combine to form a single
factor which has been dubbed the grace scale. High scores on the factor
show an inclination to the mother-spouse-lover-friend end of the scale.

In table 9.1 we note that those in their twenties and thirties have higher
scores[2] on the grace scale than those above forty. Women have higher
scores than men, northerners have higher scores than southerners, Catholics and Jews have higher scores than Protestants. Within the Protestant
denominations Methodists, Lutherans, Presbyterians, and Episcopalians
have the higher scores. Baptists, "other" Protestants, and nondenomina-
tional Protestants have the lower scores.[3]

The grace scale also correlates positively with education, with living
in the North, with liberal political views, and with propensity to identify
with the Democratic political party. It is, of course, impossible to say
whether religious imagery shapes political orientation and party affiliation or vice versa. In theory, religious symbols are the overarching images that become master templates for a person's life, but there is no
reason why these images cannot be modified in the course of life, and
political convictions might very well affect such a modification. In this
analysis, we will be constrained to test the hypothesis that the relation-

Table 9.1
Grace Scale and Background Variables
(Z scores)

Age	
18–29	.09
30–39	.03
40–49	−.07
50–59	−.02
60–69	−.06
Over 70	−.05
Sex	
Men	−.02
Women	.02
Religion	
Protestant	−.09
Catholic	.08
Jew	.12
Denomination	
Baptist	−.25
Methodist	.04
Lutheran	.05
Presbyterian	.09
Episcopalian	.07
Other	−.24
Non Denom	−.08
Education	
Ten years or less	−.05
Twelve years	−.05
More than twelve	.07
Region	
North	.05
South	−.10
Political Orientation	
Liberal	.20
Moderate	−.00
Conservative	−.13
Party Identification	
Democrat	.04
Independent	−.08
Republican	−.12

TABLE 9.2
Correlations with Grace Scale
(r)

Reagan Vote 1980	−.09
Reagan Vote 1984	−.14
Bush vote in 1988	−.08
Favor Capital Punishment	−.07
Civil Liberties Scale	.14
Gov Help Blacks	.09
Blacks Should not Push	−.12
Feminism	.17

ship between religious imagery and social and political attitudes and behavior is spurious and that the apparent correlation is merely a function of political and religious liberalism.

A high score on the grace scale does indeed (table 9.2) correlate with social and political attitudes and behaviors. Those who are more likely to picture God as a "friend," a "mother," a "spouse," and a "lover" were less likely both in 1980 and in 1984 to vote for Ronald Reagan and in 1988 to vote for George Bush. They were also more likely to oppose capital punishment, to support civil liberties, to advocate government help for blacks, to reject the notion that blacks ought not to push their way into white neighborhoods, and to support feminist attitudes on women's labor force and political participation. All of the relationships in table 9.2 are statistically significant.

Moreover, when regression equations are run in which the influence of the grace scale is standardized for age, sex, region, and education, capital punishment, feminism, civil liberties, and the two racial correlations continue to be statistically significant (table 9.3). Indeed, the grace scale is the only one of the five items in the regression equation that relates significantly to all five dependent variables. The grace scale seems to be in general a more powerful net predictor of attitudes in these five areas than region, sex, and age, though generally not so powerful as education. Thus, the effect of the grace scale on political and social attitudes is not a function of any of the demographic variables normally considered in social research. Not to examine the possibility of the religious imagination affecting social and political attitudes would make

TABLE 9.3
Standardized Correlations between Grace Scale and
Other Variables with Dependent Variables

	Grace	Age	Sex	Education	Region
			(β)		
Capital Punishment	−.07	.01*	.10	.03*	.01*
Civil Liberties	.10	.02*	.05*	.25	.08
Blacks Push	−.06	−.02*	.09	−.28	.10
Help Blacks	.07	−.01*	.02*	.12	.03*
Feminism	.12	−.23	.03*	.25	.10

*Not significant

about as much sense as excluding age, sex, and region from a questionnaire or from subsequent analysis.

Moreover, those with high scores on the grace scale (table 9.4) were 8 percentage points less likely to claim they voted for Ronald Reagan in 1980 and 12 percentage points less likely to claim to have voted for him in 1984. They were also 7 percentage points less likely to claim to have voted for George Bush in 1988.

But is this propensity to vote against Ronald Reagan a function not so much of religious imageries but of political orientation (a seven-point liberal conservative scale) or party affiliation? Table 9.5 indicates that for liberals and moderates, there is in each category of party identification a statistically significant relationship between religious imagery and the propensity to vote against Reagan. A 12 percentage point difference for liberal Democrats, a 17 percentage point difference for liberal Independents, and a 15 percentage point difference for liberal Republicans.

TABLE 9.4
Presidential Voting and Grace Scale
(% Voting Republican)

	1980	1984	1988
"Graceful"	49%	58%	56%
Not "Graceful"	57%	70%	63%

TABLE 9.5
Presidential Voting and Grace Scale by Political
Orientation and Party Identification
(% Voting for Reagan in 1984)

	Democrat	Indep.	Republican
Liberal			
"Graceful"	11%	40%	82%
Not "Graceful"	23%	57%	97%
Moderate			
"Graceful"	25%	66%	92%
Not "Graceful"	39%	77%	97%*
Conservative			
"Graceful"	39%	85%	98%*
Not "Graceful"	48%*	86%*	98%*

*Not significant

There is also a 14 percentage point difference for moderate Democrats and an 11 percentage point difference for moderate Independents. Among all conservatives and among Republican moderates, religious imagery did not affect voting in the 1984 election at levels of statistical significance.

Religious imagery then does not overcome conservative political orientation but among those who describe themselves as liberal or moderate and as Independents or Democrats, the quality of religious imagery does have a considerable effect on voting behavior. The "story" of one's relationship with God contained in religious imagery does indeed help to tell the story one writes in the ballot box.

The religious imagination then does contribute to people's social and political attitudes and behaviors and its contribution cannot be reduced to either demographic or political orientation and identification factors. The final question that must be asked, however, is whether the religious imagination as measured by the grace scale is merely a form of religious liberalism. Obviously the people with the more gracious religious imaginations cannot be written off as fundamentalists because as we noted previously those denominations that are likely to be fundamentalist have low average scores in the scale. To test the possibility, however, that religious imagery is merely a mask for religious liberalism, regression equations were written in which education, political orientation, and attitudes toward the Bible were entered as predictor variables. What impact, if any, on political and social attitudes and behaviors does religious imagery have net of education, political orientation (liberal versus conservative), and attitudes toward the Bible. The Bible item taken from the General Social Survey provides three possible responses:

> The Bible is the actual word of God and it is to be taken literally, word for word.
>
> The Bible is the inspired word of God but not everything should be taken literally word for word.
>
> The Bible is an ancient book of fables, legends, history and moral precepts recorded by man.

(Roughly speaking, about half of NORC's respondents checked the middle response, about three-eighths the first and about one-eighth the last.)

As might be expected, education and religious and political liberalism do diminish somewhat (table 9.6) the relationship between religious imagery and attitudes and behavior. However, even net of education, political orientation, and attitude toward the Bible, the religious imagination (as measured by the grace scale) continues to correlate positively with all the dependent variables used in the analysis.

Images of God as "friend" and "mother," in other words, are statistically significant and reasonably important correlates of political and social attitudes and behaviors, even when education and political and religious liberalism are taken into account.

The data in table 9.1 support a hypothesis derived from David Tracy's work on the Protestant and Catholic imaginations. Catholics indeed were

TABLE 9.6
Correlations with Grace Scale Net of Education and
Political and Religious "Liberalism"

	r	β
Voting (84)	−.14	−.09
Civil Liberties	.14	.08
Capital Punishment	−.07	−.06
Blacks Push	−.12	−.06
Help Blacks	.09	.07
Feminism	.17	.11

FIGURE 9.1
Grace Scale by Age and Denomination

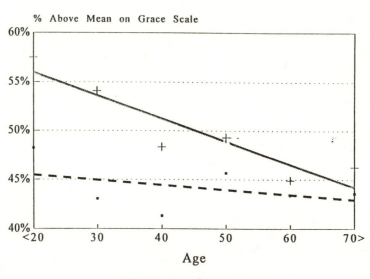

% Above Mean on Grace Scale

Age

-•- PROTESTANT + CATHOLIC

Source: GSS 1984-91 N=8,681

more likely to have "gracious" images of God than Protestants. But is this phenomenon a result of the recent changes in Catholicism inaugurated at the Second Vatican Council (which may be a return to an older Catholic religious sensibility)? The data in figure 9.1[4] demonstrate that there is a statistically significant correlation with age for Catholics but not for Protestants and that the differences between Catholics and Protestants tend to be concentrated among the younger respondents. The possibility that figure 9.1 represents real social change, perhaps due to the changes in the Church at the Vatican Council, in Catholics' religious

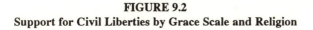

FIGURE 9.2
Support for Civil Liberties by Grace Scale and Religion

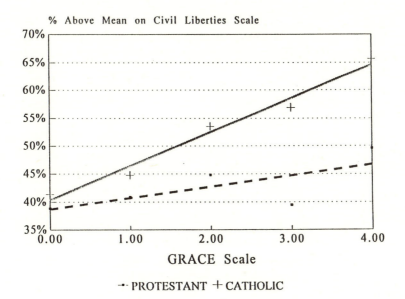

% Above Mean on Civil Liberties Scale

GRACE Scale

-·- PROTESTANT + CATHOLIC

Source: GSS 1984-91 N=8,491

Grace=Mother+Lover+Spouse+Friend

imagery and not a life cycle phenomenon seems to be strengthened by the fact that there is no age correlation for religious imagery among Protestants. In any event the conclusion that Catholics are different,[5] which one would draw from figure 9.1, will be repeatedly supported in the rest of this book.

Such support is found in figure 9.2. While the correlation between the grace scale and support for civil liberties is significant for both Catholics and Protestants, it is stronger for Catholics. There is virtually no difference between the two among those who have none of the four "graceful" images but among those who have three or four such images the difference is 15 percentage points.[6] The interaction between age and the grace scale for Catholics does not incidentally account for the higher score of Catholics on the civil liberties factor.

Perhaps the grace scale used in this analysis does not indeed measure cultural orientation at all. Perhaps it measures personality orientation. Perhaps it is a psychological rather than a religious variable. Obviously there is no way to refute that possibility. While it is possible in theory (Parsonian theory) to separate the culture system from the personality system, the two interact so powerfully in an individual from the earliest days of his life that in practice it would be very difficult to sort them out. It may be that the religious imagery questions asked in the General Social Survey are nothing more than a kind of inkblot that merely measures different personality orientations. One must note, however, that even if the grace scale merely measures personality, it is a very powerful personality measure if through four rather simple items one can provide more predictive power than do far more elaborate personality tests.

In conclusion, the implication of the present chapter is that religion can be profitably approached as a predictor variable that, given the relatively small correlations in sociology between all predictor variables and the dependent variable, is of some considerable importance in understanding social attitudes and behaviors. The way one pictures God does affect attitudes and voting patterns independently of political and religious orientations and independently of sex, age, education, and region of the country. It can no longer be reasonably said that religion is not politically and socially important enough to be considered worth investigating (beyond the simple denominational cross-tabulation) in attempts to understand the shape and the functioning of American society. People's "stories of God" do relate to their stories of political and social life. Such stories ought not to be ignored by a responsible social scientist.

Notes

1. The analysis in this chapter was originally reported in Greeley 1984. It was updated in Greeley 1988a and updated again for this chapter in 1993.
2. The "Z score" is the score on a factor scale that has been standardized so that the mean is zero and the standard deviation is one. Thus, a positive z score is the

percentage of the standard deviation above the mean, a negative score is the percentage of a standard deviation below the mean. People in their twenties are on
the average 9 percent of the standard deviation above the mean while people in
their sixties are 6 percent of the standard deviation below the mean.

3. Because of the large size of the sample, all the differences in table 9.1 are statistically significant except those among the various Protestant denominations. The
coefficients (r or eta as appropriate) are: age=-.06; South=-.07; education=.06;
liberal political views=.12; Democrat=.08; religion=.08. gender(women)=.02.

4. As in most charts in this book the grace is measured by a five-point scale from
zero to four. One point is assigned for each of the four images.

5. Or perhaps the conclusion that Protestants are different.

6. In log linear analyses of the data present in figures 7.1 and 7.2 the preferred
model for both situations was the one which was constituted by the interactions,
respectively, between Catholic and Age and Catholic and Grace.

10

Religious Stories and the Environment

In the previous chapter I tried to show how one would use the theory of religion as poetry to approach directly an issue that might falsify the theory: do religious stories predict political and social stories? In this and the next chapter I hope to show how a perspective that focuses on the poetic nature of religion provides insights into how religion works— insights that might not occur to someone who does not have the theoretical perspective available. In this chapter I will analyze the relationship between religious story and environmental story as a means of understanding the seeming relationship between biblical literalism and lack of concern for the environment. In the next chapter[1] I will address the question of religious story and AIDS victims.

Fundamentalists and Evangelicals in general and the Southern Baptists in particular suffer from a negative public image on political and social questions because both scholars and journalists assume that political conservatism and religious conservativism correlate with one another, an assumption for which precious little if any support exist in the empirical data (Hart 1992).

The Southern Baptist denomination, for example, is a large, pluralistic group in which a wide variety of political, social, and religious attitudes exist under a conviction that the Bible is the literal word of God, a conviction that is as variously interpreted as is the doctrine of Papal Infallibility by Catholics. Neither President Clinton nor Vice President Gore can fairly be called political conservatives; yet they are both, each in his own way, devout Southern Baptists who doubtless believe in their own fashion in literal interpretation, though they would explain it differently than would many of the more conservative members of their denomination.

Thus, to suggest that a belief in literal interpretation is evidence of political conservatism is a grave misunderstanding of 36 percent of the American population. Not all Fundamentalists are political conservatives. The so-called "moral majority" was never either, not even among Southern Baptists. The convictions of the so-called Christian Coalition, which appeared to dominate the Republican convention in 1992, are by no means typical of all Fundamentalists or even a majority of them.[2]

Lynn White, in an oft-cited article (1967), has argued that the Judaeo-Christian heritage is responsible for the ecological crisis because of the injunction of Genesis 1 that humans exercise "dominion" over the earth. So stated, White's thesis is at such a level of generality that it cannot be falsified and hence cannot be verified. Indeed even for the 1960s such an assertion in the absence of any proof of linkage represents the worse kind of intellectual nonsense especially in the prestigious pages of *Science*.

However, it is possible to draw hypotheses from White's model that can be tested. Eckberg and Blocker (1989) in a study of a random sample of people in Tulsa, Oklahoma, found that four "environmental concern" factors correlated with four "religion" variables: being Jewish or Christian (as opposed to having no religious affiliation); being conservative Protestant; believing that religion is important; and believing in the literal interpretation of the Bible. When background variables were taken into account and all the religious variables were entered into the equation, the crucial predictor of lower levels of environmental concern was belief in the literal interpretation of the Bible.

Eckberg and Blocker did not offer a social science theory that would explain how biblical literalism leads to lower levels of environmental concern. It may well be that the cultural value of human dominion over the earth does influence environmental attitudes but it would have to do so through mediating sociological and psychological mechanisms by which a religious value produces an opposition to environmental concerns. Eckberg and Blocker found a relationship in the predicted direction but they did not account for the relationship.

I propose in this chapter to develop a model that might account for the relationship and at the same time provide for the possibility of an alternative explanation that does not require an appeal to the Book of Genesis. To do this an investigation of the impact of religious story on environmental story is required.

Genesis and the Environment

If one believes that religion, before it becomes anything else, is a set of narrative symbols that explain the nature of human reality, might not Fundamentalists tend to have a harsher system of narrative symbols that could account in part for the correlation between a belief in a literal interpretation of the Scriptures and a negative attitude toward the environment? Might not those Fundamentalists with more benign narrative images have a more constructive view of the environment?

Moreover, Fundamentalists are known to be politically and morally conservative. Might that fact not account for their environmental attitudes without having to appeal to their doctrinal convictions about the Scripture? Might they not dismiss environmental concern as part of a liberal political agenda they reject? Or might they not be more rigid religiously and hence incapable of absorbing new moral concerns? In fact, might those Fundamentalists who are politically liberal and morally flexible be as likely to support environmental measures as anyone else? Might they not, like Southern Baptist Al Gore, then become "pro-environment"?

Thus, the narrative images are both causally and chronologically prior to other religious manifestations and to political and social orientations. Even the way one shapes one's denominational affiliation is a function of religious stories which one absorbs in the family triad at a time of life when the denomination is only a word.

The other cultural systems—science, common sense, ideology, law, ethics—are to an extent shaped by the ultimate worldview: they tell stories that are a reflection of the religious stories (Geertz 1957, 1966). I assume for the purpose of this chapter that four variables—denomination, doctrine, political attitudes, and moral attitudes—are all influenced by worldview and also relate to one another. To some extent these variables may be considered articulations of and reflections on the narrative symbols which are the poetic and experiential foundation of religion. My model suggests that once imagery and political and moral conservatism are taken into account, there will be no statistically significant paths from either denomination (Protestant) or doctrine (theism and biblical literalism) to environmental attitude.

The question then becomes whether in multiple regression equations in which a belief in literal interpretation (or religious affiliation) is entered along with measures of political conservatism, moral rigidity, and religious imagery, there continues to be a statistically significant relationship between the religious doctrine or affiliation and environmental attitudes. If there is no such relationship, than one would have to say that my model cannot be rejected: the apparent effect of Genesis 1 on environmental attitudes is in fact spurious just as differential religious attitudes toward AIDS can be accounted for by images and rigidities of style.

Eckberg and Blocker do not have a sufficient number of Catholics in their Tulsa sample of 300 (with a 55 percent response rate) to determine whether there is any difference between Catholics and Protestants in attitudes toward the Bible. As a sacramental religion with the conviction that such earthy realities as fire and water, light and darkness, bread and wine, oil and sexual love are metaphors for God and with less concern for Fundamentalist orthodoxy, Catholicism might be reasonably expected to be more concerned about the environment. If that relationship should appear, according to the model in table 10.3, it would be explained by a direct line between worldview and environmental attitude reinforced by an interaction with Catholic affiliation.

The General Social Survey (Davis and Smith 1991) has a single item on environmental concern, which, when the special religion module in the 1988 GSS is used in analysis, provides the data for examining the religious dynamics that might intervene between biblical literalism and lack of concern for the environment. The advantage of using the 1988 GSS is its national sample of respondents and extensive religious questions. The disadvantage is that there is only one environmental dependent variable: "We are faced with many problems in this country, none of which can be solved easily or inexpensively. I'm going to name each one of these problems and for each one I'd like you to tell me whether you think we're spending too much money on it, too little, or about the right amount...the environment."[3]

Findings

The correlation coefficients in table 10.1 confirm the findings of Eckberg and Blocker. Biblical literalism (the same variable wording they used)[4] correlates negatively with environment concern, as does belief in God and Christian affiliation (as opposed to a combination of Jews and

TABLE 10.1
Correlations with Support for the Environment

Christian	−.102
Literal Bible Interpretation	−.108
Belief in God	−.085
Attend	−.040*
Gracious Image of God	.104
Catholic	.067

*Not Statistically Significant

those with no religious affiliation). Those with a more gracious narrative image of God (mother, spouse, lover, and friend as opposed to father, master, judge, and king) are more likely to support increased spending on the environment. There is no significant correlation between either frequency of prayer or church attendance and environmental concern.

Catholics are indeed more likely to support increased spending on the environment than Protestants (70 percent versus 62 percent) but less than non-Christians (85 percent). There is virtually no difference among the three branches of Protestantism (Smith 1986) in their response to environmental spending. However, those who doubt the existence of God (80 percent)[5] are more likely than those who are more orthodox in their beliefs to be concerned about the environment (65 percent).

However, a benign image of God notably improves environmental support but only among Catholics (figures 10.1 and 10.2), as was tentatively suspected. Catholics with high scores on the grace scale are as likely (82 percent) as nonbelievers to favor more expenditure for the environment. Clearly much depends on what kind of religion one uses to predict environmental concern or lack thereof.

Analysis

There are four correlations in table 10.1 which require explanation: why are non-Christians, Catholics, and doctrinal liberals (on the existence of God and the inspiration of the Scriptures) more likely to support environmental spending?

FIGURE 10.1
Support Environment Denomination and Image of God

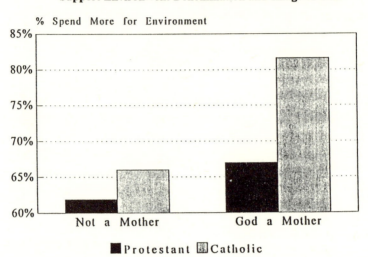

% Spend More for Environment

■ Protestant ▨ Catholic

Source: GSS 1988 N=1,481; Grace=Mother+Spouse+Lover+Friend

FIGURE 10.2
Support for Environment by Denomination and Grace Scale

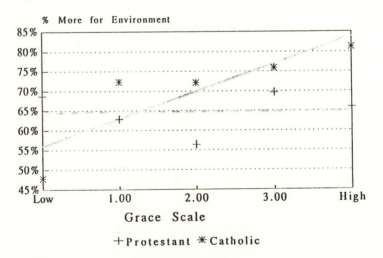

% More for Environment

Grace Scale

+ Protestant ＊ Catholic

Source: GSS 1988 N=1,481; Grace=Mother+Spouse+Lover+Friend

According to the theoretical perspective described in the introduction to this chapter, one would expect the differences to be explained by a combination of image of God and political and ethical liberalism.

As usual in this volume, religious imagery, an indicator of the narrative symbol that poetically encodes religion as a culture system, is measured by four forced choices on a seven-point scale between God as "Mother...Father," "Master...Spouse," "Judge...Lover," "Friend...King."

Political liberalism is measured by the GSS item in which the respondent locates himself/herself on a seven-point scale between "liberal" and "conservative." If this scale diminishes the relationship between doctrine (or denomination) and environmental concern it would follow that not biblical literalism as such but politically conservative biblical literalism relates to low environmental concern. Those Fundamentalists who are political liberals (and there are some since political and religious attitudes do not correlate perfectly) would have as much environmental concern as other political liberals.

Ethical liberalism is measured by a factor in GSS 1988 made up of four variables, two of which measure opinions on what is religiously important: "How important is each of the following to you...'to follow one's own conscience even if it means going against what the churches or the synagogues say and do; to believe in God without question or doubt.'" The other two items in the factor deal more directly with moral issues: "Do you agree (strongly, somewhat) or disagree (strongly, somewhat) with the following statements: 'Those who violate God's rules must be punished; Morality is a personal matter and society should not force everyone to follow one standard.'"

These four statements constitute a scale that might be said to represent a rigid and moralistic approach to religion. If such a scale diminishes the negative relationship between religious variables and environmental concern, then it would follow that not religion as such but moralistic and rigid religion is connected with less concern about the environment. Table 10.3 depicts the explanatory model which my theory of religion as poetry suggested to account for differences in environmental attitudes.

The first column[6] in table 10.2 applies this model to the differences between Christians and non-Christians with the addition of age and educational controls since the non-Christians tend to be younger and better

TABLE 10.2
Model to Explain Religious Correlations with Environmental Support

	Christian	Catholic	Belief in God	Biblical Literalism
Correlation (r)	–.071[1]	.068	–.085	–.108
Beta net of Religious Image	–.059	.001[2]*	–.058	–.086
Beta net of Religious Image and Political Views	–.038*		–.021*	–.063
Beta net of Religious Image and Polical Views and Moral Rigidity	–.020*		.000*	–.038*

* Not Significant
1. Net of Age and Education
2. Includes Interaction between "Catholic" and Image of God.

TABLE 10.3
Model to Explain Correlations between Biblical Literalism and
Opposition to Environmental Spending

Denomination
(Protestant)

Doctrine
(Biblical Literalism,
Existence of God)

World View   Environmental
(Story, Narrative Symbol,   Attitude
Image of God)

Political Conservatism

Moral Rigidity

educated (both because they are younger and include Jews). When age and education are taken into account in a multiple regression equation, the *r* of –.102 between environmental concern and Christian is reduced to a standardized correlation (beta) of –.071. A gracious image of God reduces it further to –.059. Liberal political views lower the beta even more to -.038 and statistical insignificance. Moral rigidity lowers the correlation even further to -.020.

Those who are not Christian, in other words, are more likely to support environmental concerns because they are younger, better educated, and have a more liberal political agenda and a more benign story of God. The first three variables are not specifically religious.

The second column of table 10.2 shows that the different stories of God that Catholics carry in their religious imaginations account entirely for the differences between Catholics and Protestants. Catholics are more likely to be concerned about the environment because they are more likely to have gracious images of God and because their picture of God is more likely to affect their environmental concern than is the Protestant picture of God.

Different images of God and more liberal political views eliminate the significant -.085 relationship between environmental concern and certainty about the existence of God, reducing the correlation to a beta of -.021 in the third column of table 10.2. Those who were less certain about God were also more likely to have benign images of God and to be liberal in their political perspectives. Those who were certain of the existence of God but viewed the deity more "graciously" and who were more liberal in their political orientation were as likely to be concerned about the environment as those who were less certain about the existence of God. It is not the certainty that accounts for the lower level of concern but the political and religious "story" that tends to accompany certainty .

The same explanatory model applies in the fourth column in table 10.2 to the relationship between belief in the literal interpretation of Scriptures and environmental concern, with the addition of the rigid "approach" to religion factor required to diminish the correlation to statistical insignificance, from -.108 to -.038. Thus, the relationship described by Eckberg and Blocker can be accounted for by the fact that the biblical literalists are more likely to have a stern image of God, to be conservative in their political views, and to be rigid in their "approach" to religion and morality. Those biblical literalists who are politically and religiously and ethically "liberal" are as likely to be concerned with the environment as their non-Fundamentalist counterparts.

Moral, religious, political, imaginative, biblical, and environmental liberalism do not correlate completely, or each variable would not add to the explanatory power of the models in table 10.2. But they do overlap to such an extent that biblical literalism can be understood as part of and a sign of (a story of) a more rigid and more conservative religious "style." If harsh religious images and political and ethical conservatism are removed from the "style," in real people or in a multiple regression equation, the lower level of environmental concern disappears.

The Bible, it might be argued not unreasonably, is not the cause of lower support for environmental spending, but the target of those whose rigid "style" inclines them both to resist environmental concern and insist on religious certainty.

Does religion cause this rigidity or are certain personalities inclined to gravitate toward rigid religion? The question is unanswerable unless one defines religion more precisely. Some kinds of religious orientation, like the interaction of Catholicism and benign religious imagery, seem purely religious and unaffected by political or social or ethical perspectives. How does religion correlate with environmentalism? It depends on the imaginative contents and political and ethical correlates of a person's religious story.

Conclusion

In the United States the correlations between religious and environmental attitudes seem to be spurious. A rigid religious orientation does correlate with negative attitude toward spending on the environment. But when religious imagery, and political and moral rigidity—the need for certainties in a world where certainties are fewer than religion can provide—are taken into account, the correlation disappears. Those who believe in God and in the Bible, and Christians who reject the various levels of rigidity are as likely as anyone else to support environmental spending. Catholics in particular are more likely to support it because of the impact a benign image of God has on their worldview.

Thus, a combination of rigid religious and political stories explains the apparent relationship between biblical literalism and lower levels of environmental concern. The theory of religion as poetry offers a clue as to how to explain the relationship. Moreover, using the theory as an explanatory tool uncovered another occasion where Catholics are strikingly different from Protestants (or vice versa if one wishes). It is not merely that they have somewhat higher scores on the grace index that accounts for their greater concern for the environment. In addition, the grace scale correlates with environmental attitudes for Catholics but does not do so for Protestants. Interactions of the sort portrayed in figure 10.2 will appear repeatedly in the rest of this book.[7]

Excursus: Religion and the Environment in the ISSP

This chapter was originally prepared as a memo supporting my recommendation to the International Social Survey drafting committee, which was preparing the questionnaire for the 1992 study of the environment, that the grace scale be included in the questionnaire. The drafting committee could not accept the possibility that religion, which explains what life and the world mean, might affect judgments about the environment. In particular, the committee could not accept that my four-variable religious imagery question might predict responses on the environment. Again the problem seemed to be that members of the committee could not conceive of the possibility that images of God might influence environmental images.

Nonetheless, the imagery questions are asked routinely in the General Social Survey and thus it was possible to determine whether the relationships I predicted do indeed occur at least in the United States. Or, to put the matter differently, what was the loss in predictive power from omitting the religious imagery questions from the environment questionnaire?

I created five factors (varimax rotation) from fifteen variables that measure environmental attitudes and behavior. The first measured anti-environmental attitudes toward nature and the second attitudes toward animal rights. The remaining three factors measured actual behavior: a factor measuring activities of environmental care (recycling etc.), the second affiliation with an environmental organization and the third financial contributions and environmental protest (the variable wordings are given in the footnotes to table 10.4).

The grace scale, a factor measuring benign imagery of God (mother, lover, spouse, and friend) correlated significantly with all five of the environmental factors (table 10.4). Moreover, a model designed to diminish these correlations by taking into account age, gender, education, and political views ("liberal" versus "conservative") did not reduce any of the correlations to statistical insignificance. Finally, while the betas

TABLE 10.4

Correlations between Grace[1] Scale and Environmental Concerns and Behavior

	Grace (r)	Grace (β)*	Woman (β)	Education (β)	Young (β)	Liberal (β)
Nature[2]	.15	.09	.06	.27	.04**	.16
Animal Rights[3]	.13	.09	.19	.20	.21	.14
Care[4]	.15	.11	.04**	.22	.01**	.18
Join[5]	.08	.10	.04**	.06	.01**	.07
Money[6]	.05	.06	.08	.10	.09	.01
Average β		.09	.08	.17	.07	.12

* The beta (β) statistic is the correlation between the given column variable and th row variable net of all the other column variables.

** Not statistically significant

1. God as Mother, Lover, Spouse, and Friend as opposed to Father, Judge, Master, and King.
2. Items in factor: Human beings should respect nature because it is created by God.
   People worry too much about human progress harming the environment.
   We believe too often in science and not enough in feelings of faith.
   Nature is really a fierce struggle for the survival of the fittest.
   (A positive correlation indicates rejection of this factor)
3. Items in factor: It is right to use animals for medical testing if it might save human lives.
   Animals should have the same moral rights as humans do.
   (A positive correlation indicates support for animals)
4. Items in factor: How often do you make a special effort to sort glass or cans or plastic or papers and so on for recycling?
   How often do you make a special effort to buy fruits and vegetables grown without pesticides or chemicals?
   How often do you refuse to eat meat for moral or environmental reasons?
   How often do you cut back on driving a car for environmental reasons?
5. Items in factor: In the last five years have you signed a petition on an environmental issue?
   Are you a member of any group whose main aim is to preserve or protect the environment?
6. Items in the factor: How often have you given money to an environmental group...taken part in a protest or demonstration about the environment.

for education are higher than the betas for the grace scale in four out of five cases and the betas for political views higher in three out of five cases, the betas for grace are higher than those for age and gender in three out of five comparisons.

The average beta for the grace scale (.09) is marginally higher than that for gender (.08) and for age (.07). The point here is not that grace has a stronger predictive power than either age or gender (and in some cases higher than either education or political views), the point is rather that in all five cases grace is a statistically significant predictor of environmental attitudes even when one takes into account variables that might eliminate its impact and that one can as wisely leave religious imagery out of a study of the environment as one can leave out age and gender.

The decision of the drafting committee to omit these items was unfortunate. Religious images do have an impact on environmental attitudes and behavior that social scientists can ill afford to ignore.

Notes

1. This chapter is based on and adapted from Greeley 1993a.
2. I am not a partisan of Southern Baptist theology or polity; but as a member of a denomination that is still the object of much ignorance and bigotry I believe in fair play for all denominations.
3. The policies about which respondents were asked:

   a) Space exploration program, b) Improving and protecting the environment, c) Improving and protecting the nation's health, d) Solving the problems of the big cities, e) Halting the rising crime rate, f) Dealing with drug addictions, g) Improving the nation's educational program, h) Improving the condition of blacks, i) The military, armaments and defense, j) Foreign aid, k) Welfare, l) Highways and bridges, m) Social Security, n) mass transportation, o) parks and recreation.

   In the late 1980s, the item attracting the highest proportion in favor of spending more was the improvement and protection of the environment.
4. Question wording:

   What of these statements come closest to describing your feeling about the bible: a) The bible is the actual word of God and is to be taken literally, word for word; the bible is the inspired word of God but not everything in it should be taken literally, word for word; the bible is an ancient book of fables, legends, history, and moral precepts recorded by man.
5. Question wording:

   Please look at this card and tell us which statement comes closest to expressing what you believe about God: I don't believe in God; I don't know whether there is a God and I don't believe there is any way to find out; I don't believe in a personal God but I do believe in a Higher Power of some kind; I find myself believing in God some of the time, but not at others; while I have doubts, I feel that I do believe in God; I know God really exists and I have no doubts about it.

   The first four responses were combined in an "atheist/agnostic" category for this analysis.
6. The parameters in the bottom three rows of table 10.2 are betas from three regression equations written for each of the four religious variables with environmental

11

Religious Stories and AIDS

In this chapter I continue to ask the question of whether the poetry of religion, as told in stories that recount hope renewal experiences, can shed light on the relationship between religion and political and social issues. In the analysis to be reported here I found myself asking, because the religion as poetry perspective dominates my thinking about religion, whether religious stories may have an impact on stories about AIDS.

In the modern world there is relatively little connection in ordinary circumstances between religion and public policy with regard to contagious diseases. The quarantine rules about leprosy (a much wider collection of diseases than what is now called Hansen's Disease) in the Mosaic law, rough and ready public health measures in retrospect, are now enforced by governmental agencies and not by religion.

AIDS, however, is a special case both because of the inevitably fatal outcome of the disease and because it is normally transmitted through sexual contact. It is especially likely to spread under conditions of sexual promiscuity, and in the United States has in fact spread in great part through homosexual contact. Since the traditional religions have disapproved of promiscuity and homosexuality, AIDS has become or seems to have become an issue of morality as well as of public health. Indeed some religious leaders have pronounced it a punishment of God on immorality and especially homosexual immorality.[1]

Thus, the question arises as to whether religious affiliation and devotion might have an impact on AIDS policy issues and decisions. Will the more devout have more repressive attitudes toward those who are victims of AIDS?

The 1988 General Social Survey (Davis and Smith 1988) contained two additional modules beyond the usual sets of GSS questions, the fortuitous combination of which makes it possible to address this question.[2] The first module was a battery of questions about AIDS funded by NORC;[3] the second was an extensive series of items about religion.[4]

The eight AIDS policy items[5] were as follows (the percentage in parentheses indicates the proportion of respondents who took a position that indicated hostility toward AIDS victims):

Do you support or oppose the following measures to deal with AIDS:

A) Prohibit students with AIDS virus from attending public schools (26%).

B) Develop a government information program to promote safe sex practices, such as the use of condoms (14%).

C) Permit Insurance companies to test applicants for the AIDS virus (62%).

D) Have the government pay all of the health care costs of AIDS patients (67%).

E) Conduct mandatory testing for the AIDS virus before marriage (89%).

F) Require the teaching of safe sex practices, such as the use of condoms in sex education courses in public schools (88%).

G) Require people with the AIDS virus to wear identification tags that look like those carried by people with allergies or diabetes (63%).

H) Make victims with AIDS eligible for disability benefits (40%).

The impact of denominational affiliation, frequent church attendance, and religious imagery on responses to these items will be explored in the remainder of this chapter to determine whether religious stories establish a paradigm for stories by which people cope with the tragedy of AIDS.

Denominational Affiliation

Statistically significant correlations were found between Protestant[6] affiliation and negative AIDS attitudes on three items: sex information (.10), sex education (.11), and identification tags (.16).

Seventy percent of the Protestants in the sample supported the imposition of identification tags on AIDS victims as opposed to 54 percent of the Catholics. Some of this difference was concentrated among members of Fundamentalist denominations (Smith 1986), of whose members 73 percent supported the identification tags and conservative denominations, of whose members 72 percent approved of the identity tags. However, 61 percent of Protestants in liberal denominations also supported identification tags for AIDS victims; the difference between them and Catholics is not statistically significant.

In an endeavor to explain the differences between Catholics and Protestants, I tried to reduce the .16 correlation (16 percentage points difference) between Protestant and support for identity tags to statistical insignificance through the use of multiple regression equations into which religious variables would be entered successively. My assumption was that variables associated with fundamentalist religious orientations would account for much of the differences between Protestants and Catholics.

When I inserted three items that measured attitudes toward the Bible,[7] the correlation (as measured by the beta in the regression equation) diminished to .11. Catholics, in other words, are less likely to support identification tags for AIDS victims than are conservative and Fundamentalist Protestants because they are less likely to emphasize the Bible, as literally interpreted, than are Protestants. Or, as I said in the last chapter, Catholics are less likely than Fundamentalist and moderate Protestants to have rigid stories about what life means because they focus on literal interpretation of the Scripture and hence are less likely to be rigid on the subject of AIDS.

The correlation diminished to .09 when an attitude toward formal church membership when growing up[8] was inserted in the equation and to .07 and statistical insignificance when the South as a region of the country was added.

Catholics are baptized into the Church and usually do not consciously reaffiliate in their adolescent years. However, members of the more conservative Protestant denominations are more likely to go through such a process of formal reaffiliation. It would appear that those who do are somewhat more likely to have a repressive attitude toward AIDS. Finally, Protestants, being disproportionately Southern in comparison with Catholics, may share a cultural attitude toward morality that has an impact above and beyond biblical fundamentalism.

Thus, one can account for differences between Fundamentalist and conservative Protestants and Catholics in their attitudes toward identification tags for AIDS victims by a model that takes into account explicit beliefs about the Bible, early formal relationship to a church, and region of origin, a model that gives a hint about the religious stories of these men and women.

It should be noted that 38 percent of all Americans believe in the strict literal interpretation of the Bible and 26 percent both believe in this interpretation and support prayer and Bible reading in the public schools. Forty-seven percent of Protestants believe in literal interpretation and 36 percent of Protestants believe in this interpretation and support prayer and Bible reading in public schools. The "Fundamentalist" strain in American religion is thus large. Moreover, it is not a new phenomenon. According to a Gallup index composed of the experience of being born again, belief in a literal interpretation of Scripture, and an attempt to persuade others to "decide" for Christ, a fifth of the American population has been "fundamentalist" for the last several decades with neither increase nor decrease during that period of time (Greeley 1989). Fundamentalism is a major component of American religion which did not "emerge" during the 1980s; rather, the national elites and the national media discovered (again) what had existed in the United States since the First Great Awakening in 1744! In attempting to understand the relationship between Fundamentalism and AIDS attitudes it is helpful to realize that half of the population of the South believe in the literal interpretation of the Bible as opposed to a quarter of the rest of the country.

There are also somewhat smaller relationships between Protestant affiliation and attitudes on AIDS education. Eight percent of Catholics oppose sex education about AIDS in public schools compared to 16 percent of Protestants. Ten percent of Catholics compared to 17 percent of Protestants oppose government information campaigns about "safe sex." Again there are no statistically significant differences between Catholics and liberal Protestants. Opposition among Fundamentalist Protestants is higher—20 percent oppose sex education in the public schools and 25 percent oppose government information campaigns about "safe sex."

While there is, then, a correlation between Protestantism, especially Fundamentalist Protestantism, and opposition to information campaigns about AIDS, it is nonetheless true that at least three quarters of the Fundamentalists do not oppose such campaigns.

Regression models based on the three biblical items used to account for differences between Protestants and Catholics on the issue of identification tags for AIDS victims reduce to statistical insignificance the differences between the two denominations in attitudes on information campaigns, both in the schools and outside the schools. It is precisely the story that accompanies rigid biblical literalism that accounts for greater Protestant opposition to such campaigns.

Church Attendance

Church attendance does not correlate with attitudes toward identification tags for AIDS victims, but it does correlate negatively and powerfully with attitudes on sex education in the public schools and government information campaigns: -.24 and -.32. Thirty-eight percent of those who attend church weekly or more often oppose sex education about AIDS in public schools (as opposed to 6 percent) and 29 percent oppose government campaigns about "safe sex."

Again the differences between frequent attenders and others can be diminished substantially by use in multiple regression equations of models based on biblical and moral rigidity. The -.24 relationship with opposition to sex education in public schools is reduced to -.13 by taking into account belief in biblical literalism and frequent reading of the Bible. It diminishes to -.08 (and statistical insignificance) when three attitudes on moral decision making are entered into the equation.[9] The difference in attitudes toward government informational campaigns is reduced by half by the same model: the correlation decreases from -.32 to -.16, though the difference remains statistically significant.

Those who attend church frequently are more likely to be opposed to AIDS education programs in substantial part because they accept a more literal interpretation of the Bible and because they see moral decisions in a more simplistic fashion than to those who do not attend church so frequently. Among those regular church goers who do not have such rigid religious orientations there is less difference (or no statistically significant difference) from those who do not attend church weekly.

In one sense it is not such a striking series of findings that are reported here: The religious correlation with negative attitudes toward AIDS victims or AIDS education is the result of moral and religious narrowness among certain members of the more devout population. It is what one might have expected. Nonetheless, this finding establishes that it is not religion as such but a certain highly specific type of religious story that tends to induce hostility on the subject of AIDS. While this religious orientation represents a strong component of American culture and society, it is not a majority orientation; and even among Fundamentalists the majority support AIDS education programs.

The question remains, however, whether other kinds of religious stories correlate positively with compassion on AIDS issues. Obviously more flexible attitudes on biblical inspiration and moral decision making produce greater tolerance and sympathy. But are there other indices of religious devotion that are likely to induce such positive attitudes?

Religious Stories

A person with a higher score on the grace scale, I theorized, will have experienced a more benign relationship with the powers (or Powers) that govern the cosmos and hence will be more benign in her attitudes toward and relationships with other human beings. Her religious story will shape in part the story she tells herself about AIDS.

There are modest but statistically significant positive relationships between the grace scale and tolerance on the AIDS questions; those who are more likely to have a gracious image of God are less likely to approve of identification tags for AIDS victims (-.13), of the exclusion of AIDS victims from public schools (-.14), and of premarital AIDS tests (-.09). They are also more likely to support education about "safe sex" in public schools (.11). Thus, religion measured not by affiliation nor by church attendance but by images of God correlates with tolerance and flexibility toward AIDS policy issues.

For both Catholics and Protestants tolerance increases with grace on all measures, save for attitudes toward premarital tests among Catholics. On two of the four measures, identification tags and attendance at public schools, the correlation is essentially the same for Protestants and Catholics, though on both Catholics are more tolerant than Protestants (only slightly more tolerant on the subject of public school).

On the other two measures, premarital tests and AIDS education in the schools, there is essentially no difference between Catholics and Protestants at the higher end of the grace scale because the scale leads to an increase in tolerance for Protestants and no significant changes for Catholics.

Figure 11.1 summarizes these findings. The proportion of respondents who have sympathetic attitudes toward AIDS victims on at least

FIGURE 11.1

Sympathy for AIDS Victims by Denomination and Grace Scale

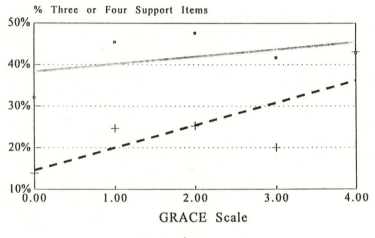

GRACE Scale

-•-Catholic +Protestant

Source: GSS 1988 N=1,481
Grace=Mother+Spouse+Lover+Friend

three items increase with grace score, more sharply for Protestants than for Catholics (and significantly for Protestants) though even at the highest levels of the grace scale Protestants are still lower in sympathy for AIDS victims than are Catholics. The grace scale causes Protestant attitudes to converge toward Catholic attitudes.

Figure 11.2, however, shows a typical interaction between Catholicism and the grace scale. There is not a significant correlation for Protestants between the grace scale and agreement that the government should

FIGURE 11.2
Sympathy for AIDS Victims by Image of God and Denomination

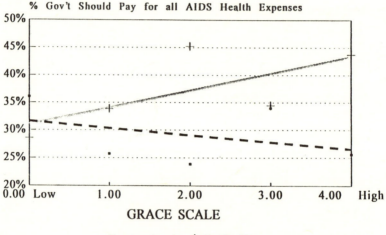

% Gov't Should Pay for all AIDS Health Expenses

GRACE SCALE

→ Protestants + Catholics

Source: GSS 1988 N=1,481
Grace=Mother+Spouse+Lover+Friend

pay for all the AIDS health care expenses. But for Catholics the correlation is statistically significant so that at the top of the grace scale Catholics are almost 25 percentage points more likely to support government payment for health care expenses of AIDS victims than are Protestants. It would seem on the basis of this and the other interactions reported in the present book that it matters not only what religious story you tell but in what community context you tell it.

Thus, images of God, codes that tell stories of a person's relationship with God and provide templates for relationships with other human beings, do correlate with AIDS policy attitudes. To understand the relationship between religion and AIDS policy attitudes, one needs to know not only about attitudes toward the Bible and moral decision making but also about the religious imagination which, according to the theory, underlies the formation and expression of such cognitive attitudes and in some cases even about your religion.[10]

Conclusion

Since 1988 Americans may have become more tolerant on such matters as identity tags for AIDS victims and premarital testing. They may also have become more consistent in their responses. Moreover, some religious denominations, especially liberal Protestant and Catholic, have insisted vigorously on the need for compassion for victims, though Catholic leaders have campaigned (with their usual success in such matters) against "safe sex" education campaigns. It would be useful to know whether these changes, should they have taken place, might also relate to religious convictions, practices, and images. One would predict that the greatest resistance to attitudinal change would come from those with rigid religious orientations and the highest likelihood of attitudinal change from those with the most gracious images of God.

Despite the findings in this chapter, originally submitted in a different form (Greeley 1991a) to one of the many task forces concerned about AIDS,[11] the impression still persists among American elites and particularly among AIDS activists that American religion is hostile to AIDS victims or potential victims. The impression has not changed because, I speculate, the people who have it do not want to change it. Any paper that raises the question of which kind of religion is hostile and which kind is not will not so much be refuted as go unread, especially when it seems to be suggesting that not all Catholics agree with the cardinal archbishop of New York on these matters.

Moreover, despite the power of the religion-as-poetry approach, as documented in the last chapter and the present chapter, to shed light on critical social and human problems, the board of governors of the General Social Survey came close to excluding the God image questions (for which the ordinary GSS funds do not pay, by the way) from future questionnaires. Moreover, the delegates to the International Social Survey Meeting in 1992 resolutely refused to include the image questions in their 1993 study of the environment. I know dogma when I see it— and rigid, dogmatic minds too.

I would like to hope that a future research project would include both the religious measures and the policy attitudes discussed in this chapter. I do not believe there is the slightest chance of that happening. Better to weaken your coalition (whether it be in support of environmental or AIDS activism) than to admit that certain kinds of religion (*grace*-full religious stories) might be on your side.

Notes

1. It is perhaps appropriate that, as a cleric, I note at the beginning of this chapter that the God I know doesn't work that way. Are children born with AIDS guilty of anything? However, it is also true that in a nonpromiscuous population, the disease would spread much less rapidly. This is a fact of epidemiology and not of divine justice.
2. The General Social Survey is funded by the National Science Foundation, which of course is not responsible for this analysis.
3. Unfortunately there was no funding available for subsequent replications of the questions so there are no data on changes in these policy attitudes since 1988.
4. This analysis was originally reported in Greeley 1991a. The present chapter is a revision and adaptation of that work.
5. The first four items were asked of one half of the sample and the other four of the second half.
6. The size of the sample permitted only comparisons between Protestants and Catholics. For the total sample N=1381. Since the items on AIDS policy were administered to only half the sample, the number of cases on each of these questions does not exceed 700.
7. The wording of the three items:

   Which of these statements comes closest to describing your feelings about the bible: a) The bible is the actual word of God and is to be taken literally word for word; b) The bible is the inspired word of God but not everything in it should be taken literally, word for word; c) The Bible is an ancient book of fables, legends, history, and moral principles recorded by men?

   The United States Supreme Court has ruled that no state or local government may require the reading of the Lord's Prayer or Bible verses in public schools. What are your views on this—do you approve or disapprove of the court ruling?

   How important is each of the following in helping you to make decisions about life—the Bible?

8. Did you ever join a church when you were growing up, that is, become a member by confirmation or such?

9. The items:

   Morality is a personal matter and society should not force anyone to follow one standard.

   Immoral actions by one person can corrupt society in general.

   Right and wrong are not usually a simple matter of black and white; there are many shades of gray.

10. The grace scale correlates negatively with all the variables in the models discussed in previous sections of this paper: literalism -.22; Bible reading -.10; Bible in public schools -.11; morality is personal, not social .08; morality is a matter of black and white, not gray -.15; immoral actions can corrupt society -.12.

11. And in response to a plea for evidence that not all religious people and especially not all Catholics were hostile to AIDS victims.

12

Religious Stories and Contact with the Dead

In the third chapter I stated as an assumption that religious experiences shaped secular experiences, that religious stories shaped secular stories, though I acknowledged that the shaping could run in the opposite direction. In this chapter I want to investigate a strange secular story, the story of contact with the dead and ask whether that experience might shape religious imagery or vice versa. The answer will be inconclusive, but it will incline slightly to the former explanation. But nonetheless the phenomenon itself, correlating as it does both with frequency of prayer and image of God, emphasizes again that both imagery and intensity are important to religious stories, as I argued in the last chapter.[1]

Olson and his colleagues (1985) reported a strikingly high incidence of "hallucinations" in which widows experienced contact with their dead spouses. The interviews on which the report based were conducted in nursing homes and do not represent a probability sample of the American population. However, it is possible, using data collected in 1984, 1988, and 1989 in NORC's annual General Social Survey, to attempt replication of the work of Olson et al., and to develop an explanatory model that will account for the higher incidence of such "contacts with the dead" (which the present author prefers to "hallucination") among those who have lost husbands or wives.

The 1984 General Social Survey questionnaire asked:

How often have you had any of the following experiences?

Thought you were somewhere you had been before but knew it was impossible.

Felt as though you were in touch with someone when they were far away from you.

Seen events that happened at a great distance as they were happening.

Felt as though you were really in touch with someone who had died.

Felt as though you were close to a powerful, spiritual force that seemed to lift you out of yourself.

The fourth item is the one on which this analysis is based. Note that it does not ask the person reporting such "contact" who the "contacted" dead person was. It is therefore entirely possible that those widows and widowers in the NORC sample who reported an experience of contact with the dead were not necessarily "in touch" with their spouse. However, it does not seem unreasonable to assume that a disproportionate incidence of such "contact" among the *widowed* (a term to be used in this analysis to include both men and women) is attributable to a contact with a departed spouse.

Forty-two percent of the respondents (N=4,490) reported "contact" with the dead; 41 percent of those who were not widowed, and 53 percent of the widowed (a statistically significant difference). Of the 397 widowed, 340 were women and 57 were men. The proportion of the widows reporting contact with the dead "at least once or twice" was 64 percent, virtually the same proportion as that recorded in the article by Olson et al. Thus, it would appear that the incidence of contact with the dead reported in the nursing home survey is not substantially different from the incidence in the general population.

That almost two-thirds of the widows in the American population have had some "contact" with a dead person (presumably their spouse) is perhaps less surprising than the fact that two-fifths of the population who are not widowed also report such contact. Olson and his colleagues note "the existence of hallucinatory experiences in a population documented at risk of increased morbidity and mortality." Indeed, yes. But also in the general population (the 40 percent reporting contact with the dead in the General Social Survey represents an increase from 25 percent in a previous NORC study in 1972 in which exactly the same questions were asked. Perhaps the respondents feel more at ease in reporting such experiences now than they did thirteen years ago).

The purpose of the present analysis, however, is not to address the rather staggering question of why and how two-fifths of the American population have experienced contact with the dead, but why this contact experience is more likely to occur among the widowed (table 12.1).

A contact with the dead experience is somewhat more likely to occur among the older respondents than among younger respondents and the correlation with age (table 12.2) is statistically significant. Nonetheless,

TABLE 12.1
"Contact with the Dead" for Widows and Widowers

	Men		Women	
	Widowed	Not	Widowed	Not
Never	55%	65%	46%	55%
Once or twice	15%	23%	19%	25%
Several Times	25%	09%	28%	14%
Often	05%	03%	07%	05%
Total	100%	100%	100%	100%
N=	20	568	129	728

TABLE 12.2
Correlates of "Contact with the Dead" Experience
Percent reporting "Contact with the Dead"

Age	
Teens	38%
Twenties	40%
Thirties	44%
Forties	39%
Fifties	42%
Sixties	50%
Seventy and Older	46%

Denomination	
Fundamentalist	42%
Moderates	38%
Liberals	26%
Catholics	44%

Race	
White	41%
Black	55%

Education	
Grammar School	50%
High School	42%
Attended College	42%
College Graduate	45%
Graduate School	32%

Sex	
Men	53%
Women	64%

38 percent of those in their teens and 40 percent of those in their twenties have had such experiences.

Catholics and Fundamentalists are the most likely to have such experiences while those Protestants with no denominational affiliation (32%) and Episcopalians (29%) are the least likely to report them. Blacks are more likely to record such experiences than whites, women more likely than men, and those who have attended graduate school less likely than the rest of the population.

The model developed for the present analysis assumes that religion might be involved in accounting for the disproportionate experience of "contact" with the dead among those who are widowed. Religion, after all, purports to explain the ultimate purposes and the final tragedies of life. It is to the stories of religion that many men and women turn in times of grief. Might it not be that in attempting to resolve the grief of a tragic loss many people develop a religious intensity that disposes them to such encounters—real or imaginary, the social scientist cannot say— with the deceased spouse?

Moreover, since it is known that religious devotion correlates with age (Hout and Greeley 1987) and since the widowed are older than the rest of the population, might it not be that the positive correlation between being widowed and "contact" with the dead can be accounted for by age and by higher levels of religious intensity or devotion?

Figure 12.1 presents such a model graphically. It proposes five significant relationships among the four variables: "widowed," "age," "religion," and "contact." If the model can be fitted into the data as it stands, without a relationship between widowed and "contact," then one can assert—in the language of log linear model fitting—that it is impossible to reject a model that accounts for the disproportionate experience of contact with the dead among the widowed by a combination of age and religion.

Contact with the dead, perhaps not surprisingly, does correlate, and significantly, with a number of different measures of religious behavior (table 12.3). It is more likely to occur among those who believe in life after death, though 30 percent of those who do not believe in life after death still report that they "felt as though they were really in touch with someone who had died," a finding that surely should be a challenge to any social scientist exploring the incidence and prevalence of paranormal experiences in the American population.

FIGURE 12.1
Model to Explain Disproportionate Contact with Dead among Widowed

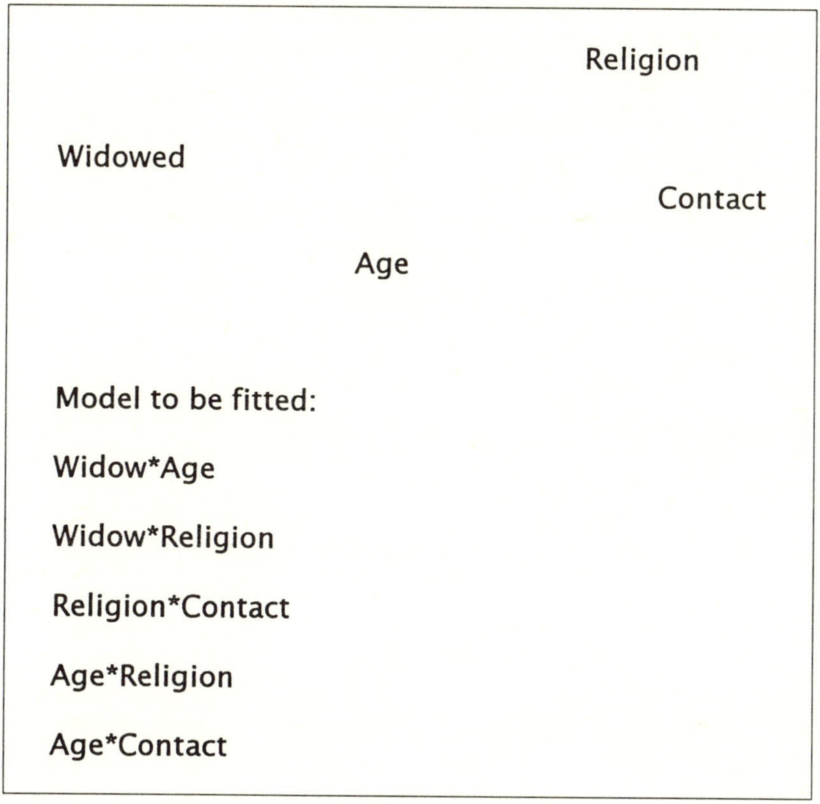

Religion

Widowed

Contact

Age

Model to be fitted:

Widow*Age

Widow*Religion

Religion*Contact

Age*Religion

Age*Contact

Those who pray frequently are more likely to have such experiences than those who do not as are those who are more likely to imagine God as a lover than as a judge. The intensity of religious commitment and the frequency of church attendance, however, do not seem to correlate with contact with the dead (though they might for widows and widowers). Finally, those who have had more than one experience of the other three kinds of psychic phenomena—dé-jà vu, extrasensory perception, and clairvoyance—are almost twice as likely to report contact with the dead as those who have had only one such experience or less. (A psychic experience may not be, strictly speaking, "religious" but the psychic

TABLE 12.3
Religion and "Contact with the Dead"

Belief in Life after Death	
Yes	47%
No	30%
Religious Commitment	
Very strong	43%
Somewhat strong	43%
Not Too strong	43%
Image of God	
Judge	41%
Lover	50%
Prayer	
Daily	48%
Weekly	35%
Less than Weekly	21%
Attendance	
Monthly or less	42%
More than once a month	43%
Psychic Experiences	
One experience or Less	24%
More than one experience	59%

measure is included in table 12.3 because the paranormal might be appropriately considered as not unrelated to the supernormal.)

Six log linear models, based on figure 12.1, were fitted to the data. Estimates were made of the distribution of respondents for each of these models. The actual distributions of the data were compared to the estimated (or "hypothesized") distribution. In the logic of log linear research, a model can be rejected if the actual distribution differs significantly from the hypothesized distribution. A high chi-square measure relative to the degrees of freedom indicates a statistically significant difference. The model then can be rejected. On the other hand, a low chi-square relative to the degrees of freedom indicates the absence of a statistically significant difference between the hypothesized distribution of respondents and the one actually observed. In the latter case it is said that the model cannot be rejected.

The statistics in table 12.5 indicate that when church attendance or prayer or psychic experience or belief in life after death are inserted in

TABLE 12.4
Explanatory Models for "Contact" Experiences Among Widowed

Variable	Chi-square	D.F.	P=
Church Attendance	41.05	26	.03
Prayer	39.34	26	.04
Psychic Experiences	31.72	26	.06
Belief in life After Death	31.02	26	.07
Religious Commitment	30.85	26	.16
God as Lover/Judge	28.62	26	.33

the "religion" slot in the model in figure 12.1, the observed distribution does differ significantly from the hypothesized distribution and therefore explanatory models containing each one of these variables can safely be rejected. Neither the religious commitment nor the religious imagination items, however, when placed in the "religion" slot can be rejected.

Since the chi-square is lower for the religious imagination item, a model that seeks to explain the higher incidence of contact with the dead among the widowed in terms of a combination of age and religious imagination becomes the preferred model.

The relationship between the image of God as a lover and contact with the dead for those who are widowed is nicely illustrated in the cross-tabulation in table 12.5. The image of God as a lover does not increase the probability of an experience of contact with the dead for those who are not widowed but for those who are. The ones who imagine God as a lover are 33 percentage points (73 percent versus 40 percent) more likely to report a contact experience.

Why then are the widowed more likely to experience contact with someone who has died? They are more likely to do so because they are older and because their religious imaginations are more likely than the imagination of others to think of God as a lover rather than a judge. The

TABLE 12.5
"Contact with the Dead" for Widowed by Image of God
(Percent Reporting Experience)

Imagine God as	Lover	Judge
Widowed	73%	40%
Not Widowed	46%	49%

larger problem of why so many Americans report contact with the dead has not been solved but the smaller question of why the widowed are more likely even than others to report it seems, tentatively at least, to be solved: the higher incidence among the widowed can be explained by their age and by a religious response to death, which falls back on stories of God as a lover instead of a judge. Or so it seems.

One assumes, in figure 12.1, that the flow of causality moves from left to right, from "widowed" to "religion" (image of God as a lover instead of a judge) to contact with the dead or, as Olson and his colleagues refer to it, a "hallucination" of the lost spouse.

But there is no absolute necessity of this upper path in the model in figure 12.1. Might not the final step in the path—a relationship between the image of God as a lover and the experience of contact with the dead—flow in the opposite direction? Might not a bereaved person first have the experience of contact with the dead and then, because of such an experience, shift upward on the judge/lover scale? Logically, at any rate, if not metaphysically or theologically, such a possibility cannot be rejected.

One can imagine in principle a way of deciding the issue. If a religious imagination scale could be administered to a sample of widowed persons shortly after the death of the spouse and then subsequently at periodic intervals administered again with other questions about how the respondent was coping with loss and about possible contact with the dead, one might be able to speak with greater confidence about the causal flow in the upper path of the chart in figure 12.1.

But even to fantasize about such research is to understand how extraordinarily complex the issues involved in such matters really are. In the absence of such an elaborate, not to say virtually impossible, experiment, one might at least ask whether the findings reported in this analysis can be replicated in another bereaved population where the grief, however intense it might be, might not normally be so powerful as the grief over the loss of a spouse.

The General Social Survey also asks whether a respondent had lost a mother, a father, a child, or a sibling at various times in their life. For the purposes of this analysis, the population was divided into two groups on each of these questions: those who had experienced such a loss within the last year, and those who either had never lost the designated relation or whose loss had been prior to the last year. As table 12.6 indicates in

TABLE 12.6
"Contact with the Dead" by Other Loss in Family
(Percent reporting contact experience)

	Yes	No
Father	48%	41%
Mother	50%	42%
Child	45%	42%
Sibling	57%	41%*

*Difference statistically significant.

each of the cases, those who have suffered the loss are more likely to report a contact experience than those who have not but the only statistically significant difference, and one of about the same order of magnitude as presented in table 12.1, is for those who have lost a sibling in recent years. The analytic question then becomes whether the same model that accounted for the higher incidence of contact with the dead among widows and widowers also will explain the higher incidence among those who have lost siblings (only 15 percent of the widowed reported a death of a sibling in the last five years). If one distributes a hypothesized population in such a fashion that age and image of God as a lover account for the relationship between the loss of a sibling and contact with the dead, how will such a hypothesized distribution relate to the actual distribution of respondents?

As table 12.7 shows, the proposition that the same model explains "sibling contact" and "spouse contact" cannot be rejected. The chi-square is 27.21 with 23 degrees of freedom and a probability of .25. In both cases then, of a higher incident of Olson et al.'s "hallucinations," age and religious imagery account for the differences. That the loss of a sibling normally would not cause as much grief as the loss of the spouse does not seem to matter.

TABLE 12.7
Model to Explain Sibling-Loss-Related Contact

Variable	Chi square	D.F.	P=
Judge/Lover	27.21	23	.25

Why sibling and spouse and not parent or child? Perhaps because both sibling and spouse are part of one's own generation and have, in the ordinary course of events, shared life longer than either a parent or a child.

Where does this finding leave us on the intricate question of the direction of the causal flow on the final step of the upper path in our analytic model? While the death of a sibling is surely a tragic experience, it does not seem likely to force a person to fall back on religious beliefs and to revise beliefs more or less permanently in the direction of more intense relationship with a God who is a lover. Or if sibling death does lead to such image modification, it would, one might presume, not exercise quite the same power as the loss of a spouse.

Obviously, one must be very cautious in suggesting even a tentative answer to the question but it would seem that the replication of the "spouse loss" story in the "sibling loss" story might inch us a little in the direction of a contact-religion causal flow. Would the loss of a sibling cause a person to revise her religious imagery? Most likely it would not. Yet those who have lost their siblings are more likely to picture God as a lover than those who have not. Whence this change? Might it be the experience of contact with the dead that causes the new imagery?

One still would be inclined to believe that it is the changing religious imagery that produces a propensity to experience contact with the dead. Yet the sibling loss phenomenon must cause us to consider more seriously that it is the actual "contact" that affects the religious imagination and not vice versa, or at least that there is an intricate reciprocal flow between the two phenomena.

Finally, it is the combination of an interaction between frequent prayer and religious imagery that accounts in part for a greater tendency to report contact with the dead among the whole American population. A religious story that combines benign imagery with intensity of interaction accounts in part for this propensity. One's stories of God relate to one's stories of death and perhaps ones experiences of death shape one's stories of God. Moreover, the difference between Catholics and Protestants in their reports of contacts with the dead is reduced to statistical insignificance when the higher score of Catholics on the God-as-Lover measure is taken into account.

To consider seriously the possibility that an experience of being in touch with a person who is dead might actually affect the imagination of the bereaved person in the direction of a more benign view of God, and presumably of the purposes of human life, is to make no suggestions at all about the "reality" of such experiences. As one of the founding fathers of modern sociology, W. I. Thomas remarked if something is defined as real, that definition itself becomes a reality to be studied. Beyond that, empirical social science as we know it must necessarily be agnostic.

The efforts of the Society for Psychic Research, alluded to briefly by Olson and his colleagues, both in its English and American manifestation have not, despite almost a century of effort, been able to resolve the issue of whether "the dead return." While a reading of the long history of that debate might lead one to conclude that those who answer "yes" have ever so slightly more evidence on their side than those who would answer "no," the issue has not been settled and is not likely ever to be settled by the techniques of empirical science.

Empirical scientists may then want to say, "since we can't measure it, it doesn't happen." But such an attitude is as dogmatic as the opposite one: "we have measured it and it does happen." A much more modest approach would be to say, "the issue is beyond the skills of our discipline"; it might happen, and then again, it might not. But, if a substantial proportion of the population thinks it *has* happened, then the incidence and the prevalence, the antecedents and the consequences of this story of their experiences are well worth studying if only so that those of us who minister in one way or another to human health might not be utterly ignorant of a widespread and quite possibly powerful phenomenon.

There is, to put it mildly, considerable bias against examining this phenomenon. When I submitted the first version of this chapter to the same journal in which Olson et al. had published their article, it was promptly rejected by its editor (presumably one who had replaced the editor that had accepted the Olson et al. article) with a stiff note saying that they didn't consider such material as appropriate for their journal. Not even as a replication of an article already published in that journal?

Dismissing an experience that seems to affect two-fifths of adult Americans as too absurd to notice is scientific dogmatism of the most intolerable sort. As I have said before I know dogma when I see it.

Note

1. The findings in this chapter were first reported in Greeley 1987. They were updated for this chapter.

13

A Story of Two Religious Imaginations

Introduction

In describing the role of a (middle range) sociological theory at the beginning of this book, I contended that one of its functions is to give the researcher a perspective with which to begin when confronted with a new data set. In this chapter I hope to illustrate this function by showing how I used my theory of religion as poetry when I discovered that there were over a thousand Southern Baptists in the NORC General Social Survey from 1983 to 1991 (while analyzing the alleged political power of the New Religious Right). Because of the perspective that my theory provided me, I found myself wondering whether the Southern Baptist religious imagination would be different from that of Catholics and whether Tracy's theory of the Two Imaginations, which emerged from the Reformation, might possibly be a useful model to explore the data. Would my model of religion as poetry be useful to account for such differences between Catholics and Protestants which I might encounter? Would it provide insights into religious diversity in America that other models might not provide?

If evangelical Reformation Protestantism survives in any large American denomination, one would expect that the denomination would be the Southern Baptist Convention. It holds to a commitment to the literal interpretation of the Bible, belief in salvation by conversion and faith, belief that participation in grace depends not on sacramental rituals but on personal faith, and insistence on "soul freedom," the right of an individual to make his own religious decisions without the intervention of an organized ecclesiastical institution. All these are solid tenets of Evangelical Reformation teaching, tenets that many "mainline" Protestant denominations no longer emphasize.[1]

Moreover, the Convention is the second largest denomination in America: one out of every ten Americans belongs to it, to say nothing of the last Democratic presidents. It is also often depicted as a bastion of political and religious reaction, a stronghold of the so-called New Christian Right. Yet one can find no sociological or demographic study of its adherents.

The Southern Baptist Convention was organized in Augusta, Georgia, in 1845 because its founders disagreed with the antislavery sentiments of the General Baptist Convention. It developed, early in its existence, a strong centralized structure, though it did not break with the Baptist home mission and publishing efforts till the end of the last century. The formal break between the two major Baptist traditions came only in 1907 when the Northern Baptist Convention (now American Baptist Convention) was organized. The Southern Baptist Convention refuses to participate in ecumenical activity and belongs neither to the National Council of Churches nor the World Council of Churches. It is reputed to be one of the fastest growing denominations in America. During the 1980s a conservative ("Fundamentalist") coalition took control of the Southern Baptist Convention (Ammerman 1990).

Like all large denominations there is considerable de facto pluralism within the Southern Baptist community, though that pluralism is not recognized by those Americans who lump all the "fundamentalist" labels together. The biblical studies published by faculty members of Southern Baptist Seminary are as professionally skilled in the art of biblical criticism as are books written by scholars of more liberal denominational backgrounds, for example, Watts (1985). However, despite some articles on the Southern Baptists (Ammerman 1991, Elifson 1976, Flynt 1981, McSwain 1980, and Thompson 1974) there exists no study based on representative national survey data of the extent of that pluralism among those who profess affiliation with the Southern Baptist Convention.

Modern sociology emerged in substantial part from a discussion of the differences between Catholics and Protestants. Weber (1958) thought that the "communitarian" ethic of the former seemed to impede educational and economic achievement while the "inner-worldly asceticism" of the latter with its emphasis on individual achievement facilitated the success of the latter. Durkheim (1961) believed, on the other hand, that the "individualism" of Protestants induced higher suicide rates among them while the "communitarian" control available to Catholics tended to reduce suicide rates.

The theories of these two giants certainly fit the pattern of religious emphasis of the two denominational traditions. For Protestantism the tendency has always been to emphasize the relationship of the individual with God while for Catholicism the tendency has always been to emphasize the individual relating to God as a member of a community. Suicide rates and educational achievement rates would be two manifestations (and perhaps not the most important) of fundamental orientations, which permeate the two traditions (Greeley 1989a, 1989b, 1991a, 1993a).

Tracy contends that two approaches to human society of the respective traditions are shaped by these imaginative pictures. The Catholic tends to see society as a "sacrament" of God, a set of ordered relationships, governed by both justice and love, which reveal, however imperfectly, the presence of God. Society is "natural" and "good" therefore for humans and their "natural" response to God is social. The Protestant on the other hand tends to see human society as "God-forsaken" and therefore unnatural and oppressive. The individual stands over against society and not integrated into it. The human becomes fully human only when he is able to break away from social oppression and relate to the absent God as a completely free individual.

Tracy's analysis complements and adds to the earlier insights of Durkheim and Weber. One may continue to speak of a "Protestant" ethic, but now one must understand the ethic as a set of fundamental world-explaining and world-shaping interpretative pictures. In this sense, ethos, as Geertz (1957) has observed, is the flip side of mythos. Formal ethical codes are derivatives of interpretative pictures. The higher suicide rates and the higher achievement rates of Protestants in turn-of-the-century Europe are the result ultimately of different symbol systems, of, if one may say it, different—though not totally different—stories of God.

Hence, the theoretical question for this chapter is whether differences between Catholics and Southern Baptists on religious, social, and political matters can be accounted for by different imaginative religious stories in the two traditions. Do "stories of God" that date to the Reformation explain different stories of human life in denominations that survive with their Reformation perspectives intact?

Demography

The analysis in this chapter will be based on data from NORC's General Social Survey, pooled from 1983 (when interviewers began to ask

FIGURE 13.1
Southern Baptists by Year

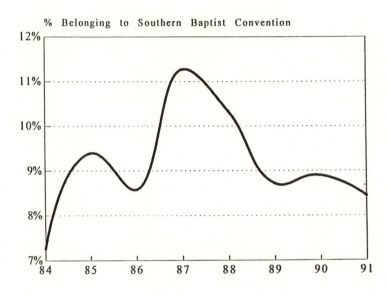

% Belonging to Southern Baptist Convention

Source: GSS 1984–91 N=12,203

about specific Protestant subdenominations) to 1991 (Davis and Smith).
In those years 1,118 respondents identified themselves as members of
the Southern Baptist Convention, approximately 9 percent of the American population. As figure 13.1 illustrates there is some evidence of significant increase and decrease in Southern Baptist membership during
those years. Thus, in a logistic regression equation the difference between
1984 and 1987 generates a "Wald" statistic of 2.36 with 1 degree of
freedom and a probability of .12. And the difference between 1987 and
1991 produces a "Wald" of 4.11 with 1 degree of freedom and a prob-

TABLE 13.1
Demography of Southern Baptists

	Southern Baptists	Other Protestants	Catholics
Black	17%	19%	4%
Hispanic	1%	1%	11%
Children	2.04	2.09	1.93
Age	45.3	46.9	44.0
Real Income	$26,502	$27,778	$30,909
College Graduate	12%	17%	18%
Professional	12%	17%	17%
White Collar	47%	53%	58%
South	78%	37%	19%
Rural	19%	17%	10%
Large City and Suburb	29%	33%	44%
Democratic	59%	47%	53%
Republican	34%	42%	33%
Liberal	22%	24%	27%
Conservative	37%	38%	31%
Liberal Democrat	15%	15%	17%
Conservative Republican	18%	22%	16%
Married to Other			
Southern Baptist	50%		
Convert	20%		
Defector	22%		

Source: GSS 1984–91 N=12,203 N (Southern Baptist Convention)=1,119

ability of .04. The Southern Baptists flourished in the middle 1980s and perhaps lost membership after that because of their internal controversies.

As table 13.1 demonstrates almost four out of five Southern Baptists still live in the Southern region of the United States (South Atlantic, East South Central, and West South Central). A little less than one out of five members is black. Their educational level, occupational prestige, and income are less than that of other American Protestants, though the difference in education and income disappears when region is taken into account and the difference in proportion professional and white collar disappears when the educational difference is taken into account. There are no statistically significant differences among Southern Baptists, other Protestants, and Catholics in family size.

FIGURE 13.2
Southern Baptists by Age

% of All Americans who are Southern Baptist

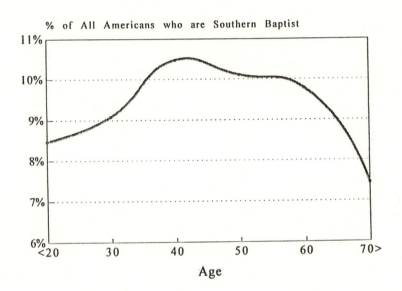

Age

Source: GSS 1984–91 N=12,203

In comparison with Catholics, Southern Baptists disproportionately live in rural areas and not in large cities. They are, nonetheless, more likely to describe themselves as Democrats[2] than other Protestants and Catholics and less likely to describe themselves as Republicans than other Protestants.[3] They are somewhat more likely than Catholics to think of themselves as conservatives and less likely to think of themselves as liberals. However, there is no difference among the three denominational groupings in the proportion that say they are liberal Democrats, and Southern Baptists are less likely than other Protestants to picture themselves as conservative Republicans.[4]

While on the average Southern Baptists are older than Catholics (45.3 versus 44.0) they are younger than other Protestants[5] (46.9). Does this average age suggest that Southern Baptists are making converts among younger people? In fact figure 13.2 suggests that the opposite might be the case. The highest proportion Southern Baptist is among those who are in their forties; the proportion slopes off among those in their twenties and thirties. Indeed in a logistic regression analysis membership among those who are in their twenties and in their thirties is significantly lower (p=.88 and p=.15) than those in their forties, which is significantly higher than those in their sixties (p=.92).

Indeed the average convert (who represents 20 percent of the Southern Baptists) is six years older than the average "cradle" Southern Baptists[6] and the surge (from 7.5 percent of the population to 10.5, a 40 percent increase) in Southern Baptist membership would seem to have occurred among those who are in their forties and fifties. Moreover, the average age of the "defector" (who represents 22 percent of those raised Southern Baptist) from the Southern Baptists is two years younger than the "cradle" Southern Baptist. One would tentatively conclude that the increase in membership in the Convention may have happened during the 1960s, 1970s, and early 1980s and has now tapered off,[7] perhaps because of the internal conflicts within the Convention in the 1980s.

In sum, Southern Baptists tend to be Southern, rural, or small town (or small city), somewhat less well-educated and affluent, more Democratic than Republican, and not disproportionately conservative Republican. They are slightly younger than other Protestants but the increase in their membership seems to have come to an end and there is a possibility, both in the advantage of defectors over converts and the somewhat lower proportion of younger Americans enrolled in the denomination, of a slight decline in membership in years to come.[8]

Religious Faith

Southern Baptists are in general substantially more likely to describe themselves as devout than Catholics and somewhat more likely to describe themselves as devout than other Protestants (table 13.2). They are, as one might expect, 15 percentage points more likely than other Protestants to believe in a literal interpretation of the Bible and 36 percentage points more likely than Catholics.[9] Nonetheless, a little more

TABLE 13.2
Religious Beliefs and Behavior of Southern Baptists

	Southern Baptists	Other Protestants	Catholics
Bible Literalists	58%	43%	22%
Member Church Organization	41%	41%	28%
Pray Daily	64%	61%	57%
"Close" to God	38%	34%	24%
Attend Regularly	49%	48%	49%
Believe in Life After Death	83%	86%	76%

Source: GSS 1984–91 N=12,203

than two out of five Southern Baptists do not believe in such literal interpretation, a smaller proportion than that of Catholics who do not accept Papal Infallibility (two out of three). If this measure of biblical "Fundamentalism" is a core doctrine of the Convention,[10] then it is one that is less likely to be accepted by younger members, even those younger members who are already devout regular church goers (figure 13.3)— 56 percent of those in their twenties who attend church several times a month accept literal interpretation as do 40 percent in the same age group who attend less regularly. While religious faith and devotion tend to increase with age, holding devotion constant, as is done in figure 13.3, suggests that the youthful decline in acceptance of literalism may be something more than a life cycle phenomenon. If to be a "Fundamentalist" you have to accept literal interpretation, than more than two out of five Southern Baptists are not "Fundamentalist." Nor are almost half of even the devout young people who affiliate with the Convention "Fundamentalist."

Southern Baptists are more likely than Catholics to pray everyday, to belong to a church-related organization, to describe themselves as close to God, and to believe in life after death. They are also more likely than other Protestants to claim closeness to God and to pray everyday. If therefore they might claim to be a "godly" people in comparison to Catholics (as the Reformers did) there is evidence in the data that they might be.

In 1988 the General Social Survey added (for one year only) a special module on religion (N=1,481) that enables one to make more detailed comparisons among the three denomination groups considered in the present analysis (table 13.3). The picture that emerges adds flesh to the

FIGURE 13.3
Inspiration by Age and Devotion
(Southern Baptists)

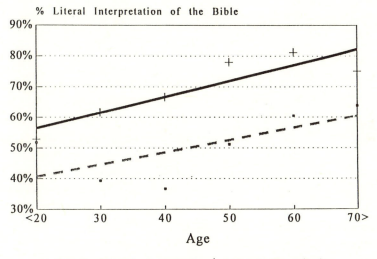

% Literal Interpretation of the Bible

Age

⁻⁻Don't Attend Regularly +Attend Regularly

Source: GSS 1984–91 N=12,203

skeleton displayed in table 13.2. Southern Baptists are more likely than both other Protestants and Catholics to be absolutely certain about the existence of God, to say they have been born again, to report efforts to persuade someone else to decide for Christ, to read the Bible weekly, and to watch religious television often.

The last four items in table 13.3 represent factor scores:

Antiscience

Science will solve our problems like crime and mental illness.

TABLE 13.3
Religious Beliefs and Behavior of Southern Baptists

	Southern Baptists	Other Protestants	Catholics
Absolutely Certain about God	84%	68%	64%
Born Again	73%	47%	15%
Win Other for Christ	77%	56%	33%
Read Bible Weekly	50%	43%	15%
Watch Religious TV	46%	35%	18%
Antiscience	48%	37%	31%
Religious Freedom	22%	37%	54%
Moral Flexibility	41%	44%	58%
Religious Dogmatism	67%	59%	50%

Source: GSS 1988 N=1,481 N(Southern Baptist Convention)=133

One trouble with science is that it makes our life change too fast.

Scientists are always prying into things they should stay out of.

One of the bad effects of science is that it breaks down people's ideas of right and wrong.

Religious Freedom

Can you tell how important each of the following is in helping you to make decisions about your life?

The Bible.

Family and friends.

The teachings of your church or synagogue.

Your own personal judgment.

Moral Flexibility

Those who violate God's law should be punished.

Right and wrong are not usually a simple matter of black and white; there are many shades of gray.

Immoral actions by one person can corrupt society in general.

Morality is a personal matter and society should not force anyone to follow one standard.

Religious Dogmatism

How important is each of the following to you:
To attend regularly religious services at church or synagogue.
To believe in God without question or doubt.
To follow faithfully the teachings of church or synagogue.
To follow one's conscience even if it means going against what the churches or synagogues say and do.

On each of the four factors the most rigid scores are those of the Southern Baptists and the least rigid are those of Catholics. (The numbers in table 13.3 represent proportions above the factor mean.) Perhaps not surprisingly, the Southern Baptists are more likely to be opposed to *science* and to be religiously *dogmatic* and Catholics least likely. Southern Baptists are also the least likely to be morally *flexible*. But surprisingly, given the Reformation emphasis on religious individualism and their own emphasis on "soul freedom" or "soul competence," Southern Baptists are also the least likely to emphasize *freedom* in decision making and Catholics the most likely. Thus, on the item about the importance of the Church in decision making, 61 percent of the Southern Baptists, 54 percent of the other Protestants, and 45 percent of the Catholics said the Church was important (44 percent, 32 percent, and 26 percent, respectively, said it was "very" important).

The stereotype of religious rigidity that many have about the Southern Baptists is confirmed by these four factor scores, but the similar stereotype about Catholics is refuted by the data. Might the reason for the latter finding be the liberalization of Catholicism after the Second Vatican Council? If that were the case, one would expect that the greater emphasis on *religious freedom* would be concentrated among younger Catholics. But in fact (figure 13.4), the "advantage" for Catholics on the *religious freedom* measure over Southern Baptists is the same at every age level, even though support for *religious freedom* declines with age for both denominations.

Perhaps the refutation of the Catholic stereotype is not all that surprising. Compared to the stern canons of the Reformation, Catholicism has always been flexible in practice when compared to Protestantism. Church-like instead of sect-like, Catholicism has often been able to include within its boundaries a substantial pluralism and a wide variety of

FIGURE 13.4
Religious Freedom by Denomination and Age

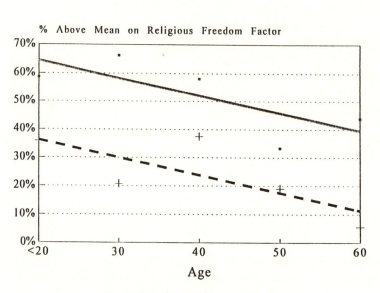

% Above Mean on Religious Freedom Factor

── Catholic   + Southern   Baptist

Source: GSS 1988 N=1,481

adherents, especially in practice and despite the solemn warnings of Church leaders. It was precisely this apparent laxity that was one of the reasons why a *reformation* was thought to be necessary. Typically, Catholicism has meant in James Joyce's phrase "HCE"—here comes everybody!

Can the differences between Catholics and Southern Baptists on these four factors be accounted for by the classic Reformation differences in religious imagination as specified by Tracy? Does the difference between analogical and dialectical religious stories account for the difference in factor scores between Catholics and Protestants? Are Baptists more rigid on morality, dogmatism, attitudes toward science, and religious freedom precisely because their religious imaginations are less "graceful" and more "harsh" than the religious imaginations of Catholics, which are more dialectical and less analogical? Or might it be that "graceful" religious imagery has greater impact on Catholics than it does on Reformation Protestants? In previous chapters about attitudes toward AIDS and toward the environment, we saw an "interaction" effect. The grace scale had a more powerful impact on Catholics than on Protestants; the story of a benign God, one who was more likely to be a mother, spouse, lover, and friend, instead of a father, master, judge, and king,[11] had a greater effect in shaping the religious and political attitudes of Catholics than the same scale did for Protestants. The Catholic score on the scale was not only higher than the Protestant score, it had greater impact.[12]

In the present analysis 40 percent of the Southern Baptists, 47 percent of the other Protestants and 54 percent of Catholics scored above the mean on the grace scale. As table 13.4 demonstrates the first set of regression equations, in which the Grace scale is entered along with denomination, reduces the correlations between Southern Baptist and the dependent variable only marginally (or not at all), save for the dogmatism factor in which the r is reduced from .24 to a β of .19.

TABLE 13.4
Explanation of Religious Differences between Catholics and Southern Baptists

	Anti Science	Religious Freedom	Moral Flexibility	Religious Dogmatism
Correlation (r) with Southern Baptist	.15	–.33	–.26	.24
β net of Grace scale	.14	–.31	–.26	.19
β net of Grace scale, and Catholic Interaction with Grace Scale	.02**	–.20	.07**	.19
Net of Grace Scale, Catholic Interaction with Grace Scale, and Religious Certainty*		–.02**		.01**

**correlation not statistically significant
Source: GSS 1988 n=1,481

FIGURE 13.5
Moral Flexibility by Image of God
(For Catholics and Southern Baptists)

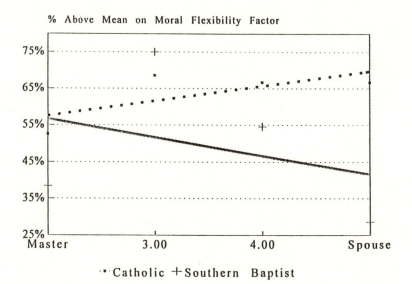

% Above Mean on Moral Flexibility Factor

·· Catholic + Southern Baptist

Source: GSS 1988 N=1,481

But when the interaction between Catholic and the grace scale is entered, the β for both the antiscience and moral flexibility factors declines to statistical insignificance. The other two correlations become statistically insignificant when a scale measuring the need for religious certainty is entered into the equation.[13]

Figure 13.5 illustrates what occurs with the moral flexibility factor. Catholic support for moral flexibility increases as Catholics are more likely to imagine God as a spouse. Southern Baptist support for the same position does not increase (the decline depicted in the chart is not statistically significant). The stories contained in religious images affect Catholic attitudes toward stern moral judgments but do not affect Southern Baptist attitudes. Stern Reformation morality is not compromised by images of a more grace-full God. This chart for all practical purposes replicates those presented in chapters on religion and the environment and religion and attitudes toward AIDS—and anticipates a subsequent chart in this chapter on religious imagery and attitudes toward civil liberties. The question arises as to why images have more effect on one side of the Reformation barrier than on the other side.

Thus, on the basis of the data from the 1988 religion study, the Reformation divide inside Christianity survives in this country when comparisons are made between Catholicism and Evangelical Reformation Protestantism. Nor does the more benign image of God among Catholics owe its origins to the Vatican Council. As figure 13.6 shows there are higher scores on the grace scale for younger Southern Baptists and Catholics than for older ones (though this pattern is not repeated among other Protestants) but the advantage of Catholics over Southern Baptists exists equally at all age levels.

Sex and Abortion

Southern Baptists are more "conservative" on family values than other Protestants and Catholics (table 13.5) but differ very little from other Christians in their attitudes toward abortion (table 13.6). Thus, the Southern Baptists are more likely to think that premarital sex, extramarital sex, and homosexual sex are always wrong and Catholics are the least likely to think that they are always wrong, perhaps because Catholics are always willing to admit the possibility of exceptions to rules, though their leadership is often not quite so flexible, especially when sex is the subject.[14]

The same response pattern persists for attitudes toward sex education in the schools (which the overwhelming majority of Americans support) and antipornography laws (which a substantial proportion of Americans also support). Southern Baptists are also most likely to have stern positions on child rearing (spanking and importance of obedience) and Catholics least likely.

However, on the emotionally charged issue of abortion, Southern Baptists think the same way as other Protestants and Catholics when

TABLE 13.5
Family Values of Southern Baptists

	Southern Baptist	Other Protestants	Catholic	Number of Cases
Premarital Sex				
Always Wrong	42%	30%	20%	7284
Extramarital Sex				
Always Wrong	84%	78%	74%	7654
Homosexuality				
Always Wrong	90%	81%	73%	7452
Ban All Porn by Law	47%	45%	39%	8957
Reject Sex Education				
in Schools	15%	16%	11%	7292
Spank Children	38%	31%	25%	4709
Obedience Most				
Important	27%	24%	17%	2125

Source: GSS 1984–91

TABLE 13.6
Abortion Attitudes for Southern Baptists

	Southern Baptists	Other Protestants	Catholics
Health	9%	10%	14%
Defect	22%	21%	24%
Rape	18%	19%	21%
Poor	66%	56%	59%
No More	67%	60%	63%
Any	71%	64%	66%

Source: GSS 1984–91 N=12,203

there is a threat to the mother's health, a chance of a defective child, and a pregnancy resulting from rape. In these three situations the overwhelming majority of Americans of all religious backgrounds support the legal possibility of abortion. On the other hand, when the situation is closer to the "abortion on demand" circumstances—the woman is poor or she wants no more children or she simply wants an abortion—the majority of all three groups oppose legal abortion, with the Southern Baptists somewhat more likely to oppose the legality of abortion than the other

FIGURE 13.6
Image of God by Denomination and Age

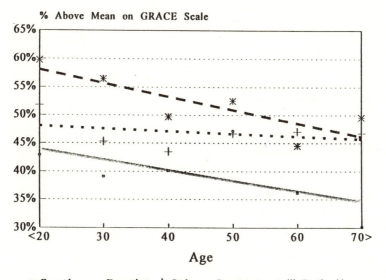

% Above Mean on GRACE Scale

Age

⊸ Southern Baptist + Other Protestant ✳ Catholic

Source: GSS 1984–91 N=7,732

two groups. Nonetheless, there is no evidence in the data in tables 13.5 and 13.6 that Southern Baptists are in general part of the New Religious Right. In fact (Greeley 1993b) no more than one out of ten (at the outside) of those who claim affiliation with the Southern Baptist Convention seem to be candidates for the New Christian Right.

Can the same model that explained the "Reformation" differences between Catholics and Southern Baptists on religious matters also account for the greater Catholic flexibility on "family values"? Table 13.7 demonstrates that a combination of higher Catholic scores on the grace

TABLE 13.7
Explanation of Differences in Family Values between
Catholics and Southern Baptists

	Premarital Sex	Extramarital Sex	Homo-sexuality	Obedience and Spanking
Correlation (r) with				
Southern Baptist	.20	.08	.18	.17
β net of Grace Scale	.17	.07	.16	.15
β net of Grace Scale, and Catholic Interaction with Grace Scale	.17	.06**	.08**	.10**

**correlation not statistically significant.
Source: GSS 1983-91

scale and the greater impact of the scale on Catholic attitudes reduce to statistical insignificance the differences between Catholics and Southern Baptists on three of the four items: extramarital sex, homosexual sex, and a child-rearing factor. The model, however, does not account for the greater tolerance of Catholics for premarital sex. It is nonetheless interesting that Catholics are more likely to think that there are exceptions to the rules on both extramarital and homosexual sex and that this greater tolerance for exceptions is the result of more gracious Catholic religious imagery.

The portrait of the affiliates of the Southern Baptist Convention that has emerged so far is more complex and intricate than one should have expected. On some matters, political affiliation and abortion attitudes, they can hardly be written off as "conservative." On the other hand, on measures of religious flexibility and sexual attitudes they are more conservative than both Catholics and other Protestants. The question remains how they might differ from other Americans on some of the other critical political and social issues in American life.

Social and Political Attitudes

Five factors were drawn from standard GSS items:

Racism

Blacks shouldn't push where they're not wanted.

White people have the right to keep blacks out of their neighbor-hoods if they want to and blacks should respect that right.

A homeowner can decide for himself whom to sell his house to, even if he prefers not to sell to blacks.

Feminism

Women should take care of their homes and leave the running of the country up to men.

Do you approve or disapprove of a married woman earning income in business or industry if she has a husband capable of supporting her?

If your party nominated a a woman for president, would you vote for her if she were qualified for the job?

Civil Liberties

Twelve items that measure tolerance for a public speech, a faculty position, and books in a library for a homosexual, a communist, a racist, or a militarist.

Trust

Three items that ask about whether people are helpful, fair, and trust-worthy.

Militarism

How much confidence do you have in the military?

Should the country be spending more money or less or about the same on the military?

In addition, a scale was composed on the subject of gun ownership. A high score was given to those who owned a pistol, a rifle, and a shotgun.

Table 13.8 shows that Southern Baptists are more likely to oppose feminism, to take racist positions, to oppose civil liberties, to distrust other people, and to support militarism than are other Protestants. More-over, the latter are more likely to agree with "conservative" stands than are Catholics (save on the militarism factor). Finally, Southern Baptists are also more likely to be fully armed with guns in their house than are

TABLE 13.8
Southern Baptist Attitudes and Behavior
(Proportion above Favor Mean)

	Southern Baptists	Other Protestants	Catholics	Number of Cases
Racism	58%	51%	40%	2459
Feminism	51%	59%	63%	2547
Civil Liberties	41%	53%	59%	2506
Trust	43%	51%	55%	3056
Militarism	55%	46%	46%	1582
Armed*	18%	13%	8%	8868

*Owned pistol, shotgun, and rifle.
Source: GSS 1984–91

the other two groups, indeed more than twice as likely to own rifles, pistols, and shotguns than are Catholics.[15]

The differences on these measures between Catholics and Southern Baptists obviously represent major cultural differences, which in substantial part would seem to stand for differences between the South and the rest of the country. But are they underpinned by differences in the religious imagination? Can the different responses to problems that American culture faces—racism, militarism, feminism, civil liberties, and trust—be attributed to fundamental differences about the meaning and purpose of human life, differences that are encoded in religious images, which are narrative symbols and hence stories?

The numbers in table 13.9 show that the differences between Catholics and Southern Baptists on all five factors can be reduced to statistical insignificance by the analytic model used in this chapter. The higher score of Catholics on the grace[16] scale and particularly the greater impact of the scale on Catholic political and social attitudes account for *all* the differences between Catholics and Southern Baptists in these five crucial dimensions of American life and culture. Differences in religious imagery, differences that date at least to the Reformation, account not only for the different religious styles but even for the different cultural values of Catholics and Southern Baptists.

Figure 13.7 portrays this the phenomenon: the line that shows the correlation between imagery and support for civil liberties is absolutely flat for Southern Baptists, while the line for Catholics shows an increase

TABLE 13.9
Explanation of Attitudinal Differences between
Catholics and Southern Baptists

	Racism	Feminism	Civil Liberties	Trust	Militarism
Correlation (r) with Southern Baptist	.15	−.12	−.19	−.13	.11
β net of Grace scale	.14	−.11	−.19	−.13	.10
β net of Grace scale, and Catholic Interaction with Grace Scale	.05**	−.01**	−.04**	−.06**	.01**

**correlation not statistically significant
Source: GSS 1984–91

of almost twenty points in support for civil liberties. Moreover, (table 13.10) within the Southern Baptist community itself, the grace scale accounts for the difference in attitudes toward feminism and civil liberties between those Southern Baptists who believe in the literal interpretation of Scripture and those who do not. The religious stories of nonliteralist Southern Baptists account for their greater sympathy for feminism and for civil liberties. The grace scale not only distinguishes Southern Baptist attitudes from those of Catholics, it also distinguishes between those within the Southern Baptist community who believe in biblical literalism and those who do not.

But why does the religious image scale not have a positive effect on Southern Baptists like it does on other Protestants and Catholics (as well as Jews and Episcopalians)?[17] Why do the stories of God in the Southern Baptist religious imagination not affect their religious styles, their sexual attitudes, "family life" values, and their political and social postures?

Might it be that Evangelical Reformation attitudes toward religious images depresses the relationship between the stories of God and the stories of daily life? In 1985 a question was asked about attitudes toward art: a seven-point choice between "Through such things as music and art we learn more about God" "It is dangerous for a human to be too concerned about worldly things like art and music." Sixty-two percent of Southern Baptists, 67 percent of other Protestants and 74 percent of Catholics chose the former reaction.

FIGURE 13.7
Support for Civil Liberties by Image of God
(For Catholics and Southern Baptists)

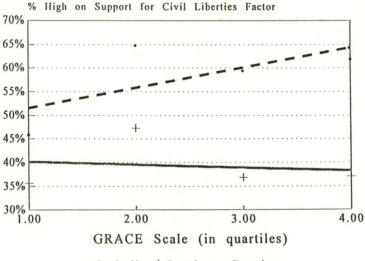

Source: GSS 1984-91 N=2,506

TABLE 13.10
Correlations with Belief in Literal Interpretation among Southern Baptists

	Racism	Feminism	Civil Liberties	Trust	Militarism
Correlation (r) with					
Literalism	.18	−.20	−.24	−.04**	.05**
β net of Grace scale	.21	−.08**	−.08**		

**correlation not statistically significant.

FIGURE 13.8
Civil Liberties by Image of God by Attitude Toward Art
(For Southern Baptists)

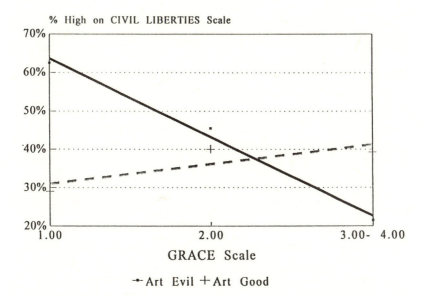

% High on CIVIL LIBERTIES Scale

GRACE Scale

-•- Art Evil + Art Good

Source: GSS 1985 N=142

When the positive reactions to music and art were dichotomized from the neutral and negative attitudes, it turned out (figure 13.8) that those Southern Baptists who had a positive attitude toward music and art displayed the .09 correlation between the grace scale and support for civil liberties, which is to be found among both other Protestants and Jews (still a little less than the .12 for Catholics), and that the elimination of the relationship is concentrated among those who rejected the religious worth of art. It therefore is at least arguable that a Reformation suspicion of religious imagery lurking in the minds of some Southern Baptists cancels out the propensity of religious stories to affect other stories of life. Indeed the Reformation endures, not only in imagery but in distrust of imagery.

Summary and Conclusion

Baptists who identify with the Southern Baptist Convention are a more complex and pluralistic group than one might have anticipated. They are indeed a national denomination, the second largest Church[18] in America, counting one out of ten Americans among its affiliates. The period of their recent spectacular growth seems to be over, and a period of slight decline may have set in. Southern Baptists are disproportionately southern and rural and not quite so affluent as other Americans, mostly because of their heavily southern location. They are more likely to be Democrats than other American Christians and no less likely to be liberal Democrats.

Their religious style, however, is both devout and profoundly Reformation, even though only three out of five of their members believe in the literal interpretation, word for word, of the Bible. They are more likely to be suspicious of science, moralistic, dogmatically rigid, and, despite their doctrine of "soul freedom," dependent on the leadership of their Church than are Catholics and other Protestants. They are also more restrained on matters of sexual morality and sterner in their ideas on child rearing, though they do not differ much from other Americans on abortion attitudes and are hardly good candidates for either the Moral Majority or the Christian Coalition.

Positions taken by the leadership and by the resolutions at the annual Convention are no more likely to represent the sentiments of many Southern Baptists than are the statements of the Catholic hierarchy reflective of the positions of ordinary Catholics.

Southern Baptists are, however, involved in a culture, both religious and political, that is profoundly different from that of other Americans and especially of American Catholics: less likely to oppose racism, more likely to oppose feminism, less likely to trust others, more likely to be militarists (and to be armed themselves), and less likely to support civil liberties for dissidents. These differences can be accounted for by their religious imagery, what Tracy would call their Dialectical Imagination, and especially by the restraints put on their religious imagery by what seems to be a Reformation skepticism about imagery. Not only do they keep alive the theology of the Reformation they also sustain the moral rigidity, the self-righteous religious style, and the harsh religious imagery that marked some of the Reformers. The differences between them and Catholics are not limited merely to faith and devotion but also extend to cultural postures. The basic axis along which Christianity split in the sixteenth century continues to exist in America.

However, the cultural differences do not cause any more religious conflicts, despite the disinterest of the Southern Baptists in ecumenism.[19] In the middle 1980s the GSS asked questions about feelings toward various groups in American society on a scale from 0 to 100. Southern Baptist feelings toward Catholics (62) did not differ from those of other Protestants or Jews and were actually "warmer" than those with no religious affiliation (51). Unfortunately, there was no feeling thermometer for reactions of Catholics to Southern Baptists. Neither group, however, is threatening to burn others at the stake, or shooting at one another in the dark as members of similar communities do in Northern Ireland. If the Reformation endures, at least in the United States it endures amiably.

This chapter also demonstrates that those who think religion is no longer important in the culture and structure of American society are not only in error but blind to the obvious facts. When the two largest heritages, both held in contempt by many of the national elite, are so profoundly different in religious style and cultural values and different indeed along lines that replicate those of the sixteenth century, and when these two Churches constitute a third of the society, religion is still a very important predictor variable indeed.

Thus, I have demonstrated in this chapter that my theory of the sociology of religion provides me with useful questions to ask and useful explanations for the differences found when answers to the questions are pursued. Neither my questions nor my explanations are necessarily the best approach to study members of the Southern Baptist Convention. I rather suspect that a Southern Baptist sociologist would ask different questions and pursue different lines of analysis. No theoretical perspective nor analytic approach is necessarily superior to an alternative perspective and approach. However, a particular perspective and approach may provide more interesting findings and explanations than others.

In this chapter I have demonstrated nothing more than that the religion-as-poetry orientation does enable me to account for many differences between Catholics and Baptists in terms not only of different religious imaginations but also of willingness to trust religious imagery. Perhaps other orientations to religion would also produce similar findings; however, all I wish to claim for the religion-as-poetry perspective is that in the case of the Southern Baptists it proved fruitful.

TABLE 13.10
Correlations with Religious and Social Attitude
(Southern Baptists Versus Catholics)*

	Correlation (r)	Net of Region and Rural (Beta)	Net of Region Rural, and, Education (Beta)
Racism	.20	.18	.15
Militarism	.10	.08	.07
Civil Liberties	−.24	−.18	−.14
People	−.09	−.08	−.06
Religious Liberty	−.19	−.14	−.10
Armed	.25	.19	.19
Feminism	−.10	−.08	−.06
Grace	−.17	−.17	−.17

*All betas are statistically significant.

Excursus

The Table above considers an alternative explanation for the differences between Catholics and Southern Baptists. Perhaps the two denominations are different because they have different demographic backgrounds. Southern Baptists are by definition from the South. They are also rural. When these two dimensions are taken into account, would not the differences between them and Catholics go away? Would not southern rural culture be a better explanation than religious imagery?

In fact when 8 variables are considered in regression equations with South and Rural added, the correlations diminish somewhat but all remain statistically significant. When education is added in a second set of equations there is an added decline in the relationships but they all continue to be significant. It will be remembered that the imagery items reduce the correlations to insignificant. Thus the demographic explanation does not eliminate the payoff of the imagery explanation. Note too that none of the demographic variables change the relationship between Southern Baptist and the "Grace" scale.

The impact of these models varies from variable to variable. Thus when cross tabulations are performed for region and college education, Catholics are significantly more likely to support "civil liberties" in all eight cells. The only significant difference in "feminism" is between Catholics in the south who did not attend college and their Southern Baptist counterparts (58% to 45%). This cell is the one which indicates the difference before either migration or education can mitigate the cultural differences between Catholics and Southern Baptists.

Notes

1. Richards (1991) traces the evolution of Southern Baptist theology away from Calvinism in the direction of what he calls "inerrantist evangelicalism." The inerrancy of the scriptures is clearly the issue around which current Southern Baptist controversy swirls.
2. The Southern Baptist advantage over other Protestants in proportion Democratic is not merely a function of the fact that one out of five is African-American. Among whites, 52 percent of the Southern Baptists are Democrats, 39 percent of the other Protestants, and 53 percent of the Catholics. Thus, racial composition accounts for the advantage of Southern Baptists over Catholics but not for their advantage over other Protestants.
3. Hart (1992) correlated thirty-nine "economic" variables in the General Social Survey's 1984 to 1998 data with belief in literal interpretation of the Scripture and found that in only four cases were the "literalists" more conservative than the "nonliteralists," and in twelve cases the former were in fact *more* liberal.
4. The three denominational groupings in this analysis represent 88 percent of all Americans.
5. The "other" Protestant category in this chapter contains all Protestants who are not members of the Southern Baptist Convention. They are lumped together because my main theoretical interest in this context is a comparison between Catholics and Southern Baptists. Most of the "others" are moderates or liberals in Smith's (1986) categorization. As data in other chapters of this book show, there are usually significant differences in the matters under discussion between Catholics and moderates but usually not between Catholics and liberals.
6. Denomination when growing up.
7. In the religious "musical chairs" during the present century the net gains have gone to the Baptists and the net losses to the Methodists.
8. Skerkat and Eatman (1993), analyzing the same NORC data on which this paper is based, suggest that the Convention is losing members from both of its compo-

nents, inerrantists to more conservative denominations and biblical moderates to more liberal denominations.

9. "The Bible is the actual word of God and is to be taken literally, word for word."
10. Richards (218) cites the "Peace Committee" (established in a vain attempt to mediate between the inerrantists, who were taking over the Convention, and their more moderate opponents) as affirming that the Bible contains "truth without any mixture of error." It then goes on to say that "most" Southern Baptists believe in four truths: Adam and Eve were real persons, the biblical books were written by the name authors, the miracles in the bible did occur as supernatural events in history, and that the historical events given by the biblical authors are accurate and reliable. The committee then goes on to admit that some of its members preferred "broader theological perspectives," and contends that the committee has learned "to live together... in mutual charity and commitment to each other."
11. These choices were presented on a card to respondents who were asked to locate themselves on a seven-point scale in terms of how they pictured God (only 2 or 3 percent of the respondents were unable to answer the questions). The responses constituted a factor that is called the grace scale, a high score indicates a propensity to imagine God as mother, spouse, lover, and friend.
12. In this section of the analysis, the most powerful item in the grace scale, the master/spouse choice, is used instead of the whole scale because the results are more clear-cut.
13. Combining a belief in biblical literalism and absolute certainty about the existence of God.
14. Because some questions were not asked in every GSS, the case base for responses is presented on each item in table 5 (and in table 8).
15. Thirty-four percent of Southern Baptists own pistols, 34 percent own rifles, and 40 percent own shotguns. For other Protestants the rates are 25 percent, 29 percent, and 30 percent. For Catholics 16 percent, 21 percent, and 19 percent.
16. The factor is split into quartiles for graphic presentation in this section of the analysis.
17. There is no statistically significant relationship among Catholics, Jews, and Episcopalians in their scores on the grace scale.
18. The term "Church" may not be inappropriate. While the ongoing "Convention" purports to be the servant of the annual convention held every spring, it constitutes a centralized and powerful bureaucracy, in some respects with even more power than the Catholic bureaucracy possesses, though the rhetoric and style of its internal politics differs from that of Catholicism.
19. A disinterest which, given their presuppositions, makes perfect sense.

14

The Development of a Religious Story

Religious stories have complicated plots. The image of God that a person has must be influenced by many factors if it is to provide the "privileged" symbol of a person's life, the story around which she/he organizes the personal quest for meaning. Not only the choice of image (usually one presumes unreflective) but the highly personal story that goes into the more general story. Where do religious stories come from? How do they develop? What are the most important influences in shaping the story?

Various Influences on One's Religious Stories

My colleagues and I at NORC during the last twenty years (Greeley, McCready, and McCourt 1974; and Fee, Greeley, McCready, and Sullivan 1980) developed a thesis of double religious socialization to explain the impact of two families, socialization by the family of origin and by the family of procreation, on religious behavior. The most powerful influences on a person's religion are the parents and the spouse, not merely or even mainly the devotion of these critical role opposites but more importantly the quality of the relationship itself. The religious story develops out of the family story. For the 1981 study we used an early and very complicated version of the grace[1] scale and administered it in 1979 to a national sample of Catholics between fifteen and thirty, 1,398 from the United States and 782 from Canada. Questions were also administered to the spouse or "significant other" of those who had such.[2] This survey design provided a unique opportunity to study religious socialization, that is, the passing on and development of religious stories.

Parents

Seven of the background variables that measured the quality of the story of the family of origin correlated with the early grace scale: closeness to parents, the quality of the mother-father relationship, the religious joy of the parents, the father's religious influence on the self, the mother's religious influence, and the frequency of the mother's reception of Holy Communion. The strongest was the father's religious influence and the second strongest the quality of family religious joy (.17 and .10 respectively). Combined into a factor, the correlation was .21. Love of nature and a personal intense religious experience also correlated significantly with the grace scale measure, the former at .16 and the latter at .21. In a multiple regression equation the standardized coefficients (β) became .17 for family, .17 for religious experiences, and .12 for love of nature. The religious quality of the life of the family of origin was therefore an important factor in shaping a young person's religious story, but no more important than an intense religious experience. Both the quality of the family life and the religious experience(s) were stories that shaped the grace story. Together these three dimensions of life accounted for 8 percent of the variance on the grace scale.

Schools

Attendance at Catholic schools as such did not affect in the slightest the grace scale. But there was a strong relationship between whether the young person gave his Catholic school high marks on quality and the grace scale[3] so that the β for school quality became .21 when entered into an equation with the love of nature, family religious environment, and religious experience. The impact of these latter variables was not diminished by the school influence so that the amount of variance explained by the model for those who attended Catholic schools went up to 19 percent, almost double the explained variance in the model for others.

The religious story then comes together for young people through their family stories, their school stories, and their experience stories (with nature or an intense religious interlude). Obviously, in the absence of data that follow a group of young people through time, it is not possible to sort out the influence of these stories on the religious story from the influence of the religious story on the other three.

Priests and Friends

For the whole sample of young people each of the three layers of influence already discussed adds between 2 and 3 percent to the explained variance. When the influence of the parish priest as measured by the quality of his sermons,[4] and of friends, is added to the regression equation the R^2 increase four more points to .12 or 12 percent of the variance explained by the five-variable model.

For those who attended Catholic schools, however, the increase is much more dramatic, from 19 percent of the variance explained to 30 percent (90 percent of the increase attributable to the quality of preaching).

It may be that quality religious instruction disposes a young person to listen more sympathetically to the sermon (or homily as it is now called) or that those who are already more *grace*-full to begin with are more benign in their attitudes toward the quality of religious instruction and preaching or it may be finally that the good fortune of having high quality religious instruction and high quality preaching while one is growing up has a powerful impact on shaping a young person's religious story.

The Spouse

As noted above, in the Study of Young Catholics we have measures of the spouse's religious story as well as the self's story. In the first year of marriage, the spouse's grace scale boosts the explained variance up to 14 percent. The religious story of the spouse, in other words, becomes a sixth explanatory layer, which adds about as much explained variance as did the other five taken separately. However, among those who have been married for more than five years the influence of the spouse boosts the explained variance in one's grace scale to 17 percent. The spouse now accounts for 5 percent additional explanatory power, which means that after the first five years of marriage the spouse becomes the most powerful influence on the religious imagination of an adult Catholic and, indeed, is almost half as powerful in his/her impact on the religious imagination as all the prior variables put together.

Finally, when one looks at marriages in which *both* partners say that the sexual fulfillment is excellent, the explanatory power of the model is doubled to 30 percent of the variance. The spouse's religious story is the crucial factor shaping the self's religious story *if both spouses are satis-*

fied with their sexual relationship. The religious story of the spouse in such a relationship is six times more powerful than any previous individual variable. The story of the couple's sex life and the story of their religious life make a very powerful combination indeed, as your story and my story become *our* story. A sexually exciting spouse who tells exciting religious stories has a tremendous impact on one's own religious stories.[5]

Religiously important friends and high quality sermons make an important contribution to the development of the religious imagination but even if the sermons are excellent and the friends are important, a gracious spouse almost doubles the influence of both friends and sermons. Combine a friend's story and high quality sermons with a sexually appealing and story-telling[6] spouse and the outcome is likely to be an extremely gracious image of God. God is like the spouse and the spouse is like God.

The correlation (r) between the spouse's religious story and the self's religious story in a sexually fulfilling relationship that has gone on for more than six years is .6 (and thus the R^2 for that factor alone is .36). One hardly ever finds that correlation in social research. The two stories have almost become the same story.[7]

So how does one acquire a religious story? From one's parents and friends and teachers and priests and from experiences of nature or grace, but especially from that story teller with whom you sleep passionately at night. How could it, one might ask in retrospect, be otherwise?

Prayer also has an effect on the young married couple's story (see Greeley 1980). In unions where both spouses pray everyday (not necessarily together), 42 percent of both husbands and wives say the sexual fulfillment is excellent while among couples where one or both do not pray everyday the proportion falls 24 percent. Moreover, among couples who have been married nine or ten years the correlation between spouses and prayers is .42. The differences between marriages that have lasted up to eight years and those that are now in their ninth or tenth year are striking. In the latter both spouses are 22 percentage points more likely to say that the sexual fulfillment is excellent than in the former. More than three quarters of this difference can be accounted for by the fact that both spouses pray everyday and both spouses have high grace scale scores.

Moreover, spouses are aware of the religious influence they have one on another. Fifty-seven percent of those couples in which one or the other acknowledges strong religious influence, both of whom pray daily and have high scores on the grace scale, say (that is, both spouses say) that their sexual fulfillment is excellent as opposed to 22 percent of those who are at the lower end of all four scales.

Does the sexual story shape the religious story or the religious story shape the sexual story? Clearly there is no possible answer to this question in the absence of longitudinal data. When NORC began its various longitudinal studies of young people, I suggested that more religious questions ought to be included in the questionnaires. I received a sympathetic hearing from people on the NORC staff but those (not from NORC) who directed the research clearly thought I was out of my mind. How could any serious sociological scholar have thought that religion and sexual behavior influence each other? So the questions weren't asked.

Anger and Religion

Another analysis of the Young Catholic Study data shows how conflicting stories, one from the past and the other from the present, work themselves out (Greeley and Durkin 1984). Those young Catholic women who in the late 1970s thought that a child would not suffer if the mother worked and that women should be ordained priests were 17 percentage points less likely to attend church services regularly than those who did not hold both those positions. Four influences seem to account for the differences. The "angry" feminists, as opposed to those who were feminist but went to church regularly, tended to be nonworking wives who were dissatisfied with their family situation, whose mothers were devout, and whose mothers did not work when their children were six years old. Apparently their mothers had communicated to these young women an image of the appropriate role of women which was incompatible with the young women's feminist principles. However, this conflict between mother's model and daughter's model was canceled out if five new circumstances were at work: the husband went to church regularly, the husband also was a feminist, the marriage was sexually satisfying, the husband was judged by the wife to be religiously influential, and God was pictured as a lover. Moreover, the picture of God as a lover was enhanced by two events outside the family context: judgment that priests in the parish were sympathetic and a report that the woman had had a serious discussion with a priest recently.

Thus, a young woman was apparently blaming the Church for what she considered to be an inappropriate role model handed on to her by her devout mother. However, the story contained in that role model was canceled out by different stories told by an affectionate, sympathetic, and devout husband, by a sympathetic priest, and by the image of God as a lover, which in turn seemed to be affected by both the priest and the husband. Family socialization, which perhaps unintentionally turned the young woman away from religion, appears to have been overcome by adult socialization with her husband and her priest. This reconstruction of a conflict among a number of different religious stories, all purporting to be Catholic, is highly speculative in the absence of longitudinal data, which would allow one to follow the process as it happened. But the statistics fit this explanation. At a minimum one would conclude that the development of one's own religious story is an intricate and complex process that involves listening to, and perhaps adopting as one's own, stories heard from many different story tellers, the most important of whom is the sympathetic and sexually fulfilling spouse. The two romances, divine and human, seem to be closely related.

Notes

1. For a description of which, see Greeley 1981, and of its weaknesses (most notably its length and complexity), see Greeley 1984.
2. The latter were not called that then and were not nearly so numerous as they are today.
3. Only 12 percent of those who attended Catholic grade schools and 17 percent of those who attended Catholic high schools rated the quality of their religious instruction as excellent, twice as high as the ratings given in Catholic religious education classes conducted outside the school context.
4. Only 14 percent of the respondents rated their parish sermon as excellent.
5. It remains to be seen whether this would also be true of Protestant young people, since spousal imagery of God seems to have no significant effect on the sex lives of Protestants as reported in the previous chapter.
6. The story is told, one presumes, more in who the spouse is and what the spouse does than in what she/he says.
7. Have the spouses conspired to tell the same story? First, why should they bother to try to duplicate answers? Second, the respondent was interviewed personally and a drop-off questionnaire was left for the spouse; why take time and energy to try to recall your answers so that your spouse could give the same answers? Third, why should this improbable conspiracy take place only in those families where the sexual fulfillment (as reported by both spouses) is rated "excellent"?

15

Conclusion

Picture, if you will, an elderly Irish woman (in Ireland for the sake of the discussion) kneeling in the back of a church devoutly moving her fingers over her rosary beads. There is a certain admirable simplicity, it would seem, in the woman's religious faith as she prays for her dead husband, her children, her grandchildren, and her great-grandchildren. For weal or woe, however, one says, such women will disappear from the Irish church as other generations of more skeptical, more secularized women replace her.

Maybe. But when the woman was young herself, "keeping company" perhaps with the man she would eventually marry, she would have never imagined herself tolling the beads in the back of the church as her grandmother was doing at that time, praying perhaps for her and her young man. The religious life cycle is remarkably durable: the more things change the more they remain the same.

The old woman in the back of church, for all her piety, it might be said, is likely to be superstitious, bigoted, and the victim of patriarchal myths. It will be good thing for Ireland (and by implication Irish America) when the religious style for which the woman stands disappears. And, say some of the Irish critics of religion in their own country, the sooner the better.

Maybe. *But,* on the average, such a woman is less likely to be superstitious, less likely to be bigoted, and less likely to adhere to patriarchal values than her counterpart across the Irish sea *or anywhere else.* She is also more likely not to be opposed to homosexual marriage ceremonies. "Sure," as one Irishman remarked to me in language appropriate for a Roddy Doyle novel, "We don't care what the poor fockers do!"

The important issue concerning her, therefore, is not whether her religious stories are going to vanish from Irish life because the available empirical data suggest that they are not. Rather the important question is what religious stories she may share (as David Tracy has asked) with the monks who produced the Book of Kells, John Scotus Erigena, and James Joyce and which distinguish her in her elderly devotion from women in other countries. The question is not whether the Irish religious heritage is vanishing (though it may well be changing) but rather what it is, that is, what experiences and images and stories are the bearers of that heritage and how they are different from other religious heritages.

The woman with the beads represents a heritage. Before the heritage is dismissed as outmoded or embarrassing, it might possibly be useful to know what it is, to understand the experiences and the images and the stories from which it is made.

The Irish religious heritage with which I end this book is like the New Mexican religious heritage with which I began it—extraordinary durable and with a durability that transcends mere prose propositions. If we want to understand New Mexico and Ireland (and every other religious heritage) we must go beyond the prose and listen to the poetry.

"Secularization" doesn't explain much variance. Religious imagery does. As long as sociology is obsessed with monitoring the assumed (dogmatically assumed) decline of religion it will never listen to the poetry. Yet I find that when I try to explain this approach to Irish sociologists (well, some of them) and other Irish intellectuals, they quite literally cannot comprehend what I am trying to say.

It is not fair to blame the Irish however. The eyes of my American colleagues glaze over too. They simply do not hear my theory and do not see my correlations. There is yet a long way to go.

My theory, put quite simply, is that religious stories, dealing with as they do the ultimate meaning of life, tend to shape more proximate stories of the meaning of events of daily life. Religious stories, particularly as they are expressed in images of God, will predict (at low to moderate levels of correlation) political, social, and familial stories. The religious stories are in their turn shaped by the most intimate experiences of life, those in the family of orientation and the family of procreation. Experiences of spouse and parent shape, and of course are shaped by, experiences of God.

I began to explicate my theory in chapter 3 with the story of the Madonna of O'Hare. If my theory has any utility, I should be able to establish that the image and story of the mother love of God ought to

predict other and more proximate stories, for example, stories of attitudes toward the civil liberties of communists, atheists, homosexuals,
and militarists. If God loves us like a loving mother, it would follow that
we should have more maternal and more loving (which is to say more
tolerant) stories (attitudes) toward those whom society defines as deviant. As I noted in subsequent chapters the grace scale correlates positively with attitudes toward civil liberties. So does the mother/father
component of that scale—.03 for Fundamentalist Protestants, .04 for
moderate Protestants, .08 for liberal Protestants, and .18 for Catholics
(who are perhaps especially likely to be influenced by Madonna images). The latter two correlations are statistically significant. As established in chapter 9, these correlations generally persist when all pertinent
social, political, educational, religious and geographic variables are taken
into account. Moreover, the standardized correlation (beta) for the grace
scale is stronger on civil liberties than correlations for age, sex, and
region. Omit religious imagery from your questionnaire, I repeat, if you
are also willing to omit age, sex, and region.

Figure 15.1 demonstrates the patterns of correlations between civil
liberties and the grace scale by denomination. The relationship is strongest for Catholics and weakest (statistically insignificant) for Fundamentalists. The liberal and moderate Protestants are in between; on this
measure the relationship for the former is significant and for the latter
insignificant.

Figure 15.1 summarizes the argument of this book—stories of God
predict stories of human life. If there were measures in the General Social survey of the socialization experiences of childhood and marriage, I
would expect that the grace scale would act as a partial conduit, a code,
a symbol connecting family stories with civil liberty stories. Figure 15.1
also demonstrates the differences between the Dialectical Imagination
in the Fundamentalists and the Analogical Imagination in Catholics:
Catholics are more tolerant of dissidents than Fundamentalist Protestants and Catholic images of God affect their stories more powerfully
than do the images of the Fundamentalists. Catholics, moderates, and
liberals do not differ in their tolerance for deviants and the grace scale
affects the images of all three at levels of statistical significance, but the
impact is greater for Catholics. Catholics on the low end of the scale are
less likely to be tolerant than moderate and liberal Protestants at the low
end of the scale, perhaps because less gracious stories of God (Father,

FIGURE 15.1
Civil Liberties by Religion by Image of God

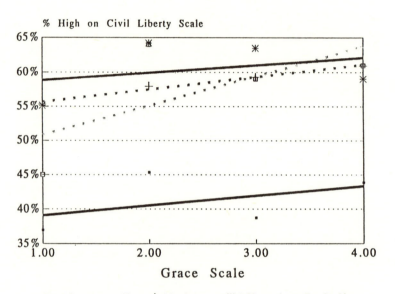

% High on Civil Liberty Scale

Grace Scale

‑‑Fundamentalist +Moderate *Liberal ⊡·Catholic

Master, Judge, King) also have a greater impact on Catholics than they do on Protestants.

Have I proved my theory that religion is poetry before it is prose? Surely not. In sociology, theories are never proved, they are only proved useful. I would like to think that in this book, which is probably too religious for the sociological voice and too sociological for the religious voice, I have proved that the theory of religion as poetry (as metaphor and story) is not completely without use. I hope I have established that it is not unreasonable for those interested in the scholarly or serious study of religion to consider my theory when they ponder the religious phenomena. If they do not do so, I think I might have proved that they would deprive themselves of a powerful tool of analysis.

Various measures of religious stories correlate positively with such public policy matters as civil liberties, racial justice, feminism, the death penalty, AIDS, environmental spending, government intervention on the side of the poor, and cheating the government. Moreover, these measures continue to relate significantly to such issues even when the relevant demographic variables are taken into account and often more powerfully than do some of these demographic variables, even in lieu of one another. Moreover, many of these relationships exist not only in the United States but in many other countries. What more could one ask of a newly proposed predictor variable, even if the International Social Survey Program will not use the religious image variables on its questionnaires and the Board of Overseers of the General Social Survey considered dropping them?

I keep expressing modest hopes for the enterprise recorded in this essay. Let anyone and everyone say that my methods are flawed, my assumptions dubious, my measurements problematic, my conclusions not cautious enough,[1] my speculations what one might expect from a person who was once dismissed by a colleague at the University of Chicago as a "loud-mouthed Irish priest."[2] All I hope is that they add, "but, you know, he seems to be onto something."

Like my other modest expectations, however, this one is falsely modest. In for an inch, in for a light year. If I'm onto anything at all, the conclusion that follows is that religion continues to an be important correlate of other behaviors, especially when one considers the experiential and narrative dimensions of religion. It also follows that predictions of the demise of religion are mistaken. If frequency of prayer affects attitudes toward the death penalty and, for Catholics, toward AIDS, one might not even want that kind of religion to disappear.

Another modest expectation is that some social science readers of this book might say that, while as a Catholic the author is clearly biased in favor of that heritage, he seems to be onto something when he says that Catholics were different, are different, and are likely to continue to be different.[3] There are too many astonishing interactions in his data to say that he's completely wrong when he argues that David Tracy's theory of the Analogical Imagination does account in part for why Catholics are different.

Once more the expectation is not modest at all. In for an inch, in for a galaxy. If Catholics are truly different and if I am onto something about them in this essay, no matter how slight it may be, then maybe some of the paradigms about that heresy are ill-conceived. Catholicism then would not be a phenomenon about which everything is known that needs to be known, but an unexplored continent about which little is known, a wonderland full of counter-intuitive surprises.

It is, in other words, gentle critics, a zero-sum game. Either this essay is the work or a charlatan or a fool or, to use the game metaphor a little differently (to tell a different story), it is a whole new game.

As I was finishing up the book I attended a seminar in which findings were reported about young people returning to religion in the life-cycle process. It was hardly a revolutionary notion, but the work was well done. There was solid evidence that marriage and especially children correlated with a return to religion. One of the students made the usual observation: churches provided activities for children and friends for young parents. So of course they would reaffiliate.

She was not wrong in what she said, so much as in what she did not say. Churches in this country are indeed centers for every conceivable kind of activity (though, mutatis mutandis, that sort of activity took place in the Middle Ages too). But her explanation, typical of the purportedly hard-headed and cynical functionalism with which sociologists tend to approach religion, ignored the possibility that young parents might also be returning to the churches precisely for what the churches uniquely offer—meaning and community and meaning-supporting community. A place to tell your stories to people who will listen and where you listen to other people's stories.

Stories of meaning today are as unmentionable as sex is alleged to have been in Victorian drawing rooms, perhaps because if one admits that large numbers of people are looking for meaning it follows perhaps that one might do it oneself. In for an inch, in for a cosmos.

If a sociologist does not need or want a religion, that is his privilege. But why does the security of that decision require that he proclaim that religion isn't important to anyone else anymore and that it doesn't have any effect on human life anymore, and make that proclamation in the teeth of the data? Why is it necessary to claim majority support for his own agnosticism? Should it not be enough for him to assert that he doesn't need or want religion and that sociology cannot answer religious questions?

Normally a sociologist would not end a book on this highly personal note. But this is a different kind of book, one in which the writer (none too subtly, it might be said) contends that the profession has missed the boat completely on three important phenomena: the predictive power of religion, the importance of religious imagery, and the Catholic heritage. Having been dismissed before when I argued this position—backed up by many of the data gathered in the present essay—this time I am not about to go silently into that good night. Rather, I will rant against not the failing of the light but the fact that the light never went on in the first place.

I have somewhat less to say to the theological voice to which I have listened as I wrote this book. It is too busy either attempting to dialogue with secular humankind (the faculty member down the corridor) or abasing itself to anyone who claims to speak for politically correct "minorities" or wondering whether any kind of faith is possible after Jacques Derrida. The sociologist might at least read this book, the theologian never.

But anyway I would say to the unlikely theologian who picks up the book (maybe at a remainder sale) and the even more unlikely hierarch that you should be quiet for a little while and listen to the stories your people, like the elderly Irish woman saying her rosary, are telling about their experiences of grace. It might just be possible that the Holy Spirit (assuming that there is one) is speaking through them too, especially because by reputation She blows where She will. Maybe, just maybe, the vividness and the intensity of their stories would be a useful counterweight to your frequently dry as dust (though never unnecessary) prosaic wisdom. Maybe.

From one perspective this essay might be much ado about nothing, without, alas, Emma Thompson. For most of human history (at least that about which we know) human religion was almost entirely story and ritual and community. Why should it be any different now? To argue that poetic religion is less important today and prosaic religion more important assumes that humankind has gone through a profound change in its constitution since, let us say, the Enlightenment.

Social scientists may not need or want religion in their own lives, but it is the worst kind of dogmatism to say that therefore it is not a subject that matters anymore in the human condition and may be taken to be sociologically uninteresting, especially when the available data call that conclusion into serious question.

References

Abrams, M., D. Gerard, and N. Timms. 1985. *Values and Social Change in Britain.* London: Macmillan.

Allport, Gordon W. 1954. *The Nature of Prejudice.* Cambridge, MA: Addison-Wesley.

Alwin, D. 1986. "Religion and Parental Child-Rearing Orientations: Evidence of a Catholic-Protestant Convergence." *American Journal of Sociology* 92:412-20.

Ammerman, Nancy T. 1990. *Baptist Battles: Social Change and Religious Conflict in the Southern Baptist Convention.* New Brunswick, NJ: Rutgers University Press.

———. 1991. "Southern Baptists and the New Christian Right." *Review of Religious Research* 32 (March): 213-36.

Barstow, Anne L. 1986. *Joan or Arc: Heretic, Mystic, Shaman.* Lewiston, NY: The Edwin Mellen Press.

Bossy, John. 1985. *Christianity in the West 1400-1700.* New York: Oxford University Press.

Boyle, Leonard. 1981. "Montaillou Revisited: *Mentalité* and Methology." In *Pathways to Medieval Peasants,* edited by J. A. Raftis. Toronto: Pontifical Institute of Medieval Studies.

Brundage, James A. 1987. *Law, Sex, and Christian Society in Medieval Europe.* Chicago: The University of Chicago Press.

Butler, Jon. 1990. *Awash in a Sea of Faith.* Cambridge, MA: Harvard University Press.

Byrd, Randolph C. "Positive Therapeutic Effects of Intercessory Prayer in a Coronary Care Unit Population." *Southern Medical Journal* 81:826-29.

Calvaruso, C., and S. Abbruzzese. 1985. *Indagine sui valori in Italia.* Torino: SEI.

Carroll, Michael. 1992. *Madonnas that Maim.* Baltimore: Johns Hopkins University Press.

Christian, William. 1981. *Apparitions in Late Medieval and Renaissance Spain.* Princeton, NJ: Princeton University Press.

Cipriani, Roberto. 1989. "Diffused Religion and New Values In Italy." In *The Changing Face of Religion,* edited by James A. Beckford and Thomas Luckmann, Newbury Park, CA: Sage Publications, 24-48.

Connolly, S. J. 1982. *Priest and People in Pre-Famine Ireland.* Dublin: Gill and Macmillan.

Davis, James A., and Tom Smith. 1991. *General Social Surveys 1972-1989.* Chicago: NORC.

Delumeau, Jean. 1977. *Catholicism between Luther and Voltaire: A New View of the Counter-Reformation.* Philadelphia: Westminster Press.

Duffy, Eamon. 1992. *Stripping of the Altars.* New Haven, CT: Yale University Press.

Durkheim, Emile 1915. The Elementary Forms of Religious Life; a study in religious sociology. Translated by Joseph Ward Swain. London: G. Allen & Unwin, Ltd.; New York: The Macmillan Company.

———. 1961. *Suicide,* translated by John Spaulding and George Simpson. Glencoe, IL: The Free Press.

Durkin, John, and Andrew Greeley. 1991. "A Model of Religious Choice Under Uncertainty: On Responding Rationally to the Non Rational." *Rationality and Society* 3 (April): 178-96.

Eckberg, D. L., and T. Jean Blocker. 1989. "Varieties of Religions Involvement and Environmental Concern." *Journal for the Scientific Study of Religion* 28: 509-17.

Eider, Ellen. 1992. "Religion, Disability, Depression, and the Time of Death." *American Journal of Sociology* 97 (January).

Elifson, Kirk W. 1976. "Religious Behavior among Urban Southern Baptists: A Causal Inquiry." *Sociological Analysis* 37 (Spring): 32-44.

Erskine, Helen Gaudet. 1965. "The Polls: Personal Religion." *Public Opinion Quarterly* 29:147-49.

Fawcett, Thomas. 1971. *Symbolic Language*. Minneapolis: Augsburg.

Fee, Joan, Andrew Greeley, William McCready, and Teresa Sullivan. 1980. *Young Catholics in the United States and Canada*. New York: Sadlier.

Finke, Roger, and Rodney Stark. 1992. *The Churching of America, 1776-1990: Winners and Losers in Our Religious Economy*. New Brunswick, NJ: Rutgers University Press.

Flint, Valerie Irene. 1992. *The Rise of Magic in Early Medieval Europe*. Princeton, NJ: Princeton University Press.

Flynt, J. Wayne. 1981. "Southern Baptists: Rural to Urban Transition." *Baptist History and Heritage*. Nashville: Southern Baptist Convention.

———. 1993 "How Large is the Religious Right?" *Sociology of Religion* (forthcoming).

Fogerty, M., L. Ryan, and J. Lee. 1984. *Irish Values and Attitudes*. Dublin: Dominican Press.

Gallup, George. 1968. *The Gallup Poll: Public Opinion Polls 1935-1971*. New York: Random House.

Geertz, Clifford. 1957. "Ethos, World-View and the Analysis of Sacred Symbols." *The Antioch Review* 17: 424-34.

———. 1966. "Religion as a Cultural System." *Anthropological Approaches to the Study of Religion*, edited by Michael Bonton. New York: Praeger, 1-46.

———. 1968. "Religion as a Cultural System." *The Religious Situation 1968*, edited by Donald Cutler. Boston: Beacon Press.

Gentilcore, David. 1992. *Bishop to Witch*. Manchester: Manchester University Press.

Ginzburg, Carlo. 1983. *The Night Riders: Witchcraft and Agrarian Cults in the Sixteenth and Seventeenth Centuries* translated by John and Anne Tedeschi. New York: Penguin Books.

Greeley, Andrew. 1964. "The Protestant Ethic: Time for a Moratorium." *Sociological Analysis* 25:20-33.

———. 1976. *Death and Beyond*. Chicago: Thomas More Press.

———. 1980. *The Young Catholic Family: Religious Images and Marital Fulfillment*. Chicago: Thomas More Press.

———. 1981. *The Religious Imagination*. New York: Sadlier.

———. 1982. *Religion: A Secular Theory*. New York: The Free Press.

———. 1984. "Religious Imagery as a Predictor Variable in the General Social Survey." Paper Presented at a Plenary Session of the Society for the Scientific Study of Religion.

———. 1987 Hallucinations among the Widowed. Sociology and Social Research Vol. 71 No. 4 (July): 258-265.

————. 1988a. "Evidence that a Maternal Image of God Correlates with Liberal Politics." *Sociology and Social Research* 73:3–8.

————. 1988b. "The Success and Assimilation of Irish Protestants and Irish Catholics in the United States." *Sociology and Social Research* 4: 229–36.

————. 1989a. "Protestant and Catholic: Is the Analogical Imagination Extinct?" *American Sociological Review* 54, no. 4 (August): 485–502.

————. 1989b. *Religious Change in America.* Cambridge: Harvard University Press.

————. 1990. *The Catholic Myth.* New York: Charles Scribner's Sons.

————. 1991a. "Religion and Attitudes towards AIDS Policy. *Sociology and Social Research* 75, no. 3 (April):126–32.

————. 1991b. *Faithful Attraction.* New York: Tor Books.

————. 1992a. "Religion in Britain, Ireland and the United States." In *British Social Attitudes 1992.* London: SCPR.

————. 1992b. "Catholics and Sex." *America* 97, no. 3 and no. 4.

————. 1993a. "Religion and Attitudes towards the Environment. *Journal for the Scientific Study of Religion* 32 (March): 19–28.

————. 1993b. "The Faith We Have Lost." Unpublished Paper. Chicago: NORC.

————. 1993c. "Interaction with the Ultimate: Notes towards a Sociology of Prayer." Under review. Chicago: NORC.

————. 1993d. "Religion Around the World." An ISSP Report. Chicago: NORC.

Greeley, Andrew, and Mary Jule Durkin. 1984. *Angry Catholic Women.* Chicago: Thomas More Press.

Greeley, Andrew, William McCready, and Kathleen McCourt. 1974. *Catholic Schools in a Changing Church.* Kansas City: Andrews and McMeel.

Halman, L., F. Hennka, F. Moor, and H. Zanders. 1987. *Tradite, seculariastie en individualiserring.* Tilburg: Tilburg University Press.

Harding, S., and D. Phillips with M. Fogerty. 1986. *Contrasting Values in Western Europe: Diversity and Change.* London: Macmillan.

Hart, Stephen. 1992. *What Does the Lord Require?* New York: Oxford University Press.

Hatch, Nathan. 1989. *The Democratization of American Christianity.* New Haven, CT: Yale University Press.

Heiler, Friedrich. 1932. *Prayer: A Study in the History and Psychology of Religion.* New York: Oxford University Press.

Hout, Michael. 1993. "Counting the Returnees." *The Catholic World* (March/April): 52–59.

Hout, Michael, and Andrew Greeley. 1987. "The Center Does Not Hold: Church Attendance in the United States 1940-1984." *American Sociological Review* 52: 325–45.

Hull, William E. 1982. "Pluralism in the Southern Baptist Convention." *Review and Expositor* 79 (Winter): 121–46.

Iannaccone, Laurence. 1991. "The Consequences of Religious Market Structure: Adam Smith and the Economics of Religion." *Rationality and Society* 3(April): 156–77.

James, William. 1961. *The Varieties of Religious Experience.* New York: Macmillan.

Kerkhofs, J., and R. Rezohazy. 1984. *De Stille Ommekeer, Oude en Nieuwe waarden in het Belige van de jaren tachtig.* Tielt en Weexp: Lannoo.

Larkin, Emmet. 1972. "The Devotional Revolution in Ireland." *The American Historical Review* 77: 623–52.

————. 1984. *The Historical Dimensions of Irish Catholicism.* Washington D.C.: The Catholic University of America Press.

Laslett, Peter. 1981. *The World We Have Lost.* New York: Scribner.

LeRoy Ladurie, Emanuel. 1975. *Montaillou, Village Occitan de 1294–1324.* Paris: Gallimard.

Luckmann, Thomas. 1967. *The Invisible Religion: The Problem of Religion in Modern Society.* New York: Macmillan.

McCready, William, and Andrew Greeley. 1976. *The Ultimate Values of the American Population.* Beverly Hills, CA: Sage Publications.

McSwain, Larry L. 1980. "The Sociological Context for Southern Baptist Associations." *Review and Expositor* 77 (Spring): 201–12.

Martin, David 1967. *A Sociology of English Religion.* London: SCM Press.

————. 1969. *The Religious and the Secular: Studies in Secularization.* London: Routledge & K. Paul.

————. 1978. *A General Theory of Secularization.* Oxford: Blackwell.

Meissner, William. 1990. "The Role of Transitional Conceptualization in Religious Thought." *Psychoanalysis and Religion,* edited by Joseph H. Smith and Susan A. Handelman. Baltimore: Johns Hopkins University Press.

Noelle-Neumann, Elisabeth. 1981. *German Public Opinion Polls, 1967–1980.* Westport, CT: Greenwood Press.

Noelle-Neumann, E., and R. Kocher. 1987. *De Verletzte Nation.* Stuttgart: Deutsche Verlag-Anstalt.

Obelkevich, James. 1979. *Religion and the People 800–1700.* Chapel Hill: The University of North Carolina Press.

Olson, P. Richard, Joe A. Suddeth, Patricia J. Peterson, and Claudia Egelhoff. 1985. "Hallucinations of Widowhood." *Journal of Medical Geriatric Sociology* 33: 543.

Orizo, F. 1983. *Espana, entre la apatia y el cambio social.* Madrid: MAPFRE.

Otto, Rudolf. 1958. *The Idea of the Holy.* New York: Oxford University Press.

Ozment, Steven. 1992. *Protestants.* New York: Doubleday.

Parsons, Talcott. 1954. Essays in Sociological Theory. Glencoe: Free Press of Glencoe (first published in 1944).

Peterson, T. 1988. *Bakom Dubbla Las.* Stockholm: Institude for Future Studies.

Richards, W. Wiley. 1991. *Winds of Doctrine: The Origin and Development of Southern Baptist Theology.* Lanham, MD: University Press of America.

Rubin, Miri. 1992. *Corpus Christi:The Eucharist in Late Medieval Culture.* New York: Cambridge University Press.

Schneider, Jane. 1990. "Spirits and the Spirit of Capitalism." *Religious Orthodoxy and Popular Faith in European Society,* edited by Ellen Badone. Princeton, NJ: Princeton University Press.

Schank, Roger. 1990. *Tell Me A Story.* New York: Charles Scribner and Sons.

————. 1992. *A Connoisseur's Guide to the Mind.* New York: Summit Books.

Skerkat, Daren E., and Ronald Dean Eatman. 1993. "Intra-Denominational Conflict and Religious Disaffiliation: The Case of the Southern Baptists." Unpublished Paper. Nashville: Vanderbilt University.

Smith, Tom. 1986. "Classifying Protestant Denominations." *GSS Technical Report No. 67.* Chicago: NORC.

Sommerville, C. John. 1992. *The Secularization of Early Modern England.* New York: Oxford University Press.

Swimme, Brian. 1988. "The Cosmic Creation Story." *The Reenchantment of Science,* edited by David Ray Griffin. Albany: SUNY Press, 47–56.

Thompson, Robert C. 1974. "A Research Note on the Diversity among American Protestants: A Southern Baptist Example." *Review of Religious Research* 15 (Winter): 87-91.

Tiger, Lionel. 1979. *On Optimism: The Biology of Hope.* New York: Simon and Schuster.

Tomasson, Richard. 1980. *Iceland: The First New Society.* Minneapolis: The University of Minnesota Press.

Tracy, David. 1975. *Blessed Rage for Order.* New York: Seabury.

———. 1982. *The Analogical Imagination.* New York: Crossroad.

Tschannen, Oliver. 1991. "The Secularization Paradigm." *Journal for the Scientific Study of Religion* 30 (December): 396-415.

Ward, Conor, and Andrew Greeley. 1990. "Development and Tolerance: The Case of Ireland." *Erie-Ireland* 25, no. 4 (Winter).

Warner, H. Steven. 1993. "Work in Progress toward a New Paradigm for the Sociological Study of Religion in the United States." *American Journal of Sociology* 98, no. 5: 1044-93.

Watts, John D. W. 1985. *Word Biblical Commentary Isaiah 1-33.* Waco, TX: Word Books.

Weber, Max. 1958. The Protestant Ethic and the Spirit of Capitalism. Translated by Talcott Parsons. New York: Scribner's.

Whelan, Christopher. 1994. *Values and Social Change in Ireland.* Dublin: Gill and Macmillan.

White, Lynn. 1967. "The Historical Roots of Our Ecological Crisis." *Science* 155: 1203-07.

Whiting, Robert. 1989. *The Blind Devotion of the People.* Cambridge: Cambridge University Press.

Wickham, Edward R. 1957. *Church and People in an Industrial City.* London: Lutterworth Press.

Wilson, Bryan. 1969. *Religion in Secular Society.* Harmondsworth: Penguin Books.

———. 1976. *Contemporary Transformations of Religion.* London, New York: Oxford University Press.

Wright, G. E. 1964 "The Importance of Israel's Historical Symbols in Christian Faith." *The Old Testament and Christian Faith,* edited by B. W. Anderson. London: SCM Press.

Wuthnow, Robert. 1976. "Recent Patterns of Secularization: A Problem of Generations." *American Sociological Review* 41, no. 5: 850-67.

Zentralarchiv für Empirische Sozialforschung. 1986. *Role of Government: ISSP 85 Codebook.* Cologne: Die Universität zu Köln.

———. 1987. *Social Networks and Social Support Systems: ISSP 86 Codebook.* Cologne: Die Universität zu Köln.

———. 1989. *New Family Roles: ISSP 87 Codebook.* Cologne: Die Universität zu Köln.

———. 1993 *Religion. ISSP 92 Codebook (Preliminary).* Cologne: Die Universität zu Köln.

Index

Alwin, D., 137, 138, 154

Analogical imagination, 49–51, 119, 124–127, 134, 136, 143, 146, 149, 150, 154, 155, 159, 240, 165, 267

Animism and superstition: in the Middle Ages, 59, 62, 64–68, 71; in modern time, 78–79

Afterlife: belief in , 83, 84, 86–90, 92, 95,107; and contact with the dead, 220, 222

Age: and belief in afterlife, 86–89, 94, 107; and church attendance, 86, 94; and contact with the dead, 218, 223–225; and conversion from atheism to theism, 98–103; and environmental attitudes 198; and religious faith, 86, 136, 220; and religious imagination, 128, 187. *See also* Prayer

Atheism and atheists, 91

Austria: and belief in afterlife, 87, 90, 92; and belief in God, 84; and frequency of prayer, 85; and religious affiliation, 85; and support for capital punishment, 92

Baptists, 191, 192; and the grace scale, 180. *See also* Southern Baptists

Barstow, Anne, 65

Bible, 147, 148, 191; attitudes toward, 185; belief in and attitudes toward AIDS, 207, 208, 209; and environmental concerns, 192, 194, 200

Birth control: in the Middle Ages, 72; encyclical of 1968, 83

Bossy, John, 68

Britain: atheists in, 91; and belief in afterlife, 84,86,87,92; and belief in God, 86; and belief in heaven, 84; and church attendance, 84; and frequency of prayer, 85, 172; and religious affiliation, 85; and support for capital punishment, 92

Brundage, James, 73

Capital punishment: opposition to, 92, 180. *See also* Prayer

Carroll, Michael, 45, 60, 65, 75

Catholics: and attitudes toward AIDS, 206, 207, 208, 210, 211, 212; and contact with the dead, 220; and environmental attitudes, 200; and the grace scale, 241, 242, 243, 245, 248, 265; heritage, 269; and image of God 113, 116, 180, 242, 243, 265; and Madonna imagery, 24, 25, 28, 265; and the Tracy scale, 113. *See also* Analogical Imagination; Prayer; Protestants vs. Catholics.

Catholic schools, 258, 259

Christian, William, 60, 70, 71

Church attendance, 84, 115, 118; and attitudes toward AIDS, 209; and contact with the dead, 222; and environmental attitudes, 195; in Middle Ages, 60, 61, 64, 72, 74; as predictor variable, 52, 175. *See also* Age

Cipriani, Roberto, 77, 91

Clergue, Pierre, 72.

Council of Trent, 73, 75

Cullen, Cardinal Paul, 69

Death penalty. *See* Capital Punishment

Dialectical imagination, 50–51, 119, 124–127, 136, 143, 150, 153, 154, 240, 252, 265

Duffy, Eammon, 59, 70, 71, 73

Durkheim, Emile, 5, 10, 17, 21, 46, 47, 50, 125, 126, 127, 134, 230, 231; theory of religion, 9–10

Durkin, John, 20

East Germany: atheists in, 91; belief in afterlife in, 84, 87, 94; belief in God in, 84; church attendance in, 84, 98; comparison to Russia, 96–98; conversion from atheism to theism in, 97–98; decline of religion in, 91, 93–94, 97; frequency of prayer in, 98; religious affiliation in, 85, 94, 98; religious revival in, 83
Eckberg, D. L., 192
Eider, Ellen, 10, 48, 51
Eliade, Mircea, 21; theory of religion 18–19
Episcopalians: and contact with the dead, 220; and the grace scale, 180 *See also* Protestants
European Study of Values (EVSS), 86, 119, 128, 140, 146, 153, 154

Family life: quality of, 119–121, 258
Fawcett, Thomas, 27, 29, 30, 32, 116
Finke, Roger, 19, 60
Flint, Valerie, 67, 68
Freud, Sigmund, 5, 10, 17, 20, 92; theory of religion, 7–9
Fundamentalism: and attitudes toward AIDS, 206–208, 210; and contact with the dead, 220; and environmental attitudes, 191–193, 197; and the grace scale, 265; and Southern Baptists, 230, 236

Geertz, Clifford, 2, 14, 15, 21, 25, 39, 125, 231
General Social Survey, 112, 113, 138, 146, 149, 150, 154, 160, 166, 180, 185, 188, 194, 197, 201, 205, 213, 217, 218, 224, 229, 231, 236, 252, 265
Gentilcore, David, 60, 67
Ginzburg, Carlo, 62.
God: belief in , 84, 115, 195, 199, 200; closeness to, 96; concern for humans, 88, 90, 96, 106, 107, 175; image of, 112, 116, 118, 120, 124, 157, 164, 179, 180, 182, 185, 188, 195, 197, 198, 213, 217, 221–226, 257, 261,

262, 264, 265; and Madonna metaphor, 25. *See also* Religious symbols
Government: opposition to cheating the, 92: support for intervention for the poor, 92
Grace scale, 112, 113, 119, 257, 258, 261; and attitudes toward AIDS, 210–213, 241; and environmental attitudes, 200–203, 241; and impact on social attitudes, 179, 180, 182, 187, 265; and political affiliation, 180, 183; as predictor variable, 182, 188, 203

Hamilton, Bernard, 72.
Heiler, Friedrich, 158
Hope renewal experiences, 26–32, 34, 40, 42, 47, 112, 116, 205
Houser, Robert, 38
Hout, Michael, 78
Hungary: belief in afterlife in, 84, 88; church attendance in, 84, 94, 95, 97; conversion from atheism to theism in, 97; decline of religion in, 93; frequency of prayer in, 85, 172; increase in religion in, 94; and religious affiliation, 94

Iannancone, Laurence, 19
International Social Survey Project (ISSP), 136, 140, 143, 145, 146, 150, 152, 201, 214, 267; study of religion, 83–108, 172
Ireland: atheists in, 91; belief in afterlife in, 84; belief in God in, 84, 86; belief in heaven in, 84; church attendance in, 84, 95; frequency of prayer in, 84, 172; religious change in, 20; religious devotion in, 84; and the Tracy scale, 113
Israel: belief in afterlife in, 84, 88, 91; frequency of prayer in, 172; opposition to capital punishment in, 92; opposition to cheating the government in, 92
Italy: atheists in, 91; belief in afterlife in, 84; belief in God in, 84, 86; belief in heaven in, 84; church attendance in, 84, 95; frequency of prayer in 85, 172

James, William, 5, 21, 25, 29, 113; theory of religion 16-18

Jesus, 24, 25, 147

Jews, 61, 72, 129; and environmental attitudes, 194, 195; and the grace scale, 113, 180, 251; and sacred time, 48. *See also* Prayer.

Johnson, Sister Elizabeth, 42

Joyce, James, 240

Larkin, Emmet, 75

Laslett, Peter, 60, 62

Leroy, Ladurie, Emanuel, 72

Liberation theology, 7

Life after death. *See* Afterlife

Luckmann, Thomas, 58

Luther, Martin, 145

Lutherans: in the Middle Ages, 74; and the grace scale, 180. *See also* Protestants

Magic, 270; in the Middle Ages, 64-68, 71, 72, 77; in modern time, 78, 79 *See also* Animism and superstition

Malinowski, Bronislaw, 21; theory of religion, 10-11.

Marriage: in the Middle Ages, 71-74.

Marty, Martin, 42, 74

Marx, Karl, 5, 8, 9, 10, 12, 13, 17, 20, 92, 95, 98, 107; theory of religion, 2, 6-7

Methodists: in the Middle Ages, 74; and the grace scale 180. *See also* Protestants

National Opinion Research Center (NORC), 113, 116, 160, 162, 179, 185, 206, 217, 218, 229, 231, 257

Netherlands: atheists in, 91; belief in afterlife in, 86, 91; belief in God in, 84, 86; church attendance in, 84; decline in religion in, 91; frequency of prayer in, 172; religious affiliation in, 85

New Zealand: belief in afterlife in, 84; belief in heaven in, 84; church attendance in, 84, 95; conversion from atheism to theism in, 97; frequency of prayer in, 85; religious affiliation in, 85

Northern Ireland: atheists in, 91; belief in afterlife in, 84, 92; belief in heaven in, 84; church attendance in, 84; frequency of prayer in, 84, 85, 172; support for capital punishment in, 92

Norway: belief in afterlife in, 86, 87, 90; frequency of prayer in, 85, 172

Olson, P. Richard, 217, 218, 224, 225, 227

Orthodox Church, 97, 98, 101, 103-108

Otto, Rudolph, 21, 25; theory of religion, 15-16

Ozment, Stephen, 75

Parsons, Talcott, 21, 153; theory of religion, 14-15

Planissoles, Beatrice de, 72, 79

Poland: belief in afterlife in, 84, 87; belief in heaven in, 84; church attendance in, 84, 95; frequency of prayer in, 84, 172; religious devotion in, 84

Prayer: affect on attitudes, 157-177; and age, 160-162, 168; and attitudes toward AIDS, 166-168, 171; and belief in God, 162, 168, 170; and Catholics, 160, 167; and contact with the dead, 217, 221, 222, 226; and environmental attitudes, 195; frequency of, 83, 98, 260, 267; and happiness, 163, 164, 168, 170-172; and image of God, 165; importance of, 157; in schools, 91; and Jews, 162; and opposition to capital punishment, 165, 168, 170-173, 175; and opposition to cheating the government, 172, 173; as predictor variable, 159, 171, 172, 175, 177; and Protestants, 161; and relationship to God, 158; and support for government intervention for the poor, 172, 173

Presbyterians, 180. *See also* Protestants

Priests: influence of, 259, 261, 262; Jesuit, 75; in Middle Ages, 73, 75; Vincentian, 75

Protestants: and attitudes toward AIDS, 206-208, 210-212; and contact with the dead, 220; and the grace scale, 265; and image of God, 113, 116,

180; and the Tracy scale 113. *See also* Dialectical imagination; Protestants vs. Catholics

Protestants vs. Catholics, 123–155; and attitudes toward AIDS, 206, 208; and attitudes toward the Bible, 194; and communal vs. individual freedom, 50, 230; and environmental attitudes, 195, 199, 200; and the grace scale, 241, 245; and health and death, 10; and hope renewal experiences, 116; and image of God, 113, 116, 180, 186, 231; and political affiliation, 119; and relationship to God, 231; and sacred time, 48; and social control, 9; and suicide rates, 9, 123, 125, 231; and the Tracy scale, 113. *See also* Analogical imagination; Dialectical imagination

Rational choice models. *See* Sociological theories of religion

The Reformation, 13, 48, 59, 62, 63, 66, 68, 71, 73, 74, 75, 76, 79; and Southern Baptists, 229, 231, 243, 251–253

Religion: affiliation with, 85; and age, 86; and attitudes toward AIDS, 205–214; and contact with the dead, 220; decline in, 83, 86, 87, 264; definition of, 2; and environmental attitudes, 191–203; folk, 50, 62, 64–66, 75, 77; impact of socialism on, 92–107; persistence of, 91, 92; as predictor variable, 179, 188, 269; revival of, 83, 87, 97; and shaping of crucial issues, 92. *See also* Hope renewal experiences; Sociological theories of religion

Religious imagination, 52, 77, 179, 248, 259, 269; and attitudes toward AIDS, 213; and contact with the dead, 223, 225, 226; as measured by the grace scale, 185; and social attitudes, 182, 184, 185; and voting behavior, 184. *See also* Analogical imagination; Dialectical imagination; Grace scale

Religious rituals, 9, 45–48

Religious stories, 39–45, 52, 111, 112, 120, 157, 179, 193, 217, 257, 262, 263; and attitudes toward AIDS, 205, 206, 209, 210; and community rituals, 45–48; and contact with the dead, 220; development of, 257–262; and environmental attitudes, 191, 192; of the spouse, 259, 260; as predictor variable, 52, 264, 267; and story-telling community, 41–47

Religious symbols, 33, 39, 78, 180; of God, 34; differences between Catholics and Protestants, 124; of Madonna, 33, 34, 39

Religious traditions: popular and high, 48–50, 66, 77

Ricoeur, Paul, 38, 40

Russia: atheists in, 95, 97–106; belief in afterlife in, 84, 88, 92, 95, 96; belief in God in, 95, 106; belief in heaven and hell in, 95; belief in miracles in, 96; church attendance in, 98; closeness to God in, 96; comparison to East Germany, 96–98; conversion from atheism to theism, 97–106; frequency of prayer in, 98, 172; religious affiliation in, 85; religious revival in, 83, 84, 97, 105–108; support for capital punishment in, 92

Sacraments, 18

Saints, 71, 72; Augustine, 73; Joan of Arc, 66

Schank, Roger, 39, 40

Schneider, Jane, 62

Second Vatican Council, 186, 239, 243.

Secularization theory. *See* Sociological theories of religion.

Shea, John, 78

Simmel, Georg, 5, 21; theory of religion, 11–12

Slovenia: atheists in, 91; belief in afterlife in, 84, 87; belief in God in, 84; decline in religion in, 93; frequency of prayer in , 172; religious affiliation in, 85, 93, 94.

Social mobility model, 38.

Socialism, 59, 90; impact on religion, 92–107

Sociological theories of religion: classical theories, 1, 5–19, 21; rational choice models, 19–20; religion as poetry model, 23, 25, 111, 120, 179, 191, 200, 205, 213, 229, 254, 166; secularization theory, 1, 3, 19, 52, 57, 58, 63, 64, 78, 79, 91, 107, 108, 160, 264

Society for Psychic Research, 227

Sommerville, C. John, 76

Southern Baptists: and age, 235, 236; and attitudes toward abortion, 243, 244, 246; and belief in afterlife, 236; and belief in God, 237; and the Bible, 229, 235, 237, 249; and church attendance, 236; comparison to Catholics, 29, 231, 234, 255; comparison to other Protestants, 234, 235, 241, 246; and the grace scale, 241, 249, 251, 255; and image of God, 243; membership, 232, 235; and political affiliation, 234, 235, 246, 252; and prayer, 236; and religious imagination, 229; and sexual attitudes, 243, 249, 252; and social attitudes, 246–252

Soviet Union, 92.

Stark, Rodney, 19, 59, 60.

Stories, 35–41. *See also* Religious stories

Study of Young Catholics, 259, 261.

Sullivan, Andrew, 32.

Symbols, 32, 33, 35. *See also* Religious symbols

Thomas, Keith, 59, 71.

Thomas, W. I., 158, 227

Tillich, Paul, 92

Tomasson, Richard, 74

Tracy, David: theory of analogical and dialectical imaginations, 27, 50, 51, 112, 113, 124–127, 136, 155, 185, 229, 231, 240, 252, 264, 267

Tracy scale, 112–113

Trollope, Anthony, 60

Tuchman, Barbara, 79

United States of America: atheists in, 91; belief in afterlife in, 84, 86, 87; belief in God in, 84; belief in heaven in, 84; church attendance in, 84, 86, 95; prayer in, 84, 85, 160–168, 172, 175; religious devotion in, 84; and Tracy scale, 113

Saint Vladimir of Kiev, 95, 98, 107

Warner, H. Steven, 19.

Weber, Max, 5, 21, 25, 50, 125, 126, 127, 131, 134, 154, 230, 231; theory of religion, 12–14

West Germany: atheists in, 91; belief in afterlife in, 86, 87, 90, 94; belief in God in, 86; church attendance in, 84; frequency of prayer in, 85, 172; religious affiliation in, 85

Whelan, Christopher, 20

White, Lynn, 192

Wright, G. E., 32

Whiting, Robert, 76

Zionism, 90